GREEK PHILOSOPHY

GREEK PHILOSOPHY

THALES TO PLATO

BY

JOHN BURNET

LONDON
MACMILLAN & CO LTD
NEW YORK · ST MARTIN'S PRESS
1964

MACMILLAN AND COMPANY LIMITED
St Martin's Street London WC 2
also Bombay Calcutta Madras Melbourne

THE MACMILLAN COMPANY OF CANADA LIMITED
Toronto

ST MARTIN'S PRESS INC
New York

PRINTED IN GREAT BRITAIN

PREFACE

THE preparation of this volume was undertaken some years ago, but was interrupted by my work on the *Lexicon Platonicum*, which has proved a more formidable task than was at first anticipated. I have to thank the editor of this series and the publishers for their generous indulgence in the circumstances.

It is unfortunate in some respects that I have been obliged to deal with certain parts of the subject in a form which does not admit of detailed argument and still less of controversy. The second edition of my *Early Greek Philosophy* (referred to as *E. Gr. Ph.*²) makes this in large measure unnecessary in Book I., but there are certain parts of Book III. where I have had to state my conclusions baldly in the hope that I may have a later opportunity of discussing their grounds. My chief aim for the present has been to assist students who wish to acquire a firsthand knowledge of what Plato actually says in the dialogues of his maturity. So long as they are content to know something of the *Republic* and the earlier dialogues, Platonism must be a sealed book to them.

I have not thought it well to present Greek names in a Latin dress. I see no advantage, and many disadvantages, in writing Herakleitos as *Heraclitus*. It often leads to his being called out of his name, as the Emperor Herakleios usually is when disguised as *Heraclius*. On the other hand, the Latin titles of Plato's dialogues are English words. Theaitetos of Athens is best left with the beautiful name chosen for him by his father Euphronios, but 'the' *Theaetetus* is as much English as *Thessalonians*. We shall never, it seems, reach agreement on this matter; I only wish to explain my own practice.

I have to thank my friend and former colleague, Sir Henry Jones, for many valuable suggestions and, above all, for his constant encouragement. Mr. Hetherington of Glasgow University was good enough to verify most of my references, and the proofs have been carefully read by Mr. W. L. Lorimer, Lecturer in Greek at the University of St. Andrews. For the imperfections which remain I am solely responsible.

J. B.

CONTENTS

CHAPTER X

CHAPTER XI

BOOK III. PLATO

CHAPTER XII

CHAPTER XIII

CHAPTER XIV

INTRODUCTION

I

No one will ever succeed in writing a history of philosophy; for philosophies, like works of art, are intensely personal things. It was Plato's belief, indeed, that no philosophical truth could be communicated in writing at all; it was only by some sort of immediate contact that one soul could kindle the flame in another. Now in dealing with the philosophy of an earlier age, we are wholly confined to written records, and these are usually fragmentary and often second-hand or of doubtful authority. They are written, too, in a language which at best we only half understand, and have been moulded by influences for the most part beyond our ken. It will only, therefore, be in so far as the historian can reproduce the Platonic contact of souls that his work will have value. In some measure this is possible. Religious faith often seems able to break through the barriers of space and time, and so to apprehend its object directly; but such faith is something personal and incommunicable, and in the same way the historian's reconstruction of the past is primarily valid for himself alone. It is not a thing he can hand over ready-made to others. There is nothing mysterious about this aspect either of religious faith or of philological interpretation. On the contrary, all knowledge has the same character. In the present case it only means that a man who tries to spend his life in sympathy with the ancient philosophers[1] will sometimes find a direct conviction forcing itself upon him, the grounds of which can only be represented very imperfectly by a number of references in a footnote. Unless the enumeration of passages is complete — and it can never be complete — and unless each passage tells exactly in the same way, which depends on its being read in the light of innumerable other passages not consciously present to memory, the so-called proofs will not produce the same effect on any two minds. That is the sense in which philological inquiry, like every other inquiry, requires an act of faith. It is clear,

---

[1] This is what Plato calls τὸ συζῆν (*Ep.* vii. 341 c), but he is thinking of the living, not the dead.

however, that no one whose experience has not been identical can be called on to repeat this act after another, and for this reason professed histories of philosophy are often more of a hindrance than a help. They seem only to interpose another obstacle where there are obstacles enough already.

But though a history of philosophy is impossible, there are some humbler tasks that can in a measure be performed, and of which the performance may help to prepare the way for a more direct vision. In the first place, there are certain external matters that may be determined with considerable accuracy and which are not without importance. We are more likely to understand a philosopher rightly if we know the time he lived at and the surroundings that may have helped to shape his thought, even though these can never wholly explain him. It is particularly useful to know what other philosophers he was acquainted with, either directly or through their writings. In the second place, the development of Greek philosophy depends on the progress of scientific, and especially mathematical, discovery more than on anything else, and it is possible to ascertain pretty accurately the stage Greek science had reached by a given time. The records are full, and, when critically used, trustworthy. It is for these reasons that this work deals so largely with matters which may appear at first to lie outside the province of philosophy. That is, in fact, its chief justification. It is an attempt to lead the reader to the right point of view, from which he may then see for himself. Lastly, there is what may be called the cathartic or purgative function of history. The greatest of all the obstacles we have to surmount is just the mass of scholastic explanation and dogma which so soon overwhelm the teaching of any original genius. To clear that away is perhaps the greatest service that can be rendered in this field. We do not wish to see Plato with the eyes of Aristotle, or even of Plotinos, but if possible, face to face, and anyone who can help us here deserves our thanks. It may seem a purely negative service, but that lies in the nature of the case. In the long run the positive construction must be left to the individual student, and no two students will see quite alike. All the historian can do is to point the way, and warn others off tracks which have already been found to lead nowhere.

Even this, however, implies that we know already what philosophy is, and clearly, unless we have some notion of that, we shall be in danger of losing the thread of our story. We can nevertheless dispense with such a definition as would be applicable to the philosophy of all ages and peoples, for we shall find a pretty clear notion of what philosophy was during the Hellenic period emerging as we go on. This will at least do justice to one aspect of the subject, and that the one we are immediately concerned with. It will be convenient to state at once, however, that for the purpose of this work, I mean by philosophy all Plato meant by it, and nothing he did not mean by it. The latter point is important; for it means that philosophy is not mythology, and, on the other hand, that it is not positive science, however closely it may be related to both of these.

II

In the first place, philosophy is not mythology. It is true that there is plenty of mythology in Plato, and we shall have to consider the meaning of that later. It is also true that we shall have to take account from the first of a mass of cosmogonical and eschatological speculation which influenced philosophy in many ways. These things, however, are not themselves philosophy, and it cannot even be said that they are the germ from which philosophy developed. It is important to be quite clear about this; for in some quarters Oriental cosmogonies are still paraded as the source of Greek philosophy. The question is not one of cosmogonies at all. The Greeks themselves had cosmogonies long before the days of Thales, and the Egyptians and Babylonians had cosmogonies that may be older still. Even savages have cosmogonies, and they are nearly as advanced as those of more civilised peoples. It is possible, though it has certainly not been proved, that the oldest Greek cosmogonies, or some of them, came from Egypt or Babylon. It is still more probable that systems such as that of Pherekydes have preserved fragments of 'Minoan' speculation, which may be of indefinite antiquity. These things, however, have nothing directly to do with philosophy. From the Platonic point of view, there can be no philosophy where there is no rational science. It is true that not much is required — a few propositions of elementary geometry will do to begin with — but rational science of some sort there must be. Now rational science is the creation of the Greeks, and we know when it began. We do not count as philosophy anything anterior to that.

III

It is true, of course, that science originated at the time when communication with Egypt and Babylon was easiest, and just where the influence of these countries was likely to be felt, and it is a perfectly fair inference that this had something to do with its rise. On the other hand, the very fact that for two or three generations Greek science remained in some respects at a very primitive stage affords the strongest presumption that what came to Hellas from Egypt and Babylon was not really rational science. If the Egyptians had possessed anything that could rightly be called mathematics, it is hard to understand how it was left for Pythagoras and his followers to establish the most elementary propositions in plane geometry; and, if the Babylonians had really any conception of the planetary system, it is not easy to see why the Greeks had to discover bit by bit the true shape of the earth and the explanation of eclipses. It is clear that these things were not known at Babylon; they were gradually worked out in South Italy, where we can hardly assume Oriental influences. Of course everything depends on what we mean by science. If we are prepared to give that name to an elaborate record of celestial phenomena made for purposes of divination, then the Babylonians had science and the Greeks borrowed it from them. Or, if we are prepared to call rough rules of thumb for measuring fields and pyramids science, then the Egyptians had science, and it came from them to Ionia. But, if we mean by science what Copernicus and Galileo and Kepler, and Leibniz and Newton meant, there is not the slightest trace of that in Egypt or even in Babylon, while the very earliest Greek ventures are unmistakably its forerunners. Modern science begins just where Greek science left off, and its development is clearly to be traced from Thales to the present day. Copernicus says himself that he was put on the track by what he read of the Pythagoreans in the *Placita* ascribed to Plutarch.[1]

The only remains that have come down to us show that the Egyptians were not without a certain ingenuity in the solution of particular arithmetical and geometrical problems, but there is not the slightest trace of anything like general methods.[2] If incon-

---

[1] *E. Gr. Ph.*[2] p. 349, *n.* 2. It was 'the Pythagorean doctrine, taught also by Nicolas Copernicus', that was condemned by the Congregation of the Index in 1616.

[2] For the Rhind papyrus, see *E. Gr. Ph.*[2] pp. 22 ff., and, for a later discussion, see v. Bissing in *Neue Jahrbücher*, xxv. (1912), pp. 81 ff.

venient remainders occur, they are simply dropped. In the same way, the rules given for reducing triangles to rectangles are only correct if the triangles are right-angled, though those given in the diagrams are apparently meant to be equilateral. In fact the whole system resembles the rough and ready methods of the Roman *agrimensores* far more than anything we should call scientific. Nor is there the slightest ground for the statement sometimes made that the Egyptians had a more highly developed geometry which they guarded as a mystery. That is based mainly on the story that Plato went to Memphis to study under the priests, a story for which there is no good evidence. In any case we know Plato's opinion of Egyptian mathematics, and it is that there was an element of illiberality in it due to its preoccupation with merely practical ends.[1] It is stated that, though hexagons are common on the Egyptian monuments, the pentagon is never found.[2] If that is so, it is very significant. Anyone can make hexagons, but the construction of the regular pentagon is a different matter. We shall see that it was known to the Pythagoreans, to whom the pentagon was of interest as the side of the regular dodecahedron, the most important figure in their system. It should be added that all mathematical terms, 'pyramid' included, are of pure Greek origin.[3]

It is true, of course, that in Hellenistic times, a certain number of Egyptian priests applied the methods of Greek science to the traditional lore of their own country. The Hermetic literature proves it, and so does the elaborate astrological system the later Egyptians erected on a Stoic foundation. All that, however, throws no light on the origins of Greek science. On the contrary, if the Egyptians of these days adopted the contemporary Greek science and philosophy, it is only another indication of their own poverty in such things.

IV

In the case of Babylon it is even more important to distinguish the times before and after Alexander the Great. In the latter period Babylon had become a Hellenistic city, and there was free intercourse between the astronomers of Mesopotamia and Alexan-

---

[1] Plato, *Laws*, 747 b, 6 *sqq.*
[2] Zeuthen, *Histoire des mathématiques* (Paris 1902), p. 5.
[3] The words πυραμίς, πυραμοῦς, which mean a cake made of wheat and honey, are clearly derived from πυροί, 'wheat', though their form has been influenced by the analogy of σησαμίς, σησαμοῦς. See also *E. Gr. Ph.*[2] p. 25, n. 1.

dria. It is certain that Hipparchos, for instance, made use of Babylonian observations. But Greek science was fully constituted before
his time, and there can hardly be any doubt that Babylonian
astronomy attained its highest development under Greek influence.[1]
What we have really to consider is whether there is any trace of it
in Hellas at a much earlier date. Now we know a few facts about
this, and they are instructive. According to Herodotos (ii. 109),
it was from Babylon the Greeks got the instrument called the
gnomon, which indicated the solstices and equinoxes by a shadow.
Whether that is a scientific instrument or not depends on what you
do with it. The Greeks were also familiar at an early date with the
Babylonian duodecimal and sexagesimal systems of numeration,
but the use of these was limited to weights, measures, and currency,
or, in other words, to commercial purposes. They were not employed in science till Hellenistic times, when the circle was divided
into degrees. Arithmetic proper used only the decimal system. If
they had cared, the Greeks might have learned from the Babylonians to distinguish the planets. These were of the greatest
importance for purposes of divination, but the Greeks paid no
attention to astrology before the third century B.C.[2] So long as there
was no cosmological system in which the 'tramp-stars' ($\pi\lambda\alpha\nu\hat{\eta}\tau\alpha\iota$),
as the Greeks irreverently called them, could find a place, they did
not strike them as of more consequence than shooting stars and the
like. The Pythagoreans appear to have worked out their planetary
theory quite independently after discovering the real nature of the
earth. It was said to be Pythagoras or Parmenides that first
identified the evening and the morning star. The Greek equiva-
lents for the Babylonian names of the planets, which we still use
in their Latin form, appear for the first time in the Platonic
Epinomis (987 b *sq.*). Evidently, then, the Greeks did not learn
from the Babylonians the single piece of real astronomical knowledge they possessed.

---

[1] For recent statements on this subject, see Jastrow in *Enc. Brit.* (11th edition),
vol. ii. pp. 796 f.; Boll in *Neue Jahrbücher*, xxi. (1908), p. 116.
[2] See Cumont in *Neue Jahrbücher*, xxiv. (1911), pp. 1 ff. He says (p. 4): 'The
universal curiosity of the Hellenes by no means ignored astrology, but their
sober understanding rejected its adventurous doctrines. Their acute critical
sense knew well how to distinguish between the scientific observations of the
Chaldeans and their erroneous inferences. It remains their everlasting glory
that they discovered and made use of the serious, scientific elements in the
confused and complex mass of exact observations and superstitious ideas, which
constitutes the priestly wisdom of the East, and threw all the fantastic rubbish
on one side.'

They did, however, make use of one important achievement of theirs in this field, namely, their records of eclipses, and the various cycles established on the basis of these records. They used these for the purposes of the calendar, and, as we shall see, for the prediction of eclipses. Whether such observations and calculations are scientific or not depends wholly on the purpose with which they are made and the uses to which they are put. In itself an eclipse of the sun is a phenomenon of purely local interest, and it is no more scientific to record it than it would be to record rainbows. If the record suggests that something has really happened to the sun, and that something may therefore happen to the King, it is not only not science, but an instrument of positive nescience. That, however, was the view taken by the astronomers of Babylon.

The only eastern people that can bear comparison with the Greeks in science and philosophy are the Indians. How much of Indian science is original, and how much may be traced to Greek influence, is a very difficult question in view of the uncertainty of Indian chronology. It does seem certain, however, that no Indian scientific work, and therefore nothing we count as philosophy, can be dated with probability before the time of Alexander. In particular, there is no ground for believing that the mathematical book entitled the *Śulva-sutras*, or 'rules of the cord', is of earlier date, and it is in any case far below the level of Greek science.[1] The analogy of Egypt and Babylon certainly suggests that this reached India from the Hellenistic kingdom of the North West.

V

The truth is that we are far more likely to underrate the originality of the Greeks than to exaggerate it, and we do not always remember the very short time they took to lay down the lines scientific inquiry has followed ever since. By the early part of the sixth century B.C. they had learnt the rough and ready system of mensuration which was all Egypt could teach them, and a hundred years later we find the study of arithmetical and geometrical progressions, plane geometry and the elements of harmonics firmly established on a scientific basis. Another century saw the rise of

---

[1] See A. B. Keith in the *Journal of the Royal Asiatic Society*, 1909, pp. 589 ff. It is a pity that M. Milhaud has been persuaded to accept an early date for the *Śulva-sutras* in his *Nouvelles études* (1911), pp. 109 *sqq*.

solid and spherical geometry, and the sections of the cone were
soon added. The Greeks learnt, directly or indirectly, from Babylon that certain celestial phenomena recur in cycles, and may therefore be predicted. Within fifty years they had discovered that the
earth swings free in space, and the knowledge of its spherical
shape soon followed. A century saw the true account of eclipses
clearly stated, and this led up to the discovery that the earth was a
planet. A little later some Greeks even taught that the sun was not
a planet, but the centre of the planetary system. Nor must we
forget that hand in hand with this remarkable development of
mathematical and astronomical science there went an equally
striking advance in the study of the living organism. Most of the
writings that have come down to us under the name of Hippokrates
belong to the fifth century B.C., and, while some of them show a
tendency to the speculative interpretation of vital phenomena
natural in an age of rapid scientific progress, there are others which
display in an almost perfect form the method of minute and pains-
taking observation that is alone appropriate in dealing with facts
of such complexity. The physicians of Alexandria discovered the
nervous system, but the native Egyptians, though accustomed for
some thousands of years to embalm dead bodies, show astounding
ignorance of the simplest anatomical facts.

The Greeks achieved what they did, in the first place, because
they were born observers. The anatomical accuracy of their
sculpture in its best period proves that, though they never say
anything about it in their literature, apparently taking it for
granted. The Egyptians, we may remember, never learnt to draw
an eye in profile. But the Greeks did not rest content with mere
observation; they went on to make experiments of a quite modern
character. That by which Empedokles illustrated the flux and
reflux of the blood between the heart and the surface of the body
is the best known; for we have a description of it in his own words.[1]
It also established the corporeal nature of atmospheric air. We
should certainly hear of many more such experiments if our
sources were less meagre, and more intelligently compiled.
Further, the Greeks always tried to give a rational explanation
(λόγον διδόναι) of the appearances they had observed. Their
reasoning powers were exceptional, as we can see from the mathematical work they have left us. On the other hand, they were also

[1] See E. Gr. Ph.[2] p. 253.

quite conscious of the need for verification. This they expressed by
saying that every hypothesis must 'save the appearances' (σῴζειν
τὰ φαινόμενα); in other words, that it must do justice to all the
observed facts.[1] That is the method of science, as we understand it
still. It should be added that the development of mathematical and
biological science at a given time to a large extent determines the
character of its philosophy. We shall see how the mathematical
influence culminates in Plato, and the biological in Aristotle.

VI

But, while philosophy is thus intimately bound up with positive
science, it is not to be identified with it. It is true that in early
times the distinction between the two is not realised. The word
σοφία covered all we mean by science and a great deal more besides, such as the arts of making pontoons and guessing riddles.
But the distinction was there all the same. If we look at Greek
philosophy as a whole, we shall see that it is dominated from
beginning to end by the problem of reality (τὸ ὄν). In the last
resort the question is always, 'What is real?' Thales asked it no less
than Plato or Aristotle; and, no matter what the answer given may
be, where that question is asked, there we have philosophy. It is no
part of the historian's task to decide whether it is a question that
can be answered, but there is one comment he may fairly make.
It is that the rise and progress of the special sciences depended, so
far as we can see, on its being asked. We find that every serious
attempt to grapple with the ultimate problem of reality brings
with it a great advance in positive science, and that this has always
ceased to flourish when interest in that problem was weak. That
happened more than once in the history of Greek philosophy, when
the subordinate problems of knowledge and conduct came to
occupy the first place, though at the same time it was just the
raising of these problems that did most to transform the problem
of reality itself.

And this helps to explain why philosophy cannot be simply
identified with science. The problem of reality, in fact, involves
the problem of man's relation to it, which at once takes us beyond

[1] This requirement of Greek scientific method is often ignored, but Milton's
Raphael knows all about it. See *Paradise Lost*, viii. 81: 'how build, unbuild,
contrive To save appearances.'

pure science. We have to ask whether the mind of man can have any contact with reality at all, and, if it can, what difference this will make to his life. To anyone who has tried to live in sympathy with the Greek philosophers, the suggestion that they were 'intellectualists' must seem ludicrous. On the contrary, Greek philosophy is based on the faith that reality is divine, and that the one thing needful is for the soul, which is akin to the divine, to enter into communion with it. It was in truth an effort to satisfy what we call the religious instinct. Ancient religion was a somewhat external thing, and made little appeal to this except in the 'mysteries', and even the mysteries were apt to become external, and were peculiarly liable to corruption. We shall see again and again that philosophy sought to do for men what the mysteries could only do in part, and that it therefore includes most of what we should now call religion.

Nor was this religion a quietist or purely contemplative one, at least in its best days. The mysteries had undertaken to regulate men's lives, and philosophy had to do the same. Almost from the beginning it was regarded as a life. It was no self-centred pursuit of personal holiness either. The man who believed he had seen the vision of reality felt bound to communicate it, sometimes to a circle of disciples, sometimes to the whole human race. The missionary spirit was strong from the first. The philosopher believed that it was only through the knowledge of reality that men could learn their own place in the world, and so fit themselves to be fellow-workers with God, and believing this he could not rest till he had spread the knowledge of it to others. The death of Sokrates was that of a martyr, and 'intellectualism', if there is such a thing, can have no martyrs.

BOOK I

THE WORLD

I

The Ionians

MILETOS

§ 1. Though neither the time nor the *milieu* can explain the rise of so personal a thing as philosophy, they may have considerable influence on the form it assumes. It is not, therefore, without interest to observe that Miletos, 'the pride of Ionia',[1] is just the place where the continuity of prehistoric Aegean civilisation with that of later times is most strongly marked. The Milesians themselves believed their city to be a Cretan colony, and this belief has received remarkable confirmation from recent excavations. We now know that the old town of Miletos belonged to the last period of the Late Minoan civilisation, and that here at least that civilisation passed by imperceptible gradations into what we call the Early Ionic. There is a Milatos in Crete as well as in Ionia, and the name of Thales is at home in the island too.[2] We may perhaps infer that the greatness of Miletos was in some measure due to its inheritance from that earlier age which has so recently become known to us. The Milesians kept in close touch with Egypt and the peoples of Asia Minor, especially the Lydians, and their colonial empire extended to the northern coasts of the Euxine.

§ 2. There is no reason to doubt that Thales was the founder of the Milesian school of cosmologists, and to all appearance he was the first human being who can rightly be called a man of science. The distinction between cosmologies such as the Milesian and cosmogonies such as that of Pherekydes is a fundamental one, and it is far more important to observe the points in which the Milesians differed from their predecessors, whether Greek or barbarian, than to look for survivals of primitive belief in their speculations. No doubt these exist, and there may well have been

---

[1] Herod, v. 28: τῆς Ἰωνίης ἦν πρόσχημα.
[2] See my paper, 'Who was Javan?' (*Proceedings of the Classical Association of Scotland*, 1912, pp. 91 ff.).

more of them than we know; but for all that it is true to say that with Thales and his successors a new thing came into the world.

Of Thales himself we know a great deal less than we should like to know. In popular tradition he lived mainly as one of the 'Seven Wise Men', and many tales were told of him. In one of these he is the type of the unpractical dreamer, and falls into a well while star-gazing; in another he shows himself superior to the ordinary practical man by the use he makes of his scientific knowledge. He is said to have foreseen an abundance of olives and made a corner in oil, thus proving he could be rich if he liked. It is plain that people in general had no idea of his real work, and regarded him simply as a typical 'sage', to whose name anecdotes originally anonymous might be attached. These stories, then, tell us nothing about Thales himself, but they do bear witness to the impression produced by science and scientific men when they first appeared in a world that was half inclined to marvel and half inclined to scoff.

There is, however, another set of traditions about Thales from which something may be learnt. They are not of a popular character, since they attribute to him certain definite scientific achievements. One of the most important of these, the prediction of a solar eclipse, is reported by Herodotus (i. 74). The existence at Miletos of a continuous school of cosmologists makes the preservation of such traditions quite easy to understand. As, however, Thales does not appear to have written anything, it cannot be said that our evidence is complete. What makes strongly in its favour is that the discoveries and other achievements ascribed to him are for the most part just such developments of Egyptian and Babylonian 'science' as we should expect to find. But even if the evidence is considered insufficient, it makes little difference. In that case Thales would become a mere name for us, but it would still be certain that his immediate successors laid the foundations of rational science. There can be no harm, therefore, in mentioning some of these traditions and interpreting them partly in the light of what went before and partly in that of what came after.

§ 3. We learn, then, from Herodotus[1] that the life of Thales belonged to the reigns of Alyattes and Croesus, kings of Lydia, and that he was still living shortly before the fall of Sardeis in 546 B.C. We are also told that at an earlier date he had predicted an eclipse of the sun which put an end to a battle between the Lydians

[1] References to authorities are given in *E. Gr. Ph.*[2] §§ 2–7.

and the Medes. That was on May 28th (O.S.) 585 B.C. Now there is nothing at all incredible in the story of this prediction, though it is quite certain that the true cause of eclipses was not discovered till after the time of Thales, and his successors gave quite erroneous and fantastic accounts of them. The Babylonians, however, were equally ignorant on the subject, and yet they predicted eclipses with tolerable accuracy by means of a cycle of 223 lunations. It is not even necessary to suppose that Thales had to visit Babylon to learn as much as this. In Hittite times Mesopotamian influence had been strong in Asia Minor, and Sardeis has been called an advanced post of Babylonian civilisation. There may well have been 'wise men' in Lydia who had preserved the old secret. It is interesting to note also that the Lydian king seems to have employed the Milesian as his scientific expert; for we are told that Thales accompanied Croesus on the expedition that proved fatal to his monarchy, and that he diverted the course of the river Halys for him. We know, lastly, from Herodotos that he took a prominent part in politics, and that he tried to save Ionia by urging the twelve cities to unite in a federal state with its capital at Teos.

§ 4. We are further told on the authority of Aristotle's disciple Eudemos, who wrote the first history of mathematics, that Thales introduced geometry into Hellas. It is extremely probable that he had learnt in Egypt the elementary rules of mensuration referred to in the *Introduction*; but, if we may trust the tradition, he must have advanced beyond his teachers. He is said to have *taught* the Egyptians how to measure the height of the pyramids by means of their shadows, and also to have invented a method of finding the distance of ships at sea. It was common knowledge among the peoples of the East that a triangle whose sides were as $3:4:5$ had always a right angle, and right angles were laid out by means of this triangle. What we are told of Thales suggests that he invented some further applications of this primitive piece of knowledge, and if so that was the beginning of rational science. At any rate, there is no reason to doubt that he was the pioneer of those investigations which were to bear fruit later in the hands of Pythagoras, though it is hardly safe to say more.

§ 5. According to Aristotle, Thales said that the earth floats on the water, and he doubtless thought of it as a flat disc. That, at least, was the view of all his successors except Anaximander, and it remained characteristic of Ionic as distinct from Italic cosmology down to the time of Demokritos. It sounds primitive enough, but in reality it marks a notable advance. The whole history of cosmology at this date is the story of how the solid earth was gradually loosed from its moorings. Originally sky and earth were pictured as the lid and bottom of a sort of box; but from an early date the Greeks, as was natural for them, began to think of the earth as an island surrounded by the river Okeanos. To regard it as resting on the water is a further step towards a truer view. It was something to get the earth afloat.

This was no doubt connected with what Aristotle regards as the principal tenet of Thales, namely, that everything is made out of water, or, as he puts it in his own terminology, that water is the material cause of all things. We have no trustworthy information about the grounds on which this doctrine was based; for, in the absence of any writings by Thales himself, Aristotle can only guess, and his guesses are apparently suggested by the arguments used in support of a similar theory at a later date. We are perhaps justified in interpreting it rather in the light of the doctrines afterwards held by the Milesian school, and especially by Anaximenes; and, if we try to do this, our attention is at once called to the fact that in these days, and for some time after, 'air' (ἀήρ) was identified with water in a vaporous state. In fact it was regarded as only a purer and more transparent form of mist, while a still purer form was 'aether' (αἰθήρ), which is properly the bright blue of the Mediterranean sky, and is fire rather than air. It was also believed that this fire and that of the heavenly bodies was fed by vapour rising from the sea, a view which, on these presuppositions, is the natural one to take of evaporation. On the other hand, we see that water becomes solid when it freezes, and Anaximenes at least held that earth and stones were water frozen harder still. It may well have seemed to Thales, then, that water was the original thing from which fire on the one hand and earth on the other arose. That, of course, is a more or less conjectural account; but, if Anaximenes was in any sense his follower, the views of Thales must have been something like this. His greatness, however, would lie in his having asked the question rather than in the particular answer he gave it. Henceforth the question whether everything can be regarded as a single reality appearing in different forms is the central one of Greek science, and the story we have to tell is how that in time gave rise to the atomic theory.

§ 6. The next generation of the Milesian school is represented by Anaximander.[1] We are on surer ground with regard to his doctrines; for he wrote a book which was extant in the time of Theophrastos and later. It is probable that it was the first Greek book written in prose, and it may be noted here that Ionic prose was the regular medium of philosophical and scientific writing. Two Greek philosophers, Parmenides and Empedokles, wrote in verse at a later date, but that was quite exceptional, and due to causes we can still to some extent trace. Anaximander was also the first cartographer, and this connects him with his younger fellow-citizen Hekataios, whose work formed, as has been said, the text of Anaximander's map.

Anaximander seems to have thought it unnecessary to fix upon 'air', water, or fire as the original and primary form of body. He preferred to represent that simply as a boundless something (ἄπειρον) from which all things arise and to which they all return again. His reason for looking at it in this way is still in part ascertainable. It is certain that he had been struck by a fact which dominated all subsequent physical theory among the Greeks, namely, that the world presents us with a series of opposites, of which the most primary are hot and cold, wet and dry. If we look at things from this point of view, it is more natural to speak of the opposites as being 'separated out' from a mass which is as yet undifferentiated than to make any one of the opposites the primary substance. Thales, Anaximander seems to have argued, made the wet too important at the expense of the dry. Some such thought, at any rate, appears to underlie the few words of the solitary fragment of his writing that has been preserved. He said that things 'give satisfaction and reparation to one another for their injustice, as is appointed according to the ordering of time'. This conception of justice and injustice recurs more than once in Ionic natural philosophy, and always in the same connexion. It refers to the encroachment of one opposite or 'element' upon another. It is in consequence of this that they are both absorbed once more in their common ground. As that is spatially boundless, it is natural to assume that worlds[2] arise in it elsewhere than with us. Each world

---

[1] References to authorities are given in E. Gr. Ph.[2] §§ 12 sqq.
[2] I do not use the term 'world' for the earth, but as the equivalent of what was called an οὐρανός at this date, and later a κόσμος. It means everything within the heavens of the fixed stars. From our point of view, it is a 'planetary system', though the earth and not the sun is its centre, and the fixed stars are part of it.

is a sort of vortex in the boundless mass. Our authorities attribute
this view to Anaximander, and no good reason has been given for
disbelieving them. It is obviously an idea of the greatest scientific
importance; for it is fatal, not only to the theory of an absolute up
and down in the universe, but also to the view that all heavy things
tend to the same centre. It was, in many ways, a misfortune that
Plato was led to substitute for this old doctrine the belief in a
single world, and thus to prepare the way for the reactionary
cosmology of Aristotle. The Epicureans, who took up the old
Ionic view at a later date, were too unscientific to make good use of
it, and actually combined it with the inconsistent theory of an
absolute up and down. We are told that Anaximander called his
innumerable worlds 'gods'. The meaning of that will appear
shortly.

§ 7. The formation of the world is, of course, due to the
'separating out' of the opposites. Anaximander's view of the earth
is a curious mixture of scientific intuition and primitive theory.
In the first place, he is perfectly clear that it does not rest on anything, but swings free in space, and the reason he gave was that
there is nothing to make it fall in one direction rather than in
another. He inferred this because, as has been observed, his
system was incompatible with the assumption of an absolute up and
down. On the other hand, he gives the earth a shape intermediate
between the disc of Thales and the sphere of the Pythagoreans.
He regarded it as a short cylinder 'like the drum of a pillar', and
supposed that we are living on the upper surface while there is
another antipodal to us. His theory of the heavenly bodies shows
that he was still unable to separate meteorology and astronomy.
So long as all 'the things aloft' (τὰ μετέωρα) are classed together,
that is inevitable. Even Galileo maintained that comets were
atmospheric phenomena, and he had far less excuse for doing so
than Anaximander had for taking the same view of all the heavenly
bodies. Nor was his hypothesis without a certain audacious
grandeur. He supposed that the sun, moon, and stars were really
rings of fire surrounding the earth. We do not see them as rings,
however, because they are encased in 'air' or mist. What we do
see is only the single aperture through which the fire escapes
'as through the nozzle of a pair of bellows'. We note here the
beginning of the theory that the heavenly bodies are carried
round on rings, a theory which held its ground till Eudoxos

replaced the rings by spheres. We are also told that Anaximander
noted the obliquity of these rings to what we should call the
plane of the equator. Eclipses were caused by stoppages of the
apertures.

§ 8. With regard to living beings, Anaximander held that all life
came from the sea, and that the present forms of animals were the
result of adaptation to a fresh environment. It is possible that some
of his biological theories were grotesque in detail, but it is certain
that his method was thoroughly scientific. He was much impressed
by the observation of certain viviparous sharks or dogfish, and
evidently regarded them as an intermediary between fishes and
land animals. His proof that man must have been descended from
an animal of another species has a curiously modern ring. The
young of the human species require a prolonged period of nursing,
while those of other species soon find their food for themselves. If,
then, man had always been as he is now he could never have
survived.

§ 9. The third of the Milesians was Anaximenes, whose activity
seems to fall in the period when Ionia had come under Persian
rule.[1] He too wrote a prose work of which one fragment survives.
He was not a great original genius like Anaximander, and in some
respects his cosmology falls far short of his predecessor's. His title
to remembrance is really based on his discovery of the formula
which for the first time made the Milesian theory coherent, that of
rarefaction and condensation. He regarded 'air' — the air we
breathe, but also that which thickens into mist and water — as the
primary form of body, and so far his theory resembled that we have
ascribed to Thales. On the other hand, he thought of this air as
boundless and as containing an infinite number of worlds, in this
respect following Anaximander. The solitary fragment quoted
from his work shows that he was influenced by the analogy of the
microcosm and the macrocosm. 'As our soul,' he says, 'which is
air, holds us together, so do breath and air encompass the whole
world.' The world is thought of as breathing or inhaling air
from the boundless mass outside it. This Air he spoke of as a
'god'.

The cosmology of Anaximenes was reactionary in many ways.
It was felt, no doubt, that Anaximander had gone too far, though
we shall see that his audacities contained the promise of the future.

[1] References to authorities are given in *E. Gr. Ph.*[2] §§ 23 *sqq.*

According to Anaximenes, the earth is flat and floats upon the air 'like a leaf'. The heavenly bodies also float on the air. Their paths are not oblique, but the earth is tilted up, so that most of them are hidden when they get behind the higher side of it. It is unfortunate that Anaximenes did not know the spherical shape of the earth; for this line of thought might have led him to discover the inclination of its axis. As it was, he regarded it as a disc, and said the heavens surrounded it 'like a hat'. Ionia was never able to accept the scientific view of the earth, and even Demokritos continued to believe it was flat. The suggestive theory of Anaximander was to be developed in another region.

§ 10. It has recently been maintained that the Milesian cosmology was based on the primitive and popular theory of 'the four elements'. It is not meant, of course, that the scientific conception of an 'element' existed at this date. We shall see later that this was due to Empedokles, and it is only the place that the old quaternion of Fire, Air, Earth, and Water occupied in his system, and afterwards in that of Aristotle, that has led to these being called 'the four elements'. It is an unfortunate confusion, but it is very difficult to avoid it, and we must perforce continue to use the word 'element' in two senses which have very little to do with one another. It is undeniable that, from an early date, a fourfold or threefold division of this kind was recognised. It can be traced in Homer and Hesiod, and it has been plausibly suggested that it is connected with the myth of the 'portions' (μοῖραι) assigned to Zeus, Poseidon, and Hades. We are tempted, then, to say that the early cosmologists simply took one of these 'portions' after the other and regarded it as primary. But, when we look closer, we shall be more inclined to conclude that the originality of these men consisted precisely in their ignoring the old popular view completely. In particular, we hear nothing whatever of earth as a primary form of body, though earth is never passed over in any popular list of so-called 'elements'.[1] This is still more striking if we remember the importance of Mother Earth in early cosmogonies, an importance which she still retains in Pherekydes. Here once more the breach between the Milesian cosmology and everything that had gone before is really the striking thing about it.

Indeed, if we take a broad view of it, we shall see that it depends

[1] This is pointed out by Aristotle, *Met.* A, 8. 989 a, 5 *sqq.* Neither he nor Theophrastos made an exception of Xenophanes. Cf. Diels, *Vors.*³ p. 52, 28.

on the extension of the observed identity of ice, water, and steam to earth and stones on the one hand, and to air and fire on the other. In other words, it substitutes for the primitive 'four elements' something which bears a much closer resemblance to what are now called the three states of aggregation, the solid, the liquid, and the gaseous. At any rate, the Milesians believed that what appears in these three forms was one thing, and this, as I hold, they called φύσις.[1] That term meant originally the particular stuff of which a given thing is made. For instance, wooden things have one φύσις, rocks another, flesh and blood a third. The Milesians asked for the φύσις of all things. Thales said it was water, and we cannot be far wrong in guessing that he said so because, as we should put it, the liquid state is intermediate between the solid and the gaseous, and can therefore pass easily into either. Anaximander preferred to leave his Boundless as something distinct from any special form of body, so that the opposites might proceed from it. Anaximenes saw that, after all, the primary substance must have some character of its own, and identified it with 'air', that is, with the intermediate stage between water and fire. This he was able to do because he had introduced the idea of rarefaction and condensation, which alone makes the whole theory intelligible. In a word, the Milesians had drawn the outlines of the theory of matter in the physicist's sense of the word, and these outlines still survive in a recognisable form in our text-books. That, and not the particular astronomical doctrine they taught, is the central thing in the system, and that is why it is reckoned as the beginning of philosophy. It is the earliest answer to the question, 'What is reality?'

The Milesian school doubtless came to an end with the fall of Miletos in 494 B.C., but we shall see later that 'The Philosophy of Anaximenes', as it was called, continued to be taught in other Ionian cities, and that it regained its influence when Ionia was once more freed from a foreign yoke. For the present, however, what we

---

[1] Plato, *Laws*. 891 c: κινδυνεύει γὰρ ὁ λέγων ταῦτα πῦρ καὶ ὕδωρ καὶ γῆν καὶ ἀέρα πρῶτα ἡγεῖσθαι τῶν πάντων εἶναι, καὶ τὴν φύσιν ὀνομάζειν ταῦτα αὐτά. The question really is whether the original meaning of φύσις is 'growth'. Aristotle (*Met.* Δ, 4. 1014 b, 16) did not think so; for he says that, when it means 'growth', it is as if one were to pronounce it with a long υ. In other words, it did not at once suggest to him the verb φύομαι (Aeol. φυίομαι). For controversy on this subject, see Heidel, Περὶ φύσεως (*Proceedings of the American Academy of Arts and Sciences*, xlv. 4), and Lovejoy, 'The Meaning of φύσις in the Greek Physiologers' (*Philosophical Review*, xviii. 4). To my mind the fact that the Atomists called the atoms φύσις is conclusive. See Ar. *Phys.* 265 b, 25; Simpl. *Phys.* p. 1318, 34. Atoms do not 'grow'.

have to consider is the effect on philosophy of the Persian conquest
of the Hellenic cities in Asia.

THE BREAKDOWN OF IONIAN CIVILISATION

§ 11. The spirit of Ionian civilisation had been thoroughly
secular, and this was, no doubt, one of the causes that favoured the
rise of science. The origin of this secular spirit is to be found in the
world described by Homer. The princes and chiefs for whom he
sang must have been completely detached from the religious ideas
which we may infer from the monuments to have been potent
forces in the earlier Aegean civilisation. It cannot be said that the
Olympian gods are regarded with reverence in the *Iliad*, and sometimes they are not treated seriously. They are frankly human,
except that they are immortal and more powerful than men. To
the religious consciousness the word 'god' ($\theta\epsilon\acute{o}s$) always means an
object of worship, and this is just what distinguishes the gods from
other immortal and powerful beings ($\delta\alpha\acute{\iota}\mu\rho\nu\epsilon s$). In Homer, however,
the distinction is obscured. It is by no means clear that all the gods
in the *Iliad* are thought of as objects of worship, and it is only to a
certain number of them that prayers and sacrifices are actually
offered. It is very significant that when Achilles does pray in dead
earnest, it is not to the ruler of Ida or Olympos he turns, but to the
far-off Pelasgic Zeus of Dodona.

The spirit of Hesiod is very different no doubt; for he is no
Ionian, and he feels himself to be in opposition to Homer, but the
influence was too strong for him. He really did even more than
Homer to dissociate the idea of god from that of worship. It is
certain that many of the 'gods' in the *Theogony* were never worshipped by anyone, and some of them are mere personifications of
natural phenomena, or even of human passions. For our present
purpose, it is of most importance to observe that it was just this
non-religious use of the word 'god' which made it possible for the
Milesians to apply it to their primary substance and their 'innumerable worlds'. That way of speaking does not bear witness to
any theological origin of Greek science, but rather to its complete
independence of religious tradition. No one who has once realised
the utterly secular character of Ionian civilisation will ever be
tempted to look for the origins of Greek philosophy in primitive
cosmogonies.

§ 12. The feudal society pictured for us by Homer had been replaced in the Ionic cities by a commercial aristocracy, but the rhapsodes still recited Homer in the market-place, as the bards had done at the feudal prince's board. It was impossible to get away from the humanised Olympian gods, and in practice it was of these that men thought when they worshipped at the shrines founded in earlier days, when the gods were still awful beings to be approached with dread. A people brought up on Homer could hardly think of the gods as moral beings, though they were supposed to be the guardians of morality. Almost the only divine attribute they possessed was power, and even that is retained chiefly as a foil to human impotence, a thing of which the Ionians are deeply conscious. The generations of men pass away like the leaves of the forest, and there is no life to come, or at best a shadowy one, of which the departed 'soul' is itself unconscious. Only so much is left of it as will serve to explain dreams and visions; the man himself is gone for ever when he dies. So it is wise for men to think only mortal thoughts (ἀνθρώπινα φρονεῖν). The mysterious power that awards happiness and misery in this life, and is as often called 'the godhead' (τὸ θεῖον) as God, appears to be jealous of man, and brings low everyone that exalts himself. So we should eat, drink, and be merry, but take heed withal to do 'naught too much' (μηδὲν ἄγαν). The man who observes the precept 'Know thyself' will not be puffed up. For overmuch prosperity (ὄλβος) brings satiety (κόρος), which begets pride (ὕβρις), and that in turn the blindness of heart (ἄτη), which God sends on those he is resolved to ruin. A like doctrine appears in the Hebrew Wisdom literature some generations later.

§ 13. Such a view of life comes naturally to the wealthier classes in an over-civilised nation like the Ionia of the seventh and sixth centuries B.C., but it can bring no satisfaction to the people, which always demands some definite satisfaction for its religious instincts. We can still see clear traces of a very different attitude towards the gods even among the Ionians themselves. The Homeric *Hymn to Apollo* is, no doubt, sufficiently secular in tone, but the sanctuary of Delos still retained some memories of the old Aegean religion. It is not for nothing that the boat, which in prehistoric times had conveyed the 'twice seven' Ionian youths and maidens from Athens to Crete, went to Delos instead in later days, and the legend of the Hyperboreans connected Delos with still more remote and

wonderful regions. It was not, however, in Ionia itself that these
germs were to fructify; for the days of Ionian freedom were almost
at an end, and the citizens of one state after another had to seek
new homes in the far west. A new age had begun in which there
was no room for the light-hearted polytheism of Homer. When
men once more felt a real need of worship, that could not satisfy
them. It is easier to worship a tree or an animal, than a god who is
just a man freed from the restraints that keep ordinary men in
check. That is also why the worship of two agricultural gods, who
are almost unknown to Homer, Demeter and Dionysos, come to be
of such importance at this date. They had not been completely
humanised yet, though we can see the beginnings of the process in
the Homeric Hymns, so it was still possible for men to worship
them sincerely.

RELIGION

§ 14. The cult of Dionysos, in particular, had received a new
impulse from the similar Thracian and Phrygian worships of
Zagreus and Sabazios. The phenomenon of 'ecstasy', which was
prominent in all these, suggested an entirely different view of the
soul and its relation to the body from that we find in Homer, and
this was propagated by the Orphic religion, which we now find
spreading in every direction. It was distinguished from all earlier
Greek religion in two important respects. In the first place, it
appealed to a revelation which had been written down in sacred
books, and in the second place, it was organised in communities
not based on a real or fictitious tie of blood, but open to all who
became initiated and promised to obey the rule. Its teaching was
the exact opposite of the Ionian pessimism, which had widened the
gulf between its humanised gods and man so far that religion in
any real sense had become impossible. The Orphics taught, on the
contrary, that, though men were certainly fallen, they were yet
akin to the gods and might rise again by a system of 'purifications'
(καθαρμοί); they might win 'redemption' (λύσις) from sin and
death, and dwell with the gods for evermore. For the soul of the
Orpic 'saint' (ὅσιος) was immortal; it had existed before his birth,
and would exist after his death. Indeed, these words are improperly
used. What men call life is really death, and the body is the tomb
of the soul (σῶμα σῆμα), which is imprisoned successively in
animal, and even in vegetable bodies, until its final purification

liberates it from the 'wheel of birth'. Those souls, on the other hand, which are incurable (ἀνήκεστοι, ἀνίατοι) are condemned to lie in the 'Slough' (βόρβορος) for ever. The ideas of heaven and hell, salvation and damnation, were a new thing in Greek religion.

The Orphic religion was mainly the faith of obscure people. We do not know the names of its preachers and missionaries, and we only know it to have been a reality from certain gold plates buried with believers in South Italy and Crete. It is true that rulers like Peisistratos took up the religion of Orpheus for political reasons; but, on the whole, it is for us anonymous. That it was apt to degenerate into a mere superstition is natural; for there were no great Orphic teachers, so far as we know, who could have preserved its purity, and it fell an easy prey to charlatans and impostors. We shall see, however, that certain elements, which seemed to have permanent value, were taken up by the philosophers, and so preserved to later ages. In this way Orphicism has profoundly affected all subsequent religions and philosophies, and not least those which seem, at first sight, to be furthest removed from it.

ENLIGHTENMENT

§ 15. It need hardly be said that such ideas were wholly foreign to the enlightened men of the Ionian cities. The saying that 'all things are full of gods' is attributed to Thales, and belongs in any case to this period. The tendency it indicates is what we should call pantheistic, in the sense in which pantheism has been called 'a polite atheism'. This is still plainer in another form of the same saying, which is ascribed to Herakleitos. He asked his visitors to come into the kitchen, saying 'Here too are gods'. But the true spirit of Ionian science is best seen in some of the writings ascribed to Hippokrates, which are certainly not later than the fifth century B.C. In the treatise on *The Sacred Disease* (epilepsy) we read —

> 'I do not think that any disease is more divine or more sacred than others. . . . I think that those who first called this disease sacred were men such as there are still at the present day, magicians and purifiers (καθαρταί) and charlatans and impostors. They make use of the godhead (τὸ θεῖον) to cloak and cover their own incapacity.'

And again in the treatise on *Airs, Waters and Sites* —

> 'Nothing is more divine or more human than anything else, but all things are alike and all divine.'

That is the true note of 'enlightenment', and it was the note of all the Ionian schools. It is most strongly marked in an elegiac and satirical poet, who approached the question from the standpoint of the reformer rather than of the scientific investigator. I refer to Xenophanes, who is often regarded as the founder of the Eleatic school, a point we shall return to later. In any case, chronological and other considerations make it most instructive to take him up at this point in our story.

§ 16. It is difficult to determine the dates of Xenophanes' life with any accuracy; for those given by ancient authorities have been arrived at by a mere process of combination.[1] The facts of his life are also obscure. There is not the slightest evidence that he was a rhapsode, and it is most improbable. He may have visited Elea as well as other places, but no ancient authority states unambiguously that he did. He was certainly a citizen of Kolophon, and we know from his own statement that he had lived in exile from the age of twenty-five, and that he was still writing poetry when he was ninety-two. There is no doubt that he lived chiefly in Sicily, and it is practically certain that he was at the court of Hiero of Syracuse, who reigned from 478 to 467 B.C. He is also said to have been a disciple of Anaximander, and there are features in his poetry which make this probable. On the whole, it is safe to say that Xenophanes belongs mainly to the sixth century B.C., though he lived well into the fifth. Herakleitos already speaks of him in the past tense, and couples his name with that of Hekataios.

§ 17. If we look at the very considerable remains of his poetry that have come down to us, we shall see that they are all in the satirist's and social reformer's vein. There is one dealing with the management of a feast, another which denounces the exaggerated importance attached to athletic victories, and several which attack the humanised gods of Homer.[2] The problem is, therefore, to find, if we can, a single point of view from which all these fragments can be interpreted. It may be that no such point of view exists; but, if one can be found, it is likely that we shall understand Xenophanes better. Now we know that a great change came over Hellenic life at the end of the sixth century B.C. It was a reaction against the somewhat effeminate refinement and daintiness (ἀβρότης) of Ionia, which had its source in the court of Sardeis and

---

[1] References to authorities are given in E. Gr. Ph.² §§ 55 sqq.
[2] For a translation of the fragments, see E. Gr. Ph.² § 57.

had spread with Ionian colonisation even to the far West. It had reached its highest point at the court of Polykrates of Samos, and its singers were Mimnermos of Kolophon and Anakreon of Teos. It was not coarse and brutal like the luxury of later days, but there was an element of decadence in it. It was characterised at once by pessimism and frivolity. The change came when 'the Mede appeared' (Xenophanes, fr. 22), and the Ionians had no longer to do with half-Hellenised Lydians, but with a sterner foe. They then began to feel the gulf that divided the Hellene from the 'barbarian', and to accentuate the differences between them more and more. The general use of the name 'Hellenes' dates only from this time. Thucydides (i. 6) notes the change in dress which marked the new spirit, and his statement is confirmed by vase-paintings.[1] In architecture the Doric style supersedes the Ionic. Everywhere we note a return to a simpler and more virile way of life. It seems to me that Xenophanes is best understood as a pioneer of this movement.[2]

§ 18. The religious reformers of the day turned their back on the anthropomorphic polytheism of Homer and Hesiod, and Xenophanes will have none of it either. In his case, however, this revolt is based on a conviction that the tales of the poets are directly responsible for the moral corruption of the time. 'Homer and Hesiod have ascribed to the gods all things that are a shame and a disgrace among mortals, stealings and adulteries and deceiving of one another' (fr. 11). And this he held was due to the representation of the gods in human form. Men make gods in their own image; those of the Ethiopians are black and snub-nosed, those of the Thracians have blue eyes and red hair (fr. 16). If horses or oxen or lions had hands and could produce works of art, they too would represent the gods after their own fashion (fr. 15). All that must be swept away along with the tales of Titans and Giants, those 'figments of an earlier day' (fr. 1) if social life is to be reformed.

Xenophanes found the weapons he required for his attack on polytheism in the science of the time. There are traces of Anaximander's cosmology in the fragments, and Xenophanes may easily have been his disciple before he left Ionia. He seems to have taken the gods of mythology one by one and reduced them to meteorological phenomena, and especially to clouds. And he maintained

[1] See Pernice in Gercke and Norden's *Einleitung*, vol. ii. pp. 39–44.
[2] See especially fr. 3.

there was only one god — namely, the world. That is not mono-theism, as it has been called, but pantheism. It is a simple repro-duction of that special use of the term 'god' we have seen to be characteristic of the early cosmologists generally. There is no evidence that Xenophanes regarded this 'god' with any religious feeling, and all we are told about him (or rather about it) is purely negative. He is quite unlike a man, and has no special organs of sense, but 'sees all over, thinks all over, hears all over' (fr. 24). Further, he does not go about from place to place (fr. 26), but does everything 'without toil' (fr. 25). It is not safe to go beyond this; for Xenophanes himself tells us no more. It is pretty certain that if he had said anything more positive or more definitely religious in its bearing it would have been quoted by later writers.

§ 19. But while Xenophanes makes use of contemporary science to overthrow the Olympian hierarchy, it is plain that he was not himself a scientific man. In spite of Anaximander, he still believes in a flat earth extending to infinity in all directions, and boundless in depth also. Consequently it is a different sun that traverses our heaven every day. The same must apply to the moon, which he further held to be superfluous. Both sun and moon are ignited clouds. The stars, too, are clouds that go out in the day time, but glow at night like charcoal embers. That is not science as science was understood at Meletos, and it seems that Xenophanes merely made use of cosmological ideas for his own purposes. Any stick was good enough to beat the gods of Homer and Hesiod with. He says distinctly that the accounts he gives of the gods are 'guesses like the truth' (fr. 34), and he denies the possibility of certain knowledge in this field — 'Even if a man should chance to say the complete truth, he cannot know that it is the truth' (fr. 34). In all this Xenophanes is the precursor of another philosophy that came from Ionia at a later date, that of Epicurus. The difference is mainly that it was less of an anachronism in the fifth century B.C. than it was two hundred years later.

In this chapter we have seen how the traditional view of the world broke down, and how its place was taken by Orphic mysti-cism on the one hand and by enlightened scepticism on the other. Neither of these contained in itself the promise of the future. That lay in the work of the man who first united science with religion, Pythagoras of Samos.

II

Pythagoras

THE PROBLEM

§ 20. Pythagoras must have been one of the world's greatest men, but he wrote nothing, and it is hard to say how much of the doctrine we know as Pythagorean is due to the founder of the society and how much is later development.[1] We have met the same difficulty in the case of Thales, and we shall meet it again when we come to Sokrates. One general remark may be made about it at once. So far as we know, all great advances in human knowledge have been due to individuals rather than to the collective work of a school, and so it is better to take the risk of ascribing a little too much to the founder than to lose sight of him among a crowd of disciples. On the other hand, it is certain that some Pythagorean doctrines at least belong to a later generation, and it will be well to reserve these for a future chapter. Such a division is inevitable if we are to give an intelligible account of Pythagoreanism, but it must be remembered that it is often quite uncertain whether a particular doctrine belongs to the earlier period or to the later.

§ 21. It is also hard to say how much of what we are told about the life of Pythagoras is trustworthy; for a mass of legend gathered round his name at an early date. Sometimes he is represented as a man of science, and sometimes as a preacher of mystic doctrines, and we might be tempted to regard one or other of those characters as alone historical. It is quite possible to picture Pythagoras as a mere medicine-man, and to treat all Pythagorean science as the work of his successors. It is also possible to rationalise the story of his life and represent him mainly as a mathematician and statesman. In that case we have to regard the miraculous tales told of him as due to the Neopythagoreans of the early centuries of our era. There

---

[1] Aristotle never attributes any doctrine to Pythagoras himself. He generally speaks of 'the so-called Pythagoreans', and, often, still more cautiously, of 'some of the Pythagoreans'. References to authorities are given in *E. Gr. Ph.*² §§ 37 *sqq.*

is a serious difficulty here, however; for many of these wonders
were already known to Aristotle. It is equally difficult to reject the
tradition that makes Pythagoras the true founder of mathematical
science; for that science was certainly in existence by the middle of
the fifth century B.C., and it must have been the work of someone.
If the credit is really due to another than Pythagoras, it is strange
that his name should have been forgotten. Further, Herakleitos in
the next generation tells us that Pythagoras practised inquiry
(ἱστορίη) beyond all other men, and he thinks the worse of him for
it. That is practically contemporary evidence, and it can only
mean that Pythagoras was famous as a man of science. The truth
is that there is no need to reject either of the traditional views. The
union of mathematical genius and mysticism is common enough.
It was also characteristic of the seventeenth century, which took
up once more the thread of Greek science. Kepler was led to discover the laws of planetary motion by his belief in the 'harmony of
the spheres' and in planetary souls.

LIFE AND DOCTRINE

§ 22. Pythagoras was a Samian, and, as we are told, he migrated
to Italy because he disliked the rule of Polykrates. That is why his
floruit is given as 532 B.C., the year Polykrates became tyrant. No
actual dates are known, but it is safe to say that his activity belongs
mainly to the last quarter of the sixth century B.C. When he left
Samos, he founded at Kroton in southern Italy a society which was
at once a religious community and a scientific school. Such a body
was bound to excite jealousy and mistrust, and we hear of many
struggles. Pythagoras himself had to flee from Kroton to Metapontion, where he died. The chief opponent of Pythagoreanism,
Kylon, is expressly said to have been rich and noble, and there is
no evidence for the belief that Pythagoras and his followers took
the aristocratic side. That notion was based on the fancy that they
represented 'the Dorian ideal'. It is far from clear what is meant by
the Dorian ideal; but in any case Pythagoras himself was an Ionian,
and his society was established in Achaian, not Dorian, colonies.
It is also certain that the earlier Pythagoreans used the Ionic dialect.[1]

[1] It has been said that the name Pythagoras is Dorian in form. Herodotos and
Herakleitos and Demokritos call him 'Pythagores', and so no doubt he called
himself. The form 'Pythagoras' is no more Doric than 'Anaxagoras'. It is simply
Attic.

After the death of the Master, the disturbances went on more than ever, and soon after the middle of the fifth century there was a regular rising, in the course of which the Pythagorean lodges (συνέδρια) were burnt down, and many of the brethren lost their lives. Those who survived took refuge at Thebes and elsewhere, and we shall hear more of them later.

Being 'a Samian, Pythagoras would naturally be influenced by the cosmology of the neighbouring Miletos. It is stated that he was a disciple of Anaximander, which is no doubt a guess, but probably right. At any rate his astronomy was the natural development of Anaximander's theory of planetary rings, though it went far beyond that. The importance of the infinite (τὸ ἄπειρον) in the Pythagorean cosmology suggests Milesian influence, and the identification of the infinite with 'air' by at least some Pythagoreans points to a connexion with the doctrines of Anaximenes. The way in which the Pythagorean geometry developed also bears witness to its descent from that of Miletos. The great problem at this date was the duplication of the square, a problem which gave rise to the theorem of the square on the hypotenuse, commonly known still as the Pythagorean proposition (Euclid, I. 47). If we were right in assuming that Thales worked with the old 3 : 4 : 5 triangle, the connexion is obvious, and the very name 'hypotenuse' bears witness to it; for that word means the rope or cord 'stretching over against' the right angle, or, as we say, 'subtending' it.

§ 23. But this was not the only influence that affected Pythagoras in his earlier days. He is said to have been a disciple of Pherekydes as well as of Anaximander, and the mystical element in his teaching is thus accounted for. In any case, as has been indicated already, the religion of the Delian and Hyperborean Apollo had a mystical side. The legends of Abaris and Aristeas of Prokonnesos are enough to show that. There are several points of contact between this form of mysticism (which seems to be independent of the Dionysiac) and Crete. We have seen that the boat containing the seven youths and seven maidens went to Delos in historical times, though tradition remembered its original destination was Crete, and Epimenides, the great purifier, was a Cretan. There are many things, in fact, which suggest that this form of mysticism had survived from 'Minoan' times, and it is therefore quite unnecessary to seek its origin in Egypt or India. It is highly probable, then, that Pythagoras brought his ascetic practices and mystical beliefs about

PYTHAGORAS

the soul from his Ionian home, and there was a statue of Aristeas
of Prokonnesos at Metapontion, where Pythagoras died. This does
not, of course, exclude the possibility that the religion of the
Pythagoreans was also influenced by contemporary Orphicism; it
is only meant that they derived it from a genuinely Ionic source,
and that Apollo, not Dionysos, was their special god.

§ 24. Now one of the leading ideas of the Apollonian religion
which had its centre at Delos in historical times was purification
(κάθαρσις),[1] and that held an important place in the teaching of
Pythagoras. The longing for purity is something very deeply rooted
in human nature, and Catharism is always reappearing in new
forms. Of course we may mean very different things by purity. It
may be merely external, and in that case it can easily be secured by
the strict observance of certain abstinences and taboos. That these
were observed in the Pythagorean society is certain, and it is quite
likely that many members of it got no further. It is certain, however, that the leading men of the order did. There was an important
medical school at Kroton even before Pythagoras went there, and
it appears that the old religious idea of purification was early regarded in the light of the medical practice of purgation. At any
rate, Aristoxenos, who was personally acquainted with the Pythagoreans of his time, tells us that they used medicine to purge the
body and music to purge the soul. That already connects the
scientific studies of the school with its religious doctrine, since
there is no doubt that we owe the beginnings of scientific thera-
peutics and harmonics to the Pythagoreans. But that is not all. In
the *Phaedo* Sokrates quotes a saying that 'philosophy is the highest
music', which seems to be Pythagorean in origin. The purgative
function of music was fully recognised in the psychotherapy of
these days. It originated in the practice of the Korybantic priests,
who treated nervous and hysterical patients by wild pipe music,
thus exciting them to the pitch of exhaustion, which was followed
in turn by a healthy sleep from which the patient awoke cured. An
interesting light is thrown on this by what was known as 'Tarantism'
in later days.[2] Taking all these things together, there is much to be
said for the view that the originality of Pythagoras consisted in this,
that he regarded scientific, and especially mathematical, study as
the best purge for the soul. That is the theory of the early part of

---

[1] Farnell, *Cults of the Greek States*, vol. iv. pp. 295 *sqq.*
[2] See *Enc. Brit.* (11th edition) *s.v.* 'Tarantula.'

Plato's *Phaedo*, which is mainly a statement of Pythagorean doctrine, and it frequently recurs in the history of Greek philosophy. It may be added that tradition represents the word 'philosophy' as having been first used by Pythagoras. If that is so (and there is much to be said for the tradition), we need not hesitate to ascribe to him the saying mentioned in the *Phaedo* that philosophy is the 'highest music', and so, since music was certainly regarded as a soul-purge, we come to the same result in another way. We still speak of 'pure mathematics',[1] and that way of speaking has given rise in turn to the phrase 'pure scholarship'.

§ 25. Closely connected with this is the doctrine of the Three Lives, the Theoretic, the Practical, and the Apolaustic, which is probably to be referred to the founder of the society. There are three kinds of men, just as there are three classes of strangers who come to the Olympic Games. The lowest consists of those who come to buy and sell, and next above them are those who come to compete. Best of all are those who simply come to look on (θεωρεῖν). Men may be classified accordingly as lovers of wisdom (φιλόσοφοι), lovers of honour (φιλότιμοι), and lovers of gain (φιλοκερδεῖς). That seems to imply the doctrine of the tripartite soul, which is also attributed to the early Pythagoreans on good authority,[2] though it is common now to ascribe it to Plato. There are, however, clear references to it before his time, and it agrees much better with the general outlook of the Pythagoreans. The comparison of human life to a gathering (πανήγυρις) like the Games was often repeated in later days,[3] and is the ultimate source of Bunyan's 'Vanity Fair'. The view that the soul is a stranger and a sojourner in this life was also destined to influence European thought profoundly.

§ 26. There can be no doubt that Pythagoras taught the doctrine of Rebirth or transmigration,[4] which he may have learned from the contemporary Orphics. Xenophanes made fun of him for pretending to recognise the voice of a departed friend in the howls of a beaten dog (fr. 7). Empedokles seems to be referring to him when he speaks (fr. 129) of a man who could remember what happened ten or twenty generations before. It was on this that the doctrine

---

[1] Cp. the use of καθαρῶς γνῶναι, εἰδέναι, etc., in the *Phaedo*, 65 e, 66 d, e.

[2] The authority is Poseidonios. See my edition of the *Phaedo*, 68 c, 2, *note*.

[3] Cp. Menander, fr. 481 Kock (Pickard-Cambridge, p. 141. No. 68), Epictetus, ii. 14, 23.

[4] The word *metempsychosis* is not used by good writers, and is inaccurate; for it would mean that different souls entered into the same body. The older word is παλιγγενεσία, being 'born again'. See *E. Gr. Ph.*[2] p. 101, *n*. 2.

of Reminiscence, which plays so great a part in Plato's *Meno* and *Phaedo*, was based.[1] The things we perceive with the senses, we are told, *remind* us of things we knew when the soul was out of the body and could perceive reality directly. We have never seen equal sticks or stones, but we know what equality is, and it is just by comparing the things of sense with the realities of which they remind us that we judge them to be imperfect. I see no difficulty in referring this doctrine in its mathematical application to Pythagoras himself. It must have struck him that the realities he was dealing with were not perceived by the senses, and the doctrine of Reminiscence follows easily from that of Rebirth.

§ 27. As has been indicated, there is more difficulty about the cosmology of Pythagoras. Hardly any school ever professed such reverence for its founder's authority as the Pythagorean. ('The Master said so' (αὐτὸς ἔφα, *ipse dixit*) was their watchword. On the other hand, few schools have shown so much capacity for progress and for adapting themselves to new conditions. The contradiction here is doubtless more apparent than real, but it creates a difficulty for the historian, and we can hardly ever feel sure to what stage of development any given statement about Pythagoreanism refers. One thing, however, we can see distinctly. There is a form of the doctrine that precedes the rise of the Eleatic philosophy, and there is a form that is subsequent to it. We shall do well, therefore, to reserve for the present all doctrines which seem to imply the Eleatic criticism. That is really the only criterion we can apply.

§ 28. We can make out pretty clearly to begin with that Pythagoras started from the cosmical system of Anaximenes. Aristotle tells us that the Pythagoreans represented the world as inhaling 'air' from the boundless mass outside it, and this 'air' is identified with 'the unlimited'. On the other hand, Pythagoras seems to have learnt from Anaximander that the earth is not a flat disc. He still, in all probability, thought of it as the centre of the world, though his followers held otherwise at a later date, but he could no longer regard it as cylindrical. As soon as the cause of eclipses came to be understood, it was natural to infer that the earth was a sphere, and we may probably attribute that discovery to Pythagoras himself. With this exception, his general view of the world seems to have been distinctly Milesian in character.

[1] See my edition of the *Phaedo*, 72 e, 4 *note*.

When, however, we come to the process by which things are developed out of the 'unlimited', we observe a great change. We hear nothing more of 'separating out' or even of rarefaction and condensation. Instead of that we have the theory that what gives form to the Unlimited (ἄπειρον) is the Limit (πέρας). That is the great contribution of Pythagoras to philosophy, and we must try to understand it. We have seen that the Milesians had reached the conception of what we call 'matter'; it was the work of the Pythagoreans to supplement this by the correlative conception of 'form'. As this is one of the central problems of Greek philosophy, it is very important for us to ascertain if we can what was originally meant by the doctrine of the Limit.

Now the function of the Limit is usually illustrated from the arts of music and medicine, and we have seen how important these two arts were for the Pythagoreans, so it is natural to infer that the key to its meaning is to be found in them. Let us see, then, what can be safely affirmed with regard to early Pythagorean musical and medical theory. The doctrines described in the following paragraphs are all genuinely Pythagorean, but it will be remembered that our ascription of any particular statement to Pythagoras himself is conjectural. We cannot tell either whether music or medicine came first, or, in other words, whether the purge of the body was explained by the purge of the soul, or *vice versa*. It will, however, be convenient to begin with music.

MUSIC

§ 29. In the first place, it may be taken as certain that Pythagoras himself discovered the numerical ratios which determine the concordant intervals of the scale. Of course, when the Greeks called certain intervals concordant (σύμφωνα) they were thinking primarily of notes sounded in succession and not simultaneously. In other words, the term refers to melodic progressions, and not to what we call harmonious chords. The principle is ultimately the same, indeed, but it is often of importance to remember that there was no such thing as harmony in classical Greek music, and that the word 'harmony' (ἁρμονία) means in the Greek language, first 'tuning', and then 'scale'.

In the time of Pythagoras the lyre had seven strings, and it is not improbable that the eighth was added later as the result of his discoveries. All the strings were of equal length, and were tuned to the required pitch by tension and relaxation (ἐπίτασις, ἄνεσις). This was done entirely by ear, and the first thing was to make the two outside strings (*hypatē* and *nētē*)[1] concordant, in the sense explained, with one another, with the middle string (*mesē*), and with the string just above it (*tritē*, later *paramesē*). The notes (φθόγγοι) of these four strings were called 'stationary' (ἑστῶτες), and were similarly related to one another in every kind of scale; the notes of the other three (or four in the eight-stringed lyre) were 'movable' (κινούμενοι), and scales were distinguished as enharmonic, chromatic, and diatonic (with their varieties), according as these strings were tuned more or less closely to the same pitch as the nearest fixed notes. They might differ from these in pitch by as little as what we call a quarter-tone, or as much as what we call a double tone. It is obvious that none of our scales could be played on a seven-stringed lyre at all; an eight-stringed lyre, tuned to the diatonic scale, is required for them. Even in that scale, however, the Greeks did not recognise the interval we call the third as concordant.[2]

§ 30. It is quite probable that Pythagoras knew the pitch of notes to depend on the rate of vibrations which communicate 'beats' or pulsations (πληγαί) to the air. At any rate, that was quite familiar to his successors; but neither he nor they had any means of measuring the rate of vibrations. As, however, the rate of vibration of two similar strings is inversely proportional to their length, it was possible for him to transform the problem and attack it on that side. The lyre did not immediately suggest this; for its strings were of equal length, but a few experiments with strings of unequal length would establish the truth. Pythagoras doubtless used a simple apparatus, consisting of a string which could be stopped at different intervals by a movable bridge (the *monochord*), and in this way reduced the experiment to a simple comparison of lengths on a single string. The result was to show that the concordant intervals of the scale could be expressed by the simple numerical ratios 2 : 1, 3 : 2, and 4 : 3, or, taking the lowest whole numbers

[1] Observe that the terms ὑπάτη and νήτη do not refer to pitch. As a matter of fact, the ὑπάτη gave the lowest note and the νήτη the highest. The terms for 'high' and 'low' are ὀξύς (*acutus*, 'sharp'), and βαρύς (*gravis*).

[2] An elementary knowledge of the Greek lyre is essential for the understanding of Greek philosophy. A useful introduction to the subject will be found in the articles (by D. B. Monro) *Lyra* and *Musica* in Smith's *Dictionary of Antiquities*.

which have these ratios to one another, that the four stationary notes of the lyre could be expressed thus:

$$6 \qquad 8 \qquad 9 \qquad 12$$

For convenience let us represent these four notes by those of the gamut in descending order:

Nētē	*Paramesē*	*Mesē*	*Hypatē*
Mi	Si	La	Mi,

and we may explain the discovery of Pythagoras as follows:

(1) When he took a length of string double that which gave the high Mi, it gave the low Mi. That is the interval which we call the octave and the Greeks called *diapāsōn* (διὰ πασῶν, sc. χορδῶν). It is expressed by the ratio 2 : 1 (διπλάσιος λόγος).

(2) When he took a length of string half as long again as that which gave the high Mi, it gave La. That is the interval which we call the fifth and the Greeks called *dia pente* (διὰ πέντε, sc. χορδῶν). It is expressed by the ratio 3 : 2 (ἡμιόλιος λόγος).

(3) When he took a length of string one-third again as long as that which gave the high Mi, it gave Si. That is the interval which we call the fourth and the Greeks called *diatessaron* (διὰ τεσσάρων, sc. χορδῶν). It is expressed by the ratio 4 : 3 (ἐπίτριτος λόγος).

(4) The compass (μέγεθος) of the octave is a fifth and a fourth ($\frac{3}{2} \times \frac{4}{3} = \frac{12}{6}$), and the note which is a fifth from the *nētē* is a fourth from the *hypatē*, and *vice versa*.

(5) The interval between the fourth and the fifth is expressed by the ratio 9 : 8 (ἐπόγδοος λόγος). This is called the 'tone' (τόνος) or pitch *par excellence* (probably from its importance in attuning the two tetrachords to one another).

(6) As there is no (numerical) mean proportional between 1 and 2, neither the octave nor the tone can be divided into equal parts.

There is good reason for holding that Pythagoras did not go any further than this, and that no attempt was made to determine the ratios between the 'movable' notes of the tetrachord till the days of Archytas and Plato. It is by no means clear, in fact, that there was any strict rule with regard to these at this date.[1] Aristoxenos tells us that the diagrams of the older musical theorists all referred to the enharmonic scale, which proceeded by what he called quarter-tones and a double tone; but Pythagoras could not admit the possibility of quarter-tones, since the tone did not admit of equal division. The internal notes of the tetrachord must, then, have

---

[1] See Tannery, 'À propos des fragments philolaïques sur la musique' (*Rev. de philologie*, 1904, pp. 233 *sqq.*).

been regarded as of the nature of the 'unlimited', and the 'limit' was represented only by the perfect concords.

§ 31. Now if we look at the four terms ($ὅροι$) which we have discovered, we shall find that 8 and 9 are related to the extremes 6 and 12 as means. The term 9, which represents the note of the *mesē*, exceeds and is exceeded by the same number, namely 3. It is what is called the arithmetical mean ($ἀριθμητικὴ\ μεσότης$). On the other hand, the term 8, which represents the note of the *paramesē*, exceeds and is exceeded by the same fraction of the extremes; for $8 = 12 - \frac{12}{3} = 6 + \frac{6}{3}$. This was called the subcontrary ($ὑπεναντία$), or later, for obvious reasons, the harmonic mean ($ἁρμονικὴ\ μεσότης$). The geometrical mean is not to be found within the compass of a single octave.

Now this discovery of the Mean at once suggests a new solution of the old Milesian problem of opposites. We know that Anaximander regarded the encroachment of one opposite on the other as an 'injustice', and he must therefore have held there was a point which was fair to both. That, however, he had no means of determining. The discovery of the Mean suggests that it is to be found in a 'blend' ($κρᾶσις$) of the opposites, which might be numerically determined, just as that of the high and low notes of the octave had been. The convivial customs of the Greeks made such an idea natural to them. The master of the feast used to prescribe the proportions of wine and water to be poured into the mixing-bowl before it was served out to the guests. That is why the Demiourgos in Plato's *Timaeus* uses a mixing-bowl ($κρατήρ$). It may well have seemed that, if Pythagoras could discover the rule for blending such apparently elusive things as high and low notes, the secret of the world had been found.

§ 32. There remains one point of which the full significance will not appear till later, but which must be mentioned here. It is plain that the octachord scale could be increased by the addition of one or more tetrachords at either end, and that it would therefore be possible to obtain octave scales in which the smaller and larger intervals[1] occurred in a different order. We can get some rough idea of this by playing scales on the white notes of the piano alone. It is fortunately unnecessary for our present purpose to discuss the

---

[1] The example given by Aristoxenos is taken from the enharmonic tetrachord in which, according to his terminology, we may have (1) ¼ tone, ¼ tone, ditone, (2) ¼ tone, ditone, ¼ tone, or (3) ditone, ¼ tone, ¼ tone.

relation of these 'figures of the octave' (εἴδη τοῦ διὰ πασῶν), as they were called, to the 'modes' (ἁρμονίαι, τρόποι) of which we hear so much in Greek writers; for it cannot be said that this problem has been satisfactorily solved yet.[1] All that is important for us is that these scales were called 'figures' (εἴδη) just because they varied in the arrangement of their parts. We have the authority of Aristoxenos for that,[2] and we shall see that it is a matter of fundamental importance.

MEDICINE

§ 33. In Medicine we have also to do with 'opposites', such as the hot and the cold, the wet and the dry, and it is the business of the physician to produce a proper 'blend' (κρᾶσις) of these in the human body. In a well-known passage of Plato's *Phaedo* (86 b) we are told by Simmias that the Pythagoreans held the body to be strung like an instrument to a certain pitch, hot and cold, wet and dry taking the place of high and low in music. According to this view, health is just being in tune, and disease arises from undue tension or relaxation of the strings. We still speak of 'tonics' in medicine as well as in music. Now the medical school of Kroton, which is represented for us by Alkmaion, based its theory on a very similar doctrine. According to him, health depended on the 'isonomy' (ἰσονομίη) of the opposites in the body, and disease was just the undue predominance of one or the other. We need not be surprised, then, to find that Alkmaion was intimately associated with the Pythagoreans, and that he dedicated his medical treatise to some of the leading members of the society. Health, in fact, was an 'attunement' (ἁρμονία) depending on a due blend of opposites, and the same account was given of many other things with which the physician is concerned, notably of diet and climate. The word 'blend' (κρᾶσις) itself was used both of bodily *temperament*, as we still call it, and of the *temperature* which distinguished one climate from another. When we speak of 'temperance' in eating and drinking, we are equally on Pythagorean ground.

Now we find the word we have translated 'figure' (εἶδος) used more than once in the literature of the fifth century B.C. in con-

---

[1] See Monro, *Modes of Ancient Greek Music* (1894); Macran, *The Harmonics of Aristoxenus* (1902); J. D. Dennistoun, 'Some Recent Theories of the Greek Modes' (*Classical Quarterly*, vii. (1913), pp. 83 sqq.).

[2] Aristoxenos, *El. Harm.* iii. 74, is quite clear that εἴδη here means 'figures', διαφέρει δ᾽ ἡμῖν οὐδὲν εἶδος λέγειν ἢ σχῆμα· φέρομεν γὰρ ἀμφότερα τὰ ὀνόματα ἐπὶ τὸ αὐτό.

nexion with disease and death, and, as has been pointed out,[1] it occurs in many places in close connexion with a verb (καθίστασθαι) which has also a technical sense in ancient medicine. The same verb (and its substantive κατάστασις) is also applied to the individual *constitution* of a given body. It is surely natural to interpret these uses of the word in the light of the 'figures of the octave' explained above. The opposites on which health and disease depend may combine in various *patterns*, as it were, and such variation of pattern is also the explanation of the differences between the constitutions (καταστάσεις) of individual patients.

NUMBERS

§ 34. Having discovered that tuning and health were alike *means* arising from the application of Limit to the Unlimited, and that this resulted in the formation of certain 'figures' (εἴδη), it was natural for Pythagoras to look for something of the same kind in the world at large. The Milesians had taught that all things issued from the Boundless or Unlimited, though they had given different accounts of this. Anaximenes had identified it with 'air', and had explained the forms this took by rarefaction and condensation. He was thinking chiefly of 'air' as a form of mist. Pythagoras would seem to have regarded it mainly from another point of view; for the Pythagoreans, or some of them, certainly identified 'air' with the void. This is the beginning, but no more than the beginning, of the conception of abstract space or extension, and what chiefly interested Pythagoras, so far as we can see, was the problem of how it became limited so as to present the appearance of the world we know.

There is a striking confirmation of this in the Second Part of the poem of Parmenides, if, as we shall see reason for believing, that is a sketch of Pythagorean cosmology. There the two 'forms' (μορφαί), which men have erroneously assumed are Light and Darkness. Darkness was still regarded in these days as a thing, not as a mere privation of light, and 'air' was very closely associated with it. In Plato's *Timaeus* (58 d) we have what is no doubt the traditional Pythagorean view, that mist and darkness were alike forms of 'air'. Now Light and Darkness are included in the famous Pythagorean

---

[1] See A. E. Taylor, *Varia Socratica* (St. Andrews University Publications, No. ix), p. 189. Professor Taylor has not cited the εἴδη τοῦ διὰ πασῶν in confirmation of his view, but it seems to me important, seeing that we have the express authority of Aristoxenos for εἶδος = σχῆμα in that case.

table of 'opposites', where they come under the head of Limit and the Unlimited respectively.

§ 35. Briefly stated, the doctrine of Pythagoras was that all things are numbers, and it is impossible for us to attach any meaning to this statement unless we have a clear idea of what he is likely to have meant by a 'number'. Now we know for certain that, in certain fundamental cases, the early Pythagoreans represented numbers and explained their properties by means of dots arranged in certain 'figures' (εἴδη, σχήματα) or patterns. That is, no doubt, very primitive; for the practice is universal on dice and such things from the earliest times. The most celebrated of these Pythagorean figures was the *tetraktys*,[1] by which the members of the Order used to swear. This showed at a glance what the Pythagoreans conceived to be the most important property of the number ten — namely, that it is the sum of the first four natural integers $(1+2+3+4=10)$, thus —

It is obvious that this figure could be extended indefinitely, and that it takes the place of a formula for the sums of the series of successive natural integers, 3, 6, 10, 15, 21, and so on. These, therefore, were called 'triangular numbers'.

We hear in the next place of square (τετράγωνοι) and oblong (ἑτερομήκεις) numbers. A square number meant (as it still does) a number which is the product of equal factors, an oblong number, one which is the product of unequal factors. These may be presented thus —

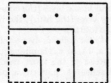 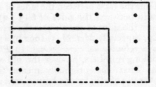

We see at once from these figures that the addition of successive odd numbers in the form of a *gnomon* produces square numbers

[1] For the form of this word cp. τρικτύς (Att. τριττύς). The forms τρικτύαρχος and τρικτυαρχεῖν occur in Delian inscriptions (Dittenberger, *Sylloge*[2], 588,19 *sqq.*).

(4, 9, 16, etc.), while the addition of successive even numbers produces oblong numbers (6, 12, 20, etc.). We might go on in the same way to study the properties of cubic numbers, but we cannot tell how far Pythagoras had advanced in this direction. The important thing to notice is that all these figures express the sums of series of different kinds. The series of integers yields triangular numbers, that of odd numbers yields square numbers, and that of even numbers yields oblong numbers. Aristotle notes further that the form (εἶδος) of the square numbers is always the same; it is the ratio 1 : 1. On the other hand, each successive oblong number has a different form (εἶδος). These correspond exactly to the concordant intervals of the octave.[1]

Our knowledge of these things comes chiefly from Neopythagorean writers, who regarded the 'figures' as more 'natural' than the ordinary notation by letters of the alphabet, but they certainly were known to Aristotle,[2] and we need have no hesitation in referring them to the very beginnings of Pythagorean science. In spite of the introduction of the Arabic (or rather Hindu) system, 'figurate numbers', as they were called, survived the Middle Ages, and the term is still used, though in a more restricted sense. It is not a little remarkable that the English language has retained the name 'figures', though it is now applied to the 'Arabic' notation.[3] In other languages the Arabic ṣifr has been adopted.

§ 36. This way of representing numbers by 'figures' would naturally lead up to problems of a geometrical nature. The dots which stood for the units were regularly called 'terms' (ὅροι, termini, 'boundary stones'), and the spaces marked out by them were called 'fields' (χῶραι). The question would naturally arise, 'How many terms are required to mark out a square which is double of a given square?' There is no reason for doubting that

---

[1] Thus the ratio between the sides of 2 (2 : 1) is the διπλάσιος λόγος (the octave); the ratio between the sides of 6 (3 : 2) is the ἡμιόλιος λόγος (the fifth); the ratio between the sides of 12 (4 : 3) is the ἐπίτριτος λόγος (the fourth).

[2] Cp. especially *Met.* N, 5. 1092 b, 8 (Eurytos and οἱ τοὺς ἀριθμοὺς ἄγοντες εἰς τὰ σχήματα τρίγωνον καὶ τετράγωνον). In *Phys.* Γ, 4. 203 a, 13, in explaining square and oblong numbers, he uses the old word εἶδος instead of the more modern σχῆμα. That εἶδος originally meant 'figure' in the sense of 'pattern' appears from the use of εἴδη for the figures on a piece of embroidery (Plut. *Them.* 29).

[3] The following quotations from the *New English Dictionary* are of interest in this connexion: 1551 RECORDE *Pathw. Knowl.*. . . . 'Formes (sc. produced by arrangements of points in rows) . . . whiche I omitte . . . considering that their knowledge appertaineth more to Arithmetike figurall than to Geometrie.' 1614 T. Bedwell, *Nat. Geom. Numbers*, i. 1, 'A rationall figurate number is a number that is made by the multiplication of numbers between themselves.'

Pythagoras discovered that the square of the hypotenuse was equal to the squares on the other two sides; but we know that he did not prove this in the same way as Euclid did later (I. 47). It is probable that his proof was arithmetical rather than geometrical; and, as he was acquainted with the 3 : 4 : 5 triangle, which is always a right-angled triangle, he may have started from the fact that $3^2 + 4^2 = 5^2$. He must, however, have discovered also that this proof broke down in the case of the most perfect triangle of all, the isosceles right-angled triangle, seeing that the relation between its hypotenuse and its sides cannot be expressed by any numerical ratio. The side of the square is incommensurable with the diagonal. That is just the same sort of difficulty we meet with when we attempt to divide the tone or the octave into two equal parts. There is no indication that Pythagoras formed any theory on the subject. He probably referred it simply to the nature of the Unlimited.

§ 37. Another problem which must have exercised him was the construction of the sphere. This he seems to have approached from the consideration of the dodecahedron, which, of all the regular solids, approaches most nearly to the sphere. Now the side of the dodecahedron is the regular pentagon; and for its construction it is necessary to divide a line in extreme and mean ratio, the so-called 'golden section' (Euclid, II. 11). That introduces us to another 'irrational magnitude',[1] and we have evidence that this too played an important part as one of the Pythagorean mysteries. The pentalpha (so-called from its shape) or pentagram was used in its construction, and the Pythagoreans are said to have appended it to

---

[1] In the scholium on Euclid, II. 11 (vol. v. p. 249, Heiberg) we have what appears to be a Pythagorean way of expressing this. This problem, we are told, οὐ δείκνυται διὰ ψήφων, 'is not to be exhibited by means of pebbles'.

their letters. It continued to be used long afterwards for magical purposes, and we meet with it in Goethe's *Faust*, and elsewhere. Tradition represented Hippasos as the man who divulged Pythagorean secrets, and one story says he was drowned at sea for revealing the incommensurability of the side and the diagonal, another that he met with the same fate for publishing the construction of the regular dodecahedron. This is one of the cases where tradition has preserved the memory of something which was real and important.

§ 38. It was natural for Pythagoras to apply his discovery to the heavenly bodies, and it is extremely probable that he regarded the intervals between the three wheels of Anaximander as corresponding to the fourth, the fifth, and the octave. That would be the most natural explanation of the doctrine generally known by the somewhat misleading name of 'the harmony of the spheres'. There is no reason to believe that the celestial spheres are older than Eudoxos, and everything points to the conclusion that the Pythagoreans retained the rings or wheels of Anaximander. They appear in the Second Part of the poem of Parmenides and also in the myth of Er in Plato's *Republic*. We must further remember that there is no question of 'harmony' in our sense of the word, but only of the concordant intervals, which seemed to express the law of the world. They yield the conception of 'form' as correlative to 'matter', and the form is always in some sense a Mean. That is the central doctrine of all Greek philosophy to the very end, and it is not too much to say that it is henceforth dominated by the idea of ἁρμονία or the tuning of a string.

III

Herakleitos and Parmenides

HERAKLEITOS

§ 39. It is above all in dealing with Herakleitos that we are made to feel the importance of personality in shaping systems of philosophy. The very style of his fragments[1] is something unique in Greek literature, and won for him in later times the epithet of 'the dark' (ὁ σκοτεινός). He is quite conscious himself that he writes an oracular style, and he justifies it by the example of the Sibyl (fr. 12) and of the God at Delphoi (fr. 11), who 'neither utters nor hides his meaning, but signifies it'. Here we see the influence of what has been called the prophetic movement of the sixth century B.C., though we are not entitled to assume without more ado that Herakleitos was influenced by that in other respects. The truth is that his central thought is quite simple, and that it is still quite possible to disentangle it from its enigmatic surroundings. Only, when we have done this, we must not suppose we have given a complete account of the man. He is much too big for our formulas.

The date of Herakleitos is roughly fixed by his reference in the past tense to Hekataios, Pythagoras, and Xenophanes (fr. 16), and by the fact that Parmenides appears to allude to him in turn (fr. 6). This means that he wrote early in the fifth century B.C. He was an Ephesian noble, and it appears that the ancient dignity of Basileus (at this date no doubt a religious office) was hereditary in his family; for we are told that he resigned it in favour of his brother. We get a glimpse of his political attitude in the quotation (fr. 114) where he says: 'The Ephesians would do well to hang themselves, every grown man of them, and leave the city to beardless lads; for they have cast out Hermodoros, the best man among them, saying, "We will have none that is best among us; if there be any such, let him be so elsewhere and among others." ' There can be no doubt

---

[1] For references to authorities and a translation of the fragments, see *E. Gr. Ph.*[2] §§ 63 *sqq.* The fragments are quoted by Bywater's numbers.

that Herakleitos was a convinced aristocrat and had a sovereign contempt for the mass of mankind.

But it was not only the common run of men that Herakleitos despised; he had not even a good word for any of his predecessors. He agrees, of course, with Xenophanes about Homer (with whom he classes Archilochos), but Xenophanes himself falls under an equal condemnation. In a remarkable fragment (fr. 16) he mentions him along with Hesiod, Pythagoras, and Hekataios as an instance of the truth that much learning (πολυμαθίη) does not teach men to think (νόον οὐ διδάσκει). The researches (ἱστορίη) of Pythagoras, by which we are to understand in the first place his harmonic and arithmetical discoveries, are rejected with special emphasis (fr. 17). Wisdom is not a knowledge of many things; it is the clear knowledge of one thing only, and this Herakleitos describes, in true prophetic style, as his Word (λόγος), which is 'true evermore', though men cannot understand it even when it is told to them (fr. 2). We must endeavour, then, to discover, if we can, what Herakleitos meant by his Word, the thing he felt he had been born to say, whether anyone would listen to him or not.

§ 40. In the first place, it is plain that the Word must be something more than the doctrine of Fire as the primary substance, or even the theory of Flux (πάντα ῥεῖ). If Herakleitos had merely substituted fire for the 'air' of Anaximenes, that would only have been a further advance on the lines of Anaximenes himself, who had substituted 'air' for the water of Thales. It is not at once obvious either that the doctrine of flux is an improvement on that of rarefaction and condensation; and, even if it were, such an improvement would hardly account for the tone in which Herakleitos speaks of his Word. It is not in this direction we must seek for his innermost thought. The doctrine of flux is, no doubt, a great scientific generalisation, but no single scientific discovery is attributed to Herakleitos. That is significant. Further, everything we are told about his cosmology shows it to have been even more reactionary than that of Xenophanes or the school of Anaximenes. On the other hand, though he uses the language of the mysteries, he condemns them in the strongest terms. The 'Night-walkers, magicians, Bakchoi, Lenai, and Mystai' of whom he speaks (fr. 124) must be the contemporary Orphics, and we are told by Clement of Alexandria, who quotes the words, that Herakleitos threatened them with the wrath to come.

Yet Herakleitos has one thing in common with the religious teachers of his time, and that is his insistence on the idea of Soul (ψυχή). To him, as to them, the soul was no longer a feeble ghost or shade, but the most real thing of all, and its most important attribute was thought (γνώμη) or wisdom (τό σοφόν). Now Anaximenes had already illustrated the doctrine of 'air' by the remark that it is breath which keeps us in life (§ 9), and we have seen how the same idea affected the Pythagorean cosmology (§ 28). The Delphic precept 'Know thyself' was a household word in those days, and Herakleitos says 'I sought myself' (ἐδιζησάμην ἐμεωυτόν, fr. 80). He also said (fr. 71): 'You cannot find out the boundaries of soul; so deep a measure hath it.' If we follow up these hints we may perhaps find ourselves on the right track.

§ 41. A glance at the fragments will show that the thought of Herakleitos was dominated by the opposition of sleeping and waking, life and death, and that this seemed to him the key to the traditional Milesian problem of the opposites, hot and cold, wet and dry. More precisely, Life, Sleep, Death correspond to Fire, Water, Earth, and the latter are to be understood from the former. Now we see that the soul is only fully alive when it is awake, and that sleep is really a stage between life and death. Sleep and death are due to the advance of moisture, as is shown by the phenomenon of drunkenness (fr. 73). 'It is death to souls to become water' (fr. 68). Waking and life are due to the advance of warmth and fire, and 'the dry soul is the wisest and the best' (fr. 74). We see further that there is a regular alternation of the two processes; sleep alternates with waking, and life with death. Fire is fed by the exhalations of water, and these exhalations are in turn produced by the warmth of the fire. If there were no water, there could be no fire; and, if there were no fire, there could be no exhalations from the water.

If we look next at the macrocosm, we shall see the explanation is the same. Night and day, summer and winter, alternate in the same way as sleep and waking, life and death, and here too it is clear that the explanation is to be found in the successive advance of the wet and the dry, the cold and the hot. It follows that it is wrong to make the primary substance an intermediate state like 'air'. It must be the most living thing in the world, and therefore it must be fire like the life of the soul; and as the fiery soul is the wisest, so will the wisdom which 'steers' the world be fire. Pure fire is to be seen best in the sun, which is lit up afresh every morning, and put out at night. It and the other heavenly bodies are just masses of pure fire ignited in a sort of basin in which they traverse the heavens, and this fire is kept up by exhalations from the earth. The phases of the moon and eclipses are due to a partial or total turning round of the basins. Darkness too is an exhalation from the earth of another kind. These last remarks prove we are not dealing with a scientific man, as science was understood in Italy.

§ 42. But, if fire is the primary form of reality, it seems that we may gain a clearer view of what Anaximander had described as 'separating out' (§ 7), and Anaximenes had explained by 'rarefaction and condensation' (§ 9). The process of combustion is the key both to human life and to that of the world. It is a process that never rests; for a flame has always to be fed by fresh exhalations as fuel, and it is always turning into vapour or smoke. The steadiness of the flame depends on the 'measures' of fuel kindled and the 'measures' of fire extinguished in smoke remaining constant. Now the world is 'an everliving fire' (fr. 20), and therefore there will be an unceasing process of 'flux'. That will apply to the world at large and also to the soul of man. 'You cannot step twice into the same river' (fr. 41), and it is just as true that 'we are and are not' at any given moment. 'The way up and the way down', which are 'one and the same' (fr. 69) are also the same for the microcosm and the macrocosm. Fire, water, earth is the way down, and earth, water, fire is the way up. And these two ways are forever being traversed in opposite directions at once, so that everything really consists of two parts, one part travelling up and the other travelling down.

Now Anaximander had held (§ 6) that all things must return to the Boundless, and so pay the penalty to one another for their injustice, and what Herakleitos regarded as his great discovery seems to attach itself to this very pronouncement. It is just the fact that the world is 'an everliving fire' which secures its stability; for the same 'measures' of fire are always being kindled and going out (fr. 20). It is impossible for fire to consume its nourishment without at the same time giving back what it has consumed already. It is a process of eternal 'exchange' (ἀμοιβή) like that of gold for wares and wares for gold (fr. 22); and 'the sun will not exceed his measures; if he does, the Erinyes, the auxiliaries of Justice, will find him out' (fr. 29). For all this strife is really justice (fr. 22), not injustice, as Anaximander had supposed, and 'War is the father of all things' (fr. 44). It is just this opposite tension that keeps things together, like that of the string in the bow and the lyre (fr. 45), and though it is a hidden attunement, it is better than any open one (fr. 47). For all his condemnation of Pythagoras, Herakleitos cannot get away from the tuned string.

But, in spite of all this, it is possible for the 'measures' to vary up to a certain point. We see that from the facts of sleeping and waking, death and life, with which we started, and also from the corresponding facts of night and day, summer and winter. These fluctuations are due to the processes of evaportion or exhalation (ἀναθυμίασις) and liquefaction (χύσις) which formed the starting-point of all early Ionian physics. Yet these fluctuations exactly balance one another, so that, in the long run, the 'measures' are not exceeded. It appears to be certain that Herakleitos inferred from this periodicity the survival of soul in some form or other. We see that day follows night and summer follows winter, and we know that waking follows sleep. In the same way, he seems to have argued, life follows death, and the soul once more begins its upward journey. 'It is the same thing in us that is quick and dead, awake and asleep, young and old' (fr. 78). That is the game of draughts that Time plays everlastingly (fr. 79).

§ 43. Such, so far as we can make it out, is the general view of Herakleitos, and now we may ask for his secret, the one thing to know which is wisdom. It is that, as the apparent strife of opposites in this world is really due to the opposite tension which holds the world together, so in pure fire, which is the eternal wisdom, all these oppositions disappear in their common ground. God is 'beyond good and bad' (fr. 57, 61). Therefore what we must do to attain wisdom is to hold fast to 'the common'. 'The waking have one and the same world, but sleepers turn aside, each into a world of his own' (fr. 95). If we keep our souls dry, we shall understand that good and evil are one, that is, that they are only passing forms of one reality that transcends them both. Such was the conclusion a man of genius drew from the Milesian doctrine of evaporation and liquefaction.

§ 44. For, with all his originality, Herakleitos remains an Ionian. He had learnt indeed the importance of soul, but his fire-soul is as little personal as the breath-soul of Anaximenes. There are certainly fragments that seem to assert the immortality of the individual soul; but, when we examine them, we see they cannot bear this interpretation. Soul is only immortal in so far as it is part of the everliving fire which is the life of the world. Seeing that the soul of every man is in constant flux like his body, what meaning can immortality have? It is not only true that we cannot step twice into the same river, but also that we are not the same for two successive instants. That is just the side of his doctrine that struck contemporaries most forcibly, and Epicharmos already made fun of it by putting it as an argument into the mouth of a debtor who did not wish to pay. How could he be liable, seeing he is not the same man that contracted the debt? And Herakleitos is an Ionian, too, in his theology. His wisdom, which is one and apart from all things, 'wills and wills not to be called by the name of Zeus' (fr. 65). That is to say, it is no more what the religious consciousness means by God than the Air of Anaximenes or the World of Xenophanes. Herakleitos, in fact, despite his prophetic tone and his use of religious languages, never broke through the secularism and pantheism of the Ionians. Belief in a personal God and an immortal soul was already being elaborated in another quarter, but did not secure a place in philosophy till the time of Plato.

PARMENIDES

§ 45. We have now to consider the criticisms directed against the fundamental assumptions of Ionian cosmology from another side. That Parmenides wrote after Herakleitos, and in conscious opposition to him, seems to be proved by what must surely be an express illusion in his poem. The words 'for whom it is and is not the same and not the same, and all things travel in opposite directions' (fr. 6, 8), cannot well refer to anyone else, and we may infer that these words were written some time between Marathon and Salamis. We know from the poem that Parmenides was a young man when he wrote it, for the goddess who reveals the truth to him addresses him as 'youth', and Plato says that Parmenides came to Athens in his sixty-fifth year and conversed with Sokrates, who was then 'very young'. That must have been in the middle of the fifth century B.C., or shortly after it. Parmenides was a citizen of Elea, for which city he legislated, and he is generally represented as a disciple of Xenophanes. It has been pointed out, however, that there is no evidence for the settlement of Xenophanes at Elea (§ 16), and the story that he founded the Eleatic school seems to be derived from a playful remark of Plato's, which would also prove

Homer to have been a Herakleitean.[1] We have much more satisfactory evidence for the statement that Parmenides was a Pythagorean. We are told that he built a shrine to the memory of his Pythagorean teacher, Ameinias, son of Diochaitas, and this appears to rest on the testimony of the inscription in which he dedicated it. The authorities Strabo followed, in referring to the legislation of Elea, expressly called Parmenides and Zeno Pythagoreans, and the name of Parmenides occurs in the list of Pythagoreans preserved by Iamblichos.[2]

§ 46. Parmenides broke with the older Ionic tradition by writing in hexameter verse. It was not a happy thought. The Hesiodic style was doubtless appropriate enough for the cosmogony he described in the second part of his poem, but it was wholly unsuited to the arid dialectic of the first. It is clear that Parmenides was no born poet, and we must ask what led him to take this new departure. The example of Xenophanes is hardly an adequate explanation; for the poetry of Parmenides is as unlike that of Xenophanes as it well can be, and his style is rather that of Hesiod and the Orphics. Now it has been clearly shown[3] that the well-known Proem, in which Parmenides describes his ascent to the home of the goddess who is supposed to speak the remainder of the verses, is a reflexion of the conventional ascents into heaven which were almost as common as descents into hell in the apocalyptic literature of those days, and of which we have later imitations in the myth of Plato's *Phaedrus* and in Dante's *Paradiso*. But, if it was the influence of such an apocalypse that led Parmenides to write in verse, it will follow that the Proem is no mere external ornament to his work, but an essential part of it, the part, in fact, which he had most clearly conceived when he began to write. In that case, it is to the Proem we must look for the key to the whole.

Parmenides represents himself as borne on a chariot and attended by the Sunmaidens who have quitted the Halls of Night to guide him on his journey. They pass along the highway till they come to the Gate of Night and Day, which is locked and barred. The key is in the keeping of *Dikē* (Right), the Avenger, who is persuaded to unlock it by the Sunmaidens. They pass in through

[1] Plato, *Soph.* 242 d. See *E. Gr. Ph.*[2] p. 140.
[2] For all this, see *E. Gr. Ph.*[2] §§ 84 *sqq.*
[3] Diels, *Parmenides Lehrgedichte*, pp. 11 *sqq.*

the gate and are now, of course, in the realms of Day. The goal of
the journey is the palace of a goddess who welcomes Parmenides
and instructs him in the two ways, that of Truth and the deceptive
way of Belief, in which is no truth at all. All this is described
without inspiration and in a purely conventional manner, so it
must be interpreted by the canons of the apocalyptic style. It is
clearly meant to indicate that Parmenides had been converted, that
he had passed from error (night) to truth (day), and the Two Ways
must represent his former error and the truth which is now
revealed to him. We have seen reason to believe that Parmenides
was originally a Pythagorean, and there are many things which
suggest that the Way of Belief is an account of Pythagorean
cosmology. In any case, it is surely impossible to regard it as
anything else than a description of some error. The goddess says
so in words that cannot be explained away. Further, this erroneous
belief is not the ordinary man's view of the world, but an elaborate
system, which seems to be a natural development of the Ionian
cosmology on certain lines, and there is no other system but the
Pythagorean that fulfils this requirement.

To this it has been objected that Parmenides would not have
taken the trouble to expound in detail a system he had altogether
rejected, but that is to mistake the character of the apocalyptic
convention. It is not Parmenides, but the goddess, that expounds
the system, and it is for this reason that the beliefs described are
said to be those of 'mortals'. Now a description of the ascent of the
soul would be quite incomplete without a picture of the region
from which it had escaped. The goddess must reveal the two ways
at the parting of which Parmenides stands, and bid him choose the
better. That itself is a Pythagorean idea. It was symbolised by the
letter Y, and can be traced right down to Christian times. The
machinery of the Proem consists, therefore, of two well-known
apocalyptic devices, the Ascent into Heaven, and the Parting of the
Ways, and it follows that, for Parmenides himself, his conversion
from Pythagoreanism to Truth was the central thing in his poem,
and it is from that point of view we must try to understand him.
It is probable too that, if the Pythagoreans had not been a religious
society as well as a scientific school, he would have been content to
say what he had to say in prose. As it was, his secession from the
school was also a heresy, and had, like all heresies, to be justified
in the language of religion.

§ 47. All the Ionians had taken for granted that the primary substance could assume different forms, such as earth, water, and fire, a view suggested by the observed phenomena of freezing, evaporation, and the like. Anaximenes had further explained these transformations as due to rarefaction and condensation (§ 9). That, of course really implies that the structure of the primary substance is corpuscular, and that there are interstices of some kind between its particles. It is improbable that Anaximenes realised this consequence of his doctrine. Even now it is not immediately obvious to the untrained mind. The problem was raised at once, however, by the use the Pythagoreans had made of the theory. According to them, as we have seen (§ 28), the world inhaled 'air', or void, from the boundless mass outside it, and this accounted for the extension of the bodies whose limits were marked out by the 'figures'. When the thing was put in this way, further questions were inevitable.

§ 48. Now the rise of mathematics in this same Pythagorean school had revealed for the first time the power of thought. To the mathematician of all men it is the same thing that can be thought (ἔστι νοεῖν) and that can be (ἔστιν εἶναι),[1] and this is the principle from which Parmenides starts. It is impossible to think what is not, and it is impossible for what cannot be thought to be. The great question, *Is it or is it not?* is therefore equivalent to the question, *Can it be thought or not?*

Parmenides goes on to consider in the light of this principle the consequences of saying that anything *is*. In the first place, it cannot have come into being. If it had, it must have arisen from nothing or from something. It cannot have arisen from nothing; for there is no nothing. It cannot have arisen from something; for there is nothing else than what *is*. Nor can anything else besides itself come into being; for there can be no empty space in which it could do so. *Is it or is it not?* If it *is*, then it is now, all at once. In this way Parmenides refutes all accounts of the origin of the world. *Ex nihilo nihil fit.*

Further, if it *is*, it simply is, and it cannot *be* more or less. There is, therefore, as much of it in one place as in another. (That makes

---

[1] This is how Zeller (*Phil. d. griech* I.⁵ p. 558, *n.* 1) took fr. 5 τὸ γὰρ αὐτὸ νοεῖν ἔστιν τε καὶ εἶναι, and it still seems to me the only possible rendering. I cannot separate εἰσὶ νοῆσαι in fr. 4, which everyone takes to mean 'are thinkable' from ἔστι νοεῖν in fr. 5. Nor do I believe that the infinitive is ever the subject of a sentence even in such places as *Il.* x. 174 (see Leaf's note). The traditional view (given *e.g.* by Goodwin, *M.T.* § 745) implies that ποιεῖν is the subject in δίκαιόν ἐστι τοῦτο ποιεῖν, which is refuted by δίκαιός εἰμι τοῦτο ποιεῖν.

rarefaction and condensation impossible.) It is continuous and indivisible; for there is nothing but itself which could prevent its parts being in contact with one another. It is therefore full, a continuous indivisible plenum. (That is directed against the Pythagorean theory of a discontinuous reality.)

Further, it is immoveable. If it moved, it must move into empty space, and empty space is nothing, and there is no nothing. Also it is finite and spherical; for it cannot *be* in one direction any more than in another, and the sphere is the only figure of which this can be said.

What *is* (τὸ ἐόν) is, therefore a finite, spherical, motionless, continuous plenum, and there is nothing beyond it. Coming into being and ceasing to be are mere 'names', and so is motion, and still more colour and the like. They are not even thoughts; for a thought must be a thought of something that *is*, and none of these can *be*.

§ 49. Such is the conclusion to which the view of the real as a single body inevitably leads, and there is no escape from it. The 'matter' of our physical text-books is just the real (τὸ ἐόν) of Parmenides; and, unless we can find room for something else than matter, we are shut up to his account of reality. No subsequent system could afford to ignore this, but of course it was impossible to acquiesce permanently in a doctrine like that of Parmenides. It deprives the world we know of all claim to existence, and reduces it to something which is hardly even an illusion. If we are to give an intelligible account of the world, we must certainly introduce motion again somehow. That can never be taken for granted any more, as it was by the early cosmologists; we must attempt to explain it if we are to escape from the conclusions of Parmenides.

IV

The Pluralists

§ 50. It was only possible to escape from the conclusions of Parmenides on two conditions. In the first place, the belief that all that *is* is one, which had been held by everyone since the days of Thales, must be given up. There was no reason why Parmenides should have denied motion except this. Motion *in pleno* is quite conceivable, though it would not explain anything on the assumption of unity. If any part of the Parmenidean One were to move, that could only mean that its place was taken at once by an equal part of it. As, however, this part would be precisely the same as that which it displaced, the result of the motion would be *nil*, and it could not be distinguished from rest. We find accordingly that both Empedokles and Anaxagoras, whose systems we have now to consider, while accepting and insisting on the Parmenidean doctrine that the real is without beginning and without end, agree in maintaining also that there are more kinds of real than one. The world we know may be explained as due to the mixture and separation of a number of primary 'elements'. The word *elementum* is a Latin translation of the Greek στοιχεῖον, 'letter of the alphabet', which does not occur in this sense till a later date, though the conception of an element was quite clearly formed. Empedokles called his elements 'roots', and Anaxagoras called his 'seeds', but they both meant something eternal and irreducible to anything else, and they both held the things we perceive with the senses to be temporary combinations of these.

The second condition that must be satisfied, if the world is to be explained in spite of Parmenides, is that some account must be given of the origin or source of the motion which had hitherto been taken for granted as something inherent in the nature of body. Accordingly, both Empedokles and Anaxagoras postulate causes of motion, which the former calls Love and Strife, and the latter calls Mind (νοῦς). What they were feeling after was obviously the later

C   B.G.P.

physical conception of *force*, but it is equally clear that they were still unable to disentangle this completely from that of body. They both use language with regard to the forces they assume which makes it plain that they were pictured as something corporeal, and this will seem quite intelligible if we remember the part played by 'fluids' in the science of fairly recent times. It is to be observed further that Empedokles felt obliged to assume two sources of motion, like the force of attraction and the force of repulsion, or the centripetal and centrifugal forces of later days, while Anaxagoras only required a single force which was capable of producing rotation. The rotatory motion itself could account for everything else.

Taking these two things together, we can understand the doctrine which is common to Empedokles and Anaxagoras, and which they both express in almost exactly the same words. It is, firstly, that there is in reality no such thing as coming into being (γένεσις) and ceasing to be (φθορά). That has been settled by Parmenides. But, secondly, it is obvious that the things in this world do come into being and cease to be. That is proved by the evidence of the senses. The only way in which these two things can be reconciled is by regarding what is commonly called coming into being as mixture, and ceasing to be as separation. From this it follows, in the first place, that the real must be such as to admit of mixture, or, in other words, that there must be different kinds of real; and, in the second place, that there must be a cause of mixture and separation.

EMPEDOKLES

§ 51. Empedokles was a citizen of Akragas in Sicily, and he played a considerable part in his native city as a democratic leader.[1] His date is roughly fixed for us by the well-attested fact that he went to Thourioi shortly after its foundation in 444/3 B.C. That was probably after his banishment from his native city. He was, therefore, contemporary with the meridian splendour of the Periklean age at Athens, and he must have met Herodotus and Protagoras at Thourioi. In his case we know for certain that he combined scientific study with a mystical religion of the Orphic type, but he differed from Pythagoras in the direction his scientific

---

[1] References to authorities are given in *E. Gr. Ph.*[2] §§ 97 *sqq.* For a translation of the fragments, see *ib.* § 105.

inquiries took. We know that Pythagoras was first and foremost a mathematician, while Empedokles was the founder of the Sicilian school of medicine. That accounts for the physiological interest that marks his speculations. It is the same difference as that between Plato and Aristotle at a later date.

We are not directly concerned here with the religious teaching of Empedokles, though we may note in passing his horror of bloody sacrifices, which he justified from the doctrine of Rebirth or transmigration. His 'Purifications' (Καθαρμοί), of which considerable fragments remain, are, indeed, our oldest and best authority for this type of religion. They are written in hexameters, and so is his more strictly philosophical poem. In this matter he imitated Parmenides, as is proved by his sometimes reproducing his actual words. The only difference is that he was a real poet, and Parmenides was not.

§ 52. As has been indicated, Empedokles unreservedly accepts the doctrine of Parmenides that 'what *is*' is uncreated and indestructible, and he only escapes from the further conclusions of the Eleatic by introducing the theory of elements or 'roots'. Of these he assumed four — fire, air, earth, and water, — and in some respects this was a return to primitive views which the Milesians had already left behind them (§ 10). In particular, it was reactionary to put earth on a level with the other three. It must be noticed, however, that Empedokles at the same time made an advance by co-ordinating air with fire and water, instead of identifying it with vapour and regarding it as a transitional form between the two. He had in fact discovered that what we call atmospheric air was a body, and was quite distinct from empty space on the one hand and from vapour or mist on the other. He was doubtless led to this discovery by the polemic of Parmenides against the existence of empty space. The plain man can imagine he has a direct perception of this, and it was necessary for Empedokles to show he was wrong. This he did by means of an experiment with the *klepsydra* or water-clock. He showed that air could keep water out of a vessel, and that the water could only enter as the air escaped. This important discovery outweighs his error in regarding air and water as elements. He had no means of discovering they were not. He might, perhaps, have got a hint of the true nature of fire from Herakleitos, but here we must remember that, so long as the sun and stars were believed to consist of fire, it was not easy to discern the truth. Even Aristotle adopted the four elements of Empedokles, though Plato and his Pythagorean friends had declared that so far from being 'letters' (στοιχεῖα), they were not even syllables.

§ 53. Besides these four 'roots', Empedokles postulated something called Love (φιλία) to explain the attraction of different forms of matter, and of something called Strife (νεῖκος) to account for their separation. He speaks of these quite distinctly as bodies. The way in which they act seems to have been suggested by the experiment with the *klepsydra* already referred to. We start with something like the sphere of Parmenides, in which the four elements are mingled in a sort of solution by Love, while Strife surrounds the sphere on the outside. When Strife begins to enter the Sphere, Love is driven towards its centre, and the four elements are gradually separated from one another. That is clearly an adaptation of the old idea of the world breathing. Empedokles also held, however, that respiration depended on the systole and diastole of the heart, and therefore we find that, as soon as Strife has penetrated to the lowest (or most central) part of the sphere, and Love is confined to the very middle of it, the reverse process begins. Love expands and Strife is driven outwards, passing out of the Sphere once more in proportion as Love occupies more and more of it, just as air is expelled from the *klepsydra* when water enters it. In fact, Love and Strife are to the world what blood and air are to the body. The physiological analogy naturally influenced the founder of a medical school, who had for the first time formulated a theory of the flux and reflux of blood from and to the heart. The conception of the attractive force as Love is also, as Empedokles says himself, of physiological origin. No one had observed, he tells us (fr. 17, 21–26) that the very same force men know in their own bodies plays a part in the life of the great world too. He does not seem to have thought it necessary to give any mechanical explanation of the cosmic systole and diastole. It was just the life of the world.

§ 54. A world of perishable things such as we know can only exist when both Love and Strife are in the world. There will, therefore, be two births and two passings away of mortal things (fr. 17, 3–5), one when Love is increasing and all the elements are coming together into one, the other when Strife is re-entering the Sphere and the elements are being separated once more. The elements alone are everlasting; the particular things we know are unstable compounds, which come into being as the elements 'run through one another' in one direction or another. They are mortal or perishable just because they have no substance (φύσις) of their own; only the 'four roots' have that. There is, therefore, no end to their death and destruction (fr. 8).[1] Their birth is a mixture and their death is but the separation of what has been mixed. Nothing is imperishable but fire, air, earth and water, with the two forces of Love and Strife.

We have little information as to how Empedokles explained the constitution of particular things. He regarded the four elements, which could be combined in an indefinite number of proportions, as adequate to explain them all, and he referred in this connexion to the great variety painters can produce with only four pigments (fr. 23). He saw, however, that some combinations are possible, while others are not. Water mixes easily with wine, but not with oil (fr. 91). This he accounted for by the presence or absence of symmetry in the 'passages' (πόροι) or 'pores' of the elements which enter into the mixture. It is unprofitable to inquire how he reconciled this view with the denial of the void he had adopted from Parmenides. For the rest, Aristotle attaches great importance to his doctrine of the 'ratio of mixture' (λόγος τῆς μείξεως), which is pretty certainly an adaptation of the Pythagorean theory of 'blending' (κρᾶσις) in fixed ratios (λόγοι). The tuned string makes itself felt once more.

§ 55. The details of the cosmology present considerable difficulties. We are told that, when the elements first separated, fire occupied the upper hemisphere and air the lower. That disturbed the equilibrium of the sphere and produced the diurnal rotation (δίνη) of the heavens. This rotation, in turn, keeps the earth in the centre. The idea was apparently that it would naturally fall into the lower hemisphere, but is prevented from doing so by the lower hemisphere constantly becoming the upper. It is clear that there is great confusion of thought here. Empedokles has reverted to the idea of an absolute up and down in the world, which Anaximander had discarded already, and he does not seem to have been consistent even in this. The fiery hemisphere is day, and the airy hemisphere is night. The sun is only the light of the fiery hemisphere reflected back from the earth and gathered in a

[1] I have adopted the interpretation of these verses suggested by Lovejoy (*Philosophical Review*, xviii. pp. 371 *sqq.*).

sort of focus. We have no means of telling how Empedokles worked out this singular theory in detail. We can only say that he was primarily a physiologist, and that astronomy was not his strong point.

And it is certainly the case that his physiology, though primitive enough, makes a far more favourable impression. We have seen the importance he attached to respiration, and how he connected it with the heart's action. It was natural, therefore, for him to regard the blood as 'what we think with' ($\hat{\omega} \phi \rho o \nu o \hat{\upsilon} \mu \epsilon \nu$),[1] and to make the heart the central sensorium. In this he departed from the theory of Alkmaion of Kroton, who had discovered the importance of the brain for sense-perception, but he adopted from him the explanation of the various senses by 'pores' or passages ($\pi \delta \rho o \iota$). Sensation was produced by 'effluences' ($\dot{\alpha} \pi o \rho \rho o \alpha \iota$) fitting into these. The origin of species was ascribed to the increasing action of Strife. At the beginning of this world there were undifferentiated living masses ($o\dot{\upsilon} \lambda o \phi \upsilon \epsilon \hat{\iota} s \tau \dot{\upsilon} \pi o \iota$), which were gradually differentiated, the fittest surviving. Empedokles also described how mortal beings arose in the period when Love was gaining the mastery, and when everything happened in just the opposite way to what we see in our world. In that case, the limbs and organs first arose in separation, and were then joined together at haphazard, so that monsters were produced, 'oxen with heads of men and men with heads of oxen.' This strange picture of a reversed evolution may possibly have been suggested by the Egyptian monuments.

ANAXAGORAS

§ 56. Anaxagoras of Klazomenai is said by Aristotle to have been older than Empedokles, but to come 'after him in his works' ($\tau o \hat{\iota} s \delta' \, \ddot{\epsilon} \rho \gamma o \iota s \, \ddot{\upsilon} \sigma \tau \epsilon \rho o s$).[2] It is not clear whether this means that he wrote later than Empedokles or that he was inferior to him in his achievement. His date is quite uncertain, but we know he settled at Athens and enjoyed the friendship of Perikles. Plato makes Sokrates attribute the eloquence of Perikles to his association with Anaxagoras. It was no doubt this very intimacy that exposed Anaxagoras to the accusation for irreligion ($\dot{\alpha} \sigma \dot{\epsilon} \beta \epsilon \iota \alpha$) which was brought against him. That is usually said to have happened just

---

[1] Plato, *Phaedo*, 96 b.
[2] References to authorities are given in *E. Gr. Ph.*[2] §§ 120 *sqq.*

before the Peloponnesian War, but we do not really know either
the date of it or the precise nature of the charge. It must have been
something more definite than his speculations about the sun. We
happen to know that even Diagoras, the typical atheist of those
days, was not tried for his opinions, but for offences in language
against the temples and festivals.¹ Perikles got Anaxagoras off in
some way, and he retired to Lampsakos, where he founded a
school. It is a remarkable fact that Plato never makes Sokrates
meet him, though he was interested in his system, and that of itself
suggests that the accusation for irreligion took place at an earlier
date than the one usually given. Like a true Ionian, Anaxagoras
wrote in prose, and considerable fragments of his book remain.

§ 57. Anaxagoras lays down that the Hellenes are wrong in
speaking of coming into being (γίνεσθαι) and ceasing to be
(ἀπόλλυσθαι). They ought to call these 'commixture' (συμμίσγεσθαι)
and 'decomposition' (διακρίνεσθαι) (fr. 17). That is almost in so
many words the doctrine of Empedokles, with which Anaxagoras
certainly seems to have been acquainted. In any case, it is certain
that he started, like Empedokles, from the Parmenidean account
of 'what is'. On the other hand, Anaxagoras was an Ionian. We are
told that he had been an adherent of 'the philosophy of Anaximenes', and it is evident from the details of his cosmology that the
statement is correct. We shall be prepared to find, then, that he
started from quite different presuppositions, though these were
also derived from medical sources. Medicine was the great interest
of the time.

Like Empedokles, Anaxagoras postulated a plurality of independent elements which he called 'seeds'. They were not,
however, the 'four roots', fire, air, earth, and water; on the contrary, these were compounds. Empedokles had supposed that bone,
for instance, could be explained as a compound of the elements in a
certain proportion, but this did not satisfy Anaxagoras. He pointed
out that from bread and water arose hair, veins, 'arteries',² flesh,
muscles, bones, and all the rest, and he asked 'How can hair be
made of what is not hair, and flesh of what is not flesh?' (fr. 10).
These words certainly read like a direct criticism of Empedokles.

¹ See the speech against Andokides preserved among the works of Lysias
(6. 17).
² The true distinction between veins and arteries was not yet known. The
arteries were supposed to contain air and were connected with the wind-pipe or
trachea (τραχεῖα, sc. ἀρτηρία).

This way of speaking, however, led to a serious misunderstanding of the theory. In Aristotle's biological works the various 'tissues', some of which Anaxagoras enumerates, are called 'homoeomerous' (ὁμοιομερῆ), a term which means that all their parts are similar to the whole. The parts of bone are bone, and the parts of blood are blood. That is just the distinction between such things as bone, flesh, and blood, and 'organs' like the heart or the lungs. There is no evidence that Anaxagoras himself used this terminology, and indeed it is incredible that no fragment containing it should have been quoted if he had. The Epicureans, however, attributed it to him, and they also understood it wrongly. They supposed it to mean that there must be minute particles in bread and water which were like the particles of blood, flesh, and bones, and the adoption of this interpretation by Lucretius has given it currency.

§ 58. We have seen that Anaxagoras had been an adherent of 'the philosophy of Anaximenes', and he kept as close to it as he could in the details of his cosmology. He could not say that everything was 'air' more or less rarefied or condensed, for that view had been destroyed by Parmenides. If the world was to be explained at all, an original plurality must be admitted. He therefore substituted for the primary 'air' a state of the world in which 'all things (χρήματα) were together, infinite both in quantity and in smallness' (fr. 1). This is explained to mean that the original mass was infinitely divisible, but that, however far division was carried, every part of it would still contain all 'things' (χρήματα), and would in that respect be just like the whole. That is the very opposite of the doctrine of 'elements', which seems to be expressly denied by the dictum that 'the things that are in one world are not separated from one another or cut off with a hatchet' (fr. 8). Everything has 'portions' (μοῖραι) of everything else in it.

But if that were all, we should be no nearer an explanation of the world than before; for there would be nothing to distinguish one 'seed' from another. The answer to this is that, though each has a 'portion' of everything in it, however minutely it may be divided, some have more of one thing and others more of another. This was to be seen already in the original undifferentiated mass where 'all things were together'; for there the portions of air and 'aether' (by which word Anaxagoras means fire) were far more numerous than the others, and therefore the whole had the appearance of air and 'aether'. Anaxagoras could not say it actually was air, as Anaximenes had done, because he had discovered for himself or learned from Empedokles the separate corporeal existence of atmospheric air. We have some references to the experiments by which he demonstrated this. He used inflated skins for the purpose. The effort to depart as little as possible from the doctrine of Anaximenes is nevertheless apparent.

§ 59. We see, then, that the differences which exist in the world as we know it are to be explained by the varying proportions in which the portions are mingled. 'Everything is called that of which it has most in it', though, as a matter of fact, it has everything in it. Snow, for instance, is black as well as white,[1] but we call it white because the white so far exceeds the black. As was natural, the 'things' Anaxagoras chiefly thought of as contained in each 'seed' were the traditional opposites, hot and cold, wet and dry, and so forth. It is of these he is expressly speaking when he says that 'the things in one world are not cut off from one another with a hatchet' (fr. 8). Empedokles had made each of these four opposites a 'root' by itself; each of the 'seeds' of Anaxagoras contains them all. In this way he thought he could explain nutrition and growth; for it is clear that the product of a number of 'seeds' might present quite a different proportion of the opposites than any one of them if they were taken severally.

§ 60. The other problem, that of the source of motion, still remains. How are we to pass from the state of the world when all things were together to the manifold reality we know? Like Empedokles, Anaxagoras looked to the microcosm for a suggestion as to the source of motion, but he found one such source sufficient for his purpose. He called it Mind ($\nu o\hat{v}s$); for that is the source of motion as well as of knowledge in us. He did not, however, succeed in forming the conception of an incorporeal force any more than Empedokles had done. For him, too, the cause of motion is a sort of 'fluid'. It is 'the thinnest of all things' (fr. 12), and, above all, it is 'unmixed', that is to say, it has no portions of other things in it, and this is what gives it the 'mastery', that is, the power both of knowing and of moving other things. Further, it enters into some things and not into others, and that explains the distinction between the animate and the inanimate. The way in which it separates and orders things is by producing a rotatory motion ($\pi\epsilon\rho\iota\chi\acute{\omega}\rho\eta\sigma\iota s$), which begins at the centre and spreads further and

---

[1] Sextus, *Pyrrh. hypot.* I. 33.

further. That is really all Anaxagoras had to say about it, and in the *Phaedo* Plato makes Sokrates complain that he made Mind a mere *deus ex machina* (98 b). Like a true Ionian he tried to give a mechanical explanation of everything he could, and, when once he had got the rotatory motion started, he could leave that to order the rest of the world.

§ 61. It is hard to believe, however, that Anaxagoras was wholly ignorant of Pythagorean science. Oinopides of Chios was introducing a more highly developed geometry into Ionia from the west, and Anaxagoras himself is credited with certain mathematical discoveries. He also knew, though he certainly did not discover, that the sun is eclipsed by the interposition of the moon, and that the moon shines by light reflected from the sun, but he cannot have been able to give the true account of lunar eclipses, seeing that he was either ignorant of or deliberately rejected the discovery that the earth was a sphere. In this respect, too, he adhered to the doctrine of Anaximenes and regarded it as a disc. That being so, he had to assume dark bodies invisible to us to account for eclipses of the moon. That is probably connected with the theory which seems to have struck his contemporaries most. His attention had been directed in some way to the huge meteoric stone which fell into the Aigospotamos in 468/7 B.C., and this suggested to him that portions of the earth might be detached and flung to a distance as from a sling by the rotatory motion. That had once been far more rapid than it is now, and so the sun, which was a mass of red-hot iron 'larger than the Peloponnesos,' and the moon, which was made of earth, had reached their present places. All this seems retrograde enough when we compare it with Pythagorean science. That was a thing the Ionians could never really assimilate. Even Demokritos was nearly as backward in these matters as Anaxagoras, and Aristotle himself could not grasp the Pythagorean conception completely.

§ 62. Though Empedokles had distinguished Love and Strife as the causes of mixture and separation from the four elements which are mixed and separated, he continued to call them all 'gods' in the sense with which we are now familiar, and he gave the name also to the Sphere in which they were all mixed together. Anaxagoras seems to have taken the step of calling only the source of motion 'god'. In that sense and to that extent it is not incorrect to call him the founder of theism. On the other hand, it seems to have been precisely for this that his contemporaries called him an atheist. In his desire to exalt Nous, he seems to have followed the lead of Xenophanes in denying the divinity of everything else, and his statements about the sun and the moon are usually mentioned in connexion with the charge of irreligion brought against him, though we cannot tell now what that referred to, or whether the charge was well founded or not. We can only say that Perikles shared the secular spirit of the Ionians, and it is quite conceivable that his immediate circle may have offended the religious suscepti-bilities of old-fashioned Athenians by ridiculing ceremonies which were still sacred in their eyes.[1]

[1] The worship of Sun and Moon was no part of Athenian religion, but Anaxagoras may have ridiculed the measures prescribed by the ἐξηγηταί on the occasion of the solar eclipse of 463 B.C. That, no doubt, would be ἀσέβεια.

V

Eleatics and Pythagoreans

ZENO

§ 63. We have seen (§ 46) how Eleaticism originated in a revolt
from Pythagoreanism, and we have now to consider its detailed
criticism of that doctrine. The great critic was Zeno. According to
Plato,[1] his work, written when he was a young man, was intended
to support the teaching of Parmenides by showing that the
hypothesis of his opponents, 'if things are a many' (εἰ πολλά ἐστι)
led up, if thoroughly worked out, to consequences at least as
paradoxical as his master's. We learn further from Plato that Zeno
was twenty-five years younger than Parmenides, and that he was
forty years old when he accompanied him on his celebrated visit to
Athens just after the middle of the fifth century B.C. All that agrees
admirably with the well-authenticated statement that Perikles
'heard' Zeno as well as Anaxagoras, and also with the accounts
which represent Zeno as engaged in controversy with Protagoras.
He also appears to have written against Empedokles.[2]

§ 64. It is significant that a work of Zeno's is cited by the title, *A
Reply to the Philosophers* (Πρὸς τοὺς φιλοσόφους); for there is reason
to believe that in these days 'philosopher' meant Pythagorean. At
any rate, it is only if we regard the arguments of Zeno as directed
against the assumption that things are a many, that is to say a
'multitude of units' (μονάδων πλῆθος), that their real significance
can be understood. According to the Pythagorean view, geometry
was simply an application of arithmetic, and the point only differs
from the arithmetical unit in so far as it is a 'unit having position'
(μονὰς θέσιν ἔχουσα). From this it ought to follow, though we need
not suppose the Pythagoreans to have said so in so many words,
that we should be able to say how many points there are in a given
terminated straight line, and further that all magnitudes must be

---

[1] *Parm.* 128 c.
[2] References to authorities are given in *E. Gr. Ph.*[2] §§ 155 *sqq.*

commensurable. The Pythagoreans themselves, however, had discovered at least two striking instances to the contrary. We have seen that neither the most perfect triangle, the isosceles right-angled triangle, nor the most perfect solid, the regular dodecahedron, can be expressed numerically; for, as we should put it, $\sqrt{2}$ and $\sqrt{5}$ are 'surds'. The Pythagoreans must have been quite well aware of these facts, though, as we have seen, they probably explained them by referring them to the nature of the 'unlimited', along with such similar cases as the impossibility of dividing the octave and the tone into equal parts.

Zeno's arguments are directed to showing that the 'unlimited' or, as the Eleatics call it, the continuous (συνεχές, lit. 'hanging together') cannot be composed of units however small and however many. We can always bisect a line, and every bisection leaves us with a line that can itself be bisected. We never come to a point or unit. It follows that, if a line is made up out of unit-points, there must be an infinite number of such points in any given terminated straight line. Now if these points have magnitude, every line will be of infinite length; if they have no magnitude, every line will be infinitely small. Again, if a point has magnitude, the addition of a point to a line will make it longer and its subtraction will make it smaller; but, if points have no magnitude, neither their addition nor their subtraction will make any difference to the line. But that of which the addition or subtraction makes no difference is nothing at all. It follows that, if number is a sum of units (and no other account of it has been suggested), there is an impassable gulf between the discrete and the continuous, between arithmetic and geometry. Things are not numbers. To put the thing in another way, geometry cannot be reduced to arithmetic so long as the number one is regarded as the beginning of the numerical series. What really corresponds to the point is what we call zero.[1]

§ 65. The celebrated arguments of Zeno concerning motion introduce the element of time, and are directed to showing that it is just as little a sum of moments as a line is a sum of points. (1) If a thing moves from one point to another, it must first traverse half the distance. Before it can do that, it must traverse a half of the half, and so on *ad infinitum*. It must, therefore, pass through an

---

[1] This is the ultimate explanation of the dispute between mathematicians and historians as to whether 1900 was the last year of the nineteenth century or the first year of the twentieth. Astronomers call the year preceding 1 A.D. the year 0, while historical chronologists make 1 A.D. the year after 1 B.C.

infinite number of points, and that is impossible in a finite time. (2) Achilles can never overtake the tortoise. Before he comes up to the point at which the tortoise started, the tortoise will have got a little way on. The same thing repeats itself with regard to this little way, and so on *ad infinitum*. (3) The flying arrow is at rest. At any given moment it is in a space equal to its own length, and therefore at rest. The sum of an infinite number of positions of rest is not a motion. (4) If we suppose three lines, one (A) at rest, and the other two (B, C) moving in opposite directions, B will pass in the same time twice the number of points in C that it passes in A. From the interpreter's point of view this last argument is the most important of all. If it is directed against the view that the line is a sum of points and time a sum of moments, it is a perfectly legitimate *reductio ad absurdum* of these views, otherwise it has no meaning at all.

§ 66. The arguments of Zeno are valid only on the assumption that the nature of number is completely expressed by the natural series of integers, but on that assumption they are unanswerable, and no other view of number had yet been suggested. Even rational fractions are unknown to Greek mathematics, and what we treat as such are expressed as ratios of one integer to another.[1] Still harder was it for the Greeks to regard a surd, for instance, as a number, and it was only in the Academy that an effort was made at a later date to take a larger view. What Zeno actually does prove is that space and time cannot consist of points or moments which themselves have magnitude, or that the elements of a continuum cannot be units homogeneous with the continuum constructed out of them. He shows, in fact, that there must be more points on the line, more moments in the shortest lapse of time, than there are members of the series of natural numbers, or, what comes to the same thing, that, though every continuum is infinitely divisible, infinite divisibility is not an adequate criterion of continuity.[2] That, however, is all he undertook to prove. We know from Plato that his work was an *argumentum ad homines*, and as such it is entirely successful.

[1] Cf. *e.g.* the ἡμιόλιος λόγος 3 : 2 and the ἐπίτριτος λόγος 4 : 3.
[2] I take this way of stating the matter from Prof. A. E. Taylor's article 'Continuity' in Hastings' *Encyclopaedia of Religion and Ethics*.

MELISSOS

§ 67. It is very significant that the next representative of the Eleatic doctrine is a Samian. As a result of the Persian wars, the Italic and Ionic philosophies had come into contact once more, and their common meeting-ground was Athens. Both Empedokles and Anaxagoras came under the influence of Parmenides, who had himself visited Athens along with Zeno, who apparently continued to reside there for some time. Anaxagoras lived at Athens for many years, and Empedokles took part in the Athenian colonisation of Thourioi. None of these men were themselves Athenians, but they had Athenian disciples, and Sokrates was already in his 'teens.

Melissos was in command of the Samian fleet that fought against Perikles in 441 B.C. We know nothing else about him. We can only guess that he had become acquainted with Eleaticism at Athens, and we can see that the modifications he introduced into it were due to 'the philosophy of Anaximenes', which still survived in Ionia.

§ 68. The main arguments of Melissos are just those of Parmenides, except that they are expressed in simple Ionic prose. His great innovation was that he regarded the real as infinite instead of making it a finite sphere. It is said that he inferred its spatial infinity from its eternity, and he does appear to have used language that might suggest such an argument. He had, however, a much more cogent reason than that. The real, he said, could only be limited by empty space, and there is no empty space. For the same reason there can be no motion and no change. The real was, of course, corporeal, as it was for Parmenides. The statement sometimes made that Melissos held it to be incorporeal is based on a misunderstanding.[1]

There can be no doubt that Melissos was looked upon in his own day as the most advanced representative of Eleaticism, and 'the thesis of Melissos' is an object of special aversion to the writer of the Hippokratean treatise on *The Nature of Man*, while Plato makes Sokrates couple his name with that of the great Parmenides himself (*Theaet.* 180 e). From a historical point of view his most remarkable saying is that, if things are a many, each one of them would have to be such as he has shown the One to be. That is just the formula of Atomism, as we shall see, and Melissos rejected it

[1] *E. Gr. Ph.*[2] § 169.

because he denied the existence of empty space. In that, too, he prepared the way for the atomic theory by making it necessary for Leukippos to affirm the existence of the Void.

THE LATER PYTHAGOREANS

§ 69. It has been said already (§ 27) that the Pythagoreans had a singular power of adapting their theories to new conditions, and it is certain that at some time or other they felt called upon to give an account of the new doctrine of elements in terms of their own system. It is probable that this was the work of Philolaos, who lived at Thebes towards the end of the fifth century B.C., but returned to South Italy as soon as it was safe for Pythagoreans to show themselves in those parts once more. From that time forward Taras (Tarentum) was the chief seat of the school, and we shall hear more of it when we come to consider the relations of Plato with Archytas. For reasons I have given elsewhere, I cannot regard the fragments which have come down to us under the name of Philolaos as authentic, but for all that they are old and contain some valuable hints as to the development of Pythagorean doctrine.[1]

§ 70. The most remarkable feature of later Pythagoreanism is the way the religious side of the doctrine was dropped and the effort that was made to clear the memory of Pythagoras himself from the imputation of mysticism. We have the echo of this in the remains of Aristoxenos and Dikaiarchos, but it must be older; for in their day scientific Pythagoreanism had ceased to exist. The statement that Hippasos of Metapontion was guilty of publishing a mystic discourse 'with the view of misrepresenting Pythagoras'[2] must go back to this generation of the school; for at a later date no one would have any interest in making it. A book by Hippasos almost certainly existed; for Aristotle is able to state that he made fire the first principle like Herakleitos. That agrees very well with what we can infer as to the earliest Pythagorean cosmology. There are all sorts of stories about this Hippasos, who is said to have been drowned at sea or to have been expelled from the order, which then made a sepulchre for him as if he were dead. Finally, the story was

---

[1] *E. Gr. Ph.*[2] §§ 138 *sqq.*
[2] Diog. viii. 7 τὸν δὲ Μυστικὸν λόγον Ἱππάσου . . . εἶναι γεγραμμένον ἐπὶ διαβολῇ Πυθαγόρου.

put about that there had from the first been two grades in the order, Mathematicians and Akousmatics, or Pythagoreans and Pythagorists, and Hippasos was represented as the leader of the lower grade. It is impossible, of course, for us to disentangle truth from falsehood in all this; but we are, I think, entitled to infer that there was a real struggle between those who held to the Pythagorist religion and those who attached themselves exclusively to the scientific side of the doctrine. In the fourth century the Pythagorean scientific school expired and its place was taken by the Academy; the Pythagorist religion, on the other hand, maintained its existence even later, as we know from the fragments of the comic poets.

§ 71. The distinctive feature of the later Pythagoreanism is its effort to assimilate the Empedoklean doctrine of the four 'elements', and there is reason for believing that the name itself (στοιχεῖον) originated at this time. If Philolaos was the author of the theory, that is natural enough. The fragment of Menon's *Iatrika* recently discovered in a London medical papyrus has revealed the fact that he belonged to the Sicilian medical school, and that the theories of that school depended on the identification of the old 'opposites', hot and cold, wet and dry, with the four elements of Empedokles.[1] The Pythagoreans had to find room for the elements in their system somehow, though they continued to resist the doctrine that they were ultimate. Plato has preserved this touch in his *Timaeus* (48 b), where he makes the Pythagorean protest that, so far from being 'letters', the four elements are not even syllables.

The view they actually took of them was that they were 'figures', or, in other words, that they were made up of particles which had the shapes of the regular solids. We need not doubt that the derivation of those figures from the elementary triangles given in Plato's *Timaeus* is in substance Pythagorean, though, as the doctrine of the five regular solids was only completed by Theaitetos, some of the constructions must belong to a later date than Philolaos.

§ 72. The later Pythagoreans appear to have said that things were *like* numbers rather than that they actually *were* numbers, and here we shall probably be right in tracing the effect of Zeno's criticism. Aristotle quotes the doctrine in both forms, and he

---

[1] The hot and cold, wet and dry are spoken of as εἴδη in Περὶ ἀρχαίης ἰατρικῆς 15, and Philistion called the four elements ἰδέαι (*E. Gr. Ph.*² p. 235, *n.* 2).

hardly seems to be conscious of any great difference between them. Further, he treats what is usually called the Platonic 'theory of ideas' as practically identical with some form of Pythagoreanism. That raises questions we shall have to deal with later; for the present, it will be enough to consider what the later Pythagoreans probably meant by saying things were 'like numbers' instead of saying that they actually were numbers. So far as we can see, it must have been something like this. For the construction of the elements we require, not merely groups of 'units having position', but plane surfaces limited by lines and capable in turn of forming the limits of solids. Now Zeno had shown that lines cannot be built up out of points or units, and therefore the elementary triangles out of which the 'figures' are constructed cannot be identical with triangular numbers such as the *tetraktys*. In particular, the isosceles right-angled triangle is of fundamental importance in the construction of the regular solids, and it cannot be represented by any arrangement of 'pebbles' ($\psi\hat{\eta}\phi o\iota$),[1] seeing that its hypotenuse is incommensurable with its other two sides. It only remains for us to say, then, that the triangles of which the elements are ultimately composed are 'likenesses' or 'imitations' of the triangular numbers. The fateful doctrine of two worlds, the world of thought and the world of sense, in fact originated from the apparent impossibility of reconciling the nature of number with continuity ($\tau\grave{o}$ $\sigma\upsilon\nu\epsilon\chi\acute{\epsilon}s$) as the Eleatics called it, or the unlimited ($\tau\grave{o}$ $\check{a}\pi\epsilon\iota\rho o\nu$) as the Pythagoreans said. There was something in the latter that seemed to resist the power of thought, and it was inferred that it could not have true reality ($o\mathring{\upsilon}\sigma\acute{\iota}a$), but was at best a process of becoming ($\gamma\acute{\epsilon}\nu\epsilon\sigma\iota s$). You may go on bisecting the side and the diagonal of a square as long as you please, but you never come to a common measure, though you are always getting nearer to it.

§ 73. The 'figures' ($\epsilon\check{\iota}\delta\eta$) are now regarded, then, not as identical with the numbers, but as likenesses of them, and we shall not be surprised to find that, once the demand for a complete identification had been given up, an attempt was made to explain other things than the elements in this way. According to Aristotle, that is exactly what happened. The Pythagoreans went on to say that justice was a square number, and to give similar accounts of marriage, opportunity, and the like. They only gave a few such

[1] Cf. p. 55, *n.* 1.

definitions, however, and Aristotle observes that they were based
on mere superficial likenesses between numbers and things. The
most valuable piece of information he gives us is that Eurytos, a
disciple of Philolaos, and therefore one of the last of the pure
Pythagoreans, went on to express the nature of horse, man, and
plant 'by means of pebbles' or counters. Theophrastos said the
same thing, and there seems to be no doubt that the statement rests
on the authority of Archytas. Alexander gives, doubtless from the
same source, an account of this extraordinary method. 'Let us
assume, for example,' he says, 'that 250 is the number which
defines man, and 360 that which defines plant. Having laid this
down, he took 250 counters, some green and some black, and others
red, and all sorts of other colours, and then, smearing the wall with
plaster and sketching on it a man and a plant, he proceeded to fix
some of the counters in the outline of the face, some in that of the
hands and some in that of other parts, and so he completed the
outline of the man he had imaged by a number of counters equal
in number to the units which he said defined the man.'

This precious testimony shows what the doctrine of 'figures'
was capable of becoming when it ventured beyond its proper
sphere, and we must remember that Eurytos was not an early
Pythagorean, but a leading man in the latest generation of the
school. According to Aristotle, it was Sokrates that directed the
theory into another channel by his study of moral (and aesthetic)
forms, and Plato represents him in the *Parmenides* (130 c–d) as
saying that at one time he had thought such things as man, fire,
and the like should have forms as well, but that he had given up
the idea of finding forms for everything from fear of falling into an
ocean of nonsense (βυθὸς φλυαρίας). We now see what that means.
Nevertheless it is quite clear that Aristotle regards all this as the
origin of what we call 'the theory of ideas', and he even seems
anxious to minimise the differences between the Platonic and the
Pythagorean form of the theory, which did not, of course, in all
cases assume such an extravagant form as Eurytos gave it. It was
also the tradition of the Academy that the doctrine in question
was of Pythagorean origin. Proklos was well read in the ancient
commentaries on Plato, some of which went back to the early days
of the Academy, and he distinctly attributes the original form of
the theory to the Pythagoreans and its elaboration to Sokrates.
His words are: 'The Pythagoreans, too, had the doctrine of forms.

Plato himself shows that by calling the wise men of Italy friends of the forms (*Soph.* 248 a). But it was Sokrates above all that held the forms in honour and most explicitly postulated them.'[1] We shall return to this when we come to Sokrates; for the present it is sufficient to point out that Proklos could hardly have spoken as he does if any other interpretation of the phrase 'friends of the forms' (εἰδῶν φίλοι) had been known in the Academy.

§ 74. To the same generation of the school belongs a remarkable advance in cosmology. It is probable that Philolaos still held the geocentric theory, for that is the only one of which we get a hint in the *Phaedo*; but there can be no doubt that the Pythagoreans in Italy made the all-important discovery that the earth was one of the planets. They did not, indeed, make it go round the sun, but they postulated a Central Fire, round which the sun, moon, and planets all revolved. This Central Fire was invisible to us because the revolution of all the heavenly bodies was naturally explained on the analogy of the moon, which is the only heavenly body that can be properly observed by the naked eye. In other words, as the moon always presents the same face to us, it was supposed that the sun and the planets, including the earth, all turned the same face to the centre. It follows that we on the earth can see the Central Fire just as little as we can see the other side of the moon. In this system there was also a body called the Counter-earth (ἀντίχθων), which is invisible to us because it is between the earth and the Central Fire. This body seems to have been assumed in order to explain eclipses of the moon. The shadow of the earth did not seem to account for them all, and another body casting a shadow was required. It will be seen that this implies the view that the moon shines by light reflected from the Central Fire, and it is not surprising that the same explanation should have been given of the sun's light. The whole cosmology of this period depends, in fact, on the extension of the observed facts regarding the moon to other bodies.

§ 75. Perhaps the most remarkable thing in the Pythagorean doctrine of this generation is that the soul has come to be regarded as an 'attunement' (ἁρμονία) of the body. That is the belief expounded by Simmias, the Theban disciple of Philolaos, in the

---

[1] Proclus *in Parm.* p. 149, Cousin: ἦν μὲν γὰρ καὶ παρὰ τοῖς Πυθαγορείοις ἡ περὶ τῶν εἰδῶν θεωρία, καὶ δηλοῖ καὶ αὐτὸς ἐν Σοφιστῇ τῶν εἰδῶν φίλους προσαγορεύων τοὺς ἐν Ἰταλίᾳ σοφούς, ἀλλ' ὅ γε μάλιστα πρεσβεύσας καὶ διαρρήδην ὑποθέμενος τὰ εἴδη Σωκράτης ἐστίν.

Phaedo (86 b *sq.*), and we are also told that it was held by those Pythagoreans who had settled at Phleious (88 d), from whom Aristoxenos adopted it at a later date. It cannot be denied that such a doctrine seems to follow quite naturally from the analogy of the tuned string; but, on the other hand, nothing can be more inconsistent with the earlier Pythagorean view of the soul as something that existed before the body, and will continue to exist after it has left the body. This doctrine, on the contrary, makes the soul a mere function of the body, and leaves no room for the belief in immortality. It is probable, therefore, that its adoption is connected with the desire, which has been noted already, to drop the religious side of the Master's teaching.

VI

Leukippos

§ 76. The first part of our story ends with Leukippos, the founder of Atomism; for it was he that really answered the question of Thales.[1] We know next to nothing about his life, and his book appears to have been incorporated in the collected works of Demokritos. No writer subsequent to Theophrastos seems to have been able to distinguish his teaching from that of his more famous disciple. Indeed his very existence has been denied, though on wholly insufficient grounds. It is certain that Aristotle and Theophrastos both regarded him as the real author of the atomic theory, and it is out of the question that they should have been decieved in such a matter, especially as Theophrastos distinguished the teaching of Leukippos from that of Demokritos on certain points.

Theophrastos was uncertain whether Leukippos was a native of Miletos or of Elea. The latter view is doubtless based on the statement that he had been a disciple of the Eleatics, and, in particular, of Zeno. We shall see that this is fully borne out by all we know of the origin of his doctrine, and we may infer with some probability that he was a Milesian who had come under the influence of Parmenides at Elea or elsewhere. It is not likely that it was at Athens; for the atomic theory does not appear to have been well known there till the time of Aristotle. Plato, in particular, does not appear to allude to it, though it would certainly have interested him if he had known it.

§ 77. Aristotle, who in default of Plato is our chief authority on the subject of atomism, gives a perfectly clear and intelligible account of the way it arose. It almost appears as if he were anxious to give a more strictly historical statement than usual just because so little was known about atomism in the Academy. According to him, it originated in the Eleatic denial of the void, from which the impossibility of multiplicity and motion had been deduced.

[1] *E. Gr. Ph.*[2] §§ 171 *sqq.*

Leukippos supposed himself to have discovered a theory which would avoid this consequence. He admitted that there could be no motion if there was no void, and he inferred that it was wrong to identify the void with the non-existent. What is not (τὸ μὴ ὄν) in the Parmenidean sense *is* just as much as what is (τὸ ὄν). In other words, Leukippos was the first philosopher to affirm, with a full consciousness of what he was doing, the existence of empty space. The Pythagorean void had been more or less identified with 'air', but the void of Leukippos was really a vacuum.[1]

Besides space there was body, and to this Leukippos ascribed all the characteristics of the Eleatic real. It was 'full' (ναστόν), or, in other words, there was no empty space in it, but it was not one. The assumption of empty space, however, made it possible to affirm that there was an infinite number of such reals, invisible because of their smallness, but each possessing all the marks of the one Eleatic real, and in particular each indivisible (ἄτομον) like it. These moved in the empty space, and their combinations can give rise to the things we perceive with the senses. Pluralism was at least stated in a logical and coherent way. As we have seen (§ 68), Melissos had already suggested that, if things were a many, each one of them must be such as he held the One to be. He intended that for a *reductio ad absurdum* of pluralism, but Leukippos accepted it, and made it the foundation of his system.

§ 78. The nature of the original motion ascribed by Leukippos to the atoms has been much discussed. At a later date the Epicureans held that all the atoms are falling eternally downwards through infinite space, and this made it very hard for them to explain how they could come in contact with one another. There is no need to attribute this unscientific conception to the early atomists. In the first place they did not, as we shall see, regard weight as a primary property of the atoms; and, in the second place, we have evidence that Demokritos said there was neither up or down, middle or end in the indefinite void.[2] Aristotle criticised all this from the point of view of his own theory of absolute weight and lightness resulting in the 'natural motions' of the elements upwards or downwards,

---

[1] The Aristotelian derivation of Atomism from Eleaticism has been contested, especially by Gomperz. It is true, of course, that the Milesian Leukippos was concerned to vindicate the old Ionic cosmology, and, in particular, to save as much of the 'philosophy of Anaximenes' as he could. So was Anaxagoras (§ 61). That, however, has no bearing on the point at issue. Theophrastos stated distinctly that Leukippos had been a member of the school of Parmenides and Zeno.

[2] Cic. *de Finibus*, i. 17; Diog. Laert. ix. 44.

as the case might be, and the Epicurean doctrine is probably the
result of this criticism. Even Epicurus, however, had the grace to
dispense with Aristotle's absolute lightness. We may therefore
regard the original motion of the atoms as taking place in all
directions, and we shall see that this alone will account for the
formation of the worlds. Demokritos compared the motions of the
atoms of the soul to that of the motes in the sunbeam which dart
hither and thither in all directions even when there is no wind,[1]
and we may fairly assume that he regarded the original motion of
the other atoms in much the same way.

§ 79. The atoms are not mathematically indivisible like the
Pythagorean monads, but they are physically indivisible because
there is no empty space in them. Theoretically, then, there is no
reason why an atom should not be as large as a world. Such an
atom would be much the same thing as the Sphere of Parmenides,
were it not for the empty space outside it and the plurality of
worlds. As a matter of fact, however, all atoms are invisible. That
does not mean, of course, that they are all the same size; for there
is room for an infinite variety of sizes below the limit of the
minimum visibile.

Leukippos explained the phenomenon of weight from the size
of the atoms and their combinations, but he did not regard weight
itself as a primary property of bodies. Aristotle distinctly says that
none of his predecessors had said anything of absolute weight and
lightness, but only of relative weight and lightness, and Epicurus
was the first to ascribe weight to atoms. Weight for the the earlier
atomists is only a secondary phenomenon arising, in a manner to
be explained, from excess of magnitude.[2] It will be observed that
in this respect the early atomists were far more scientific than
Epicurus and even than Aristotle. The conception of absolute
weight has no place in science, and it is really one of the most
striking illustrations of the true scientific instinct of the Greek
philosophers that no one before Aristotle ever made use of it, while
Plato expressly rejected it.

§ 80. The differences between groups of atoms are due to
(1) arrangement and (2) position. It is not clear whether the
illustration from the letters of the alphabet quoted by Aristotle

---

[1] Aristotle, *de Anima*, 403 b, 31.
[2] There can be no question of mass; for the φύσις of all the atoms is identical,
and each atom is a *continuum*.

was given by Leukippos or Demokritos, but in any case it is probably Pythagorean in origin, for it accounts satisfactorily for the use of the word στοιχεῖον in the sense of element, and that is found in Plato, who, as I believe, knew nothing of Atomism. However that may be, the points of resemblance between Pythagoreanism and Atomism were already noted by Aristotle, and he had direct knowledge on the subject. 'Leukippos and Demokritos', he says, 'virtually make all things numbers too and produce them from numbers.' I do not see how this statement can have any meaning unless we regard the Pythagorean numbers as patterns or 'figurate numbers', and, in that case, it is still more striking that Demokritos called the atoms 'figures' or 'forms' (ἰδέαι). The void is also a Pythagorean conception, though, as we have seen, it was not formulated with precision before Leukippos. It is hardly, then, too much to say that the atoms are Pythagorean monads endowed with the properties of Parmenidean reality, and that the elements which arise from the various positions and arrangements of the atoms are, so far, like the Pythagorean 'numbers'. Such, at any rate, seems to be the view of Aristotle, though we should have been glad if he had explained himself more fully.

§ 81. The first effect of the motion of the atoms is that the larger atoms are retarded, not because they are 'heavy', but because they are more exposed to impact than the smaller. In particular, atoms of an irregular shape become entangled with one another and form groups of atoms, which are still more exposed to impact and consequent retardation. The smallest and roundest atoms, on the other hand, preserve their original motions best, and these are the atoms of which fire is composed. It will be observed that it is simply taken for granted that an original motion will persist unless something acts upon it so as to retard it or bring it to a stop. To Aristotle that appeared incredible, and the truth had to be rediscovered and established on a firm basis by Galileo and Newton. It was really the assumption of all the earlier Greek philosophy. Before the time of Parmenides it was rest and not motion that required explanation, and now that Leukippos had discovered a way of escape from the conclusion of Parmenides, it was possible for him to revert to the older view.

§ 82. In an infinite void in which an infinite number of atoms of countless shapes and sizes are constantly impinging upon one another in all directions, there will be an infinite number of places

where a vortex motion is set up by their impact. When this
happens, we have the beginning of a world. It is not correct to
ascribe this to chance, as later writers do. It follows necessarily
from the presuppositions of the system. The solitary fragment of
Leukippos we possess is to the effect that 'Naught happens for
nothing, but all things from a ground (λόγος) and of necessity'. It
will be observed that the vortex theory is derived from that of
Anaxagoras (§ 60), which in turn was a development of the older
Ionic doctrine. So far we see that Leukippos was a Milesian, but
he has thought the matter out much more carefully than his predecessor. Anaxagoras had supposed that the analogy of a sling
would apply, and that the larger or 'heavier' bodies would,
therefore, be driven to the furthest distance from the centre.
Leukippos left weight out of account altogether, as a property
which is not primitive, but only arises when the vortex has already
been formed. He therefore looked rather to what happens in the
case of bodies in an eddy of wind or water, and he saw that the
larger bodies would tend towards the centre.

§ 83. The first effect of the vortex motion thus set up is to bring
together those atoms which are alike in shape and size, and this is
the origin of the four 'elements', fire, air, earth, and water. This
process was illustrated by the image of a sieve which brings the
grains of millet, wheat and barley together. As this image is found
also in Plato's *Timaeus* (52 e), it is probably of Pythagorean origin.
Another image was that of the waves sorting the pebbles on a
beach and heaping up long stones with long and round with round.
In this process the finer atoms are forced out towards the circumference, while the larger tend to the centre. To understand this, we
must remember that all the parts of the vortex come in contact
(ἐπίψαυσις) with one another, and it is in this way that the motion
of the outermost parts is communicated to those within them. The
larger bodies offer more resistance (ἀντέρεισις) to this communicated motion than the smaller, simply because they are larger and
therefore more exposed to impacts in different directions which
neutralise the vortex motion. In this way they make their way to
the centre where the motion is least, while the smaller bodies are
squeezed out towards the circumference where it is greatest. That
is the explanation of weight, which is not an 'occult quality', but
arises from purely mechanical causes.

§ 84. When we come to details, we find that Leukippos showed himself a true Ionian. His Eleatic teachers doubtless warned him off the Pythagorean cosmology, but they could not give him a better. It was natural, then, that he should turn to the theories of his distinguished fellow-citizen Anaximenes, and the little we know of his system shows that he did so, just as Anaxagoras had done before him. He deliberately rejected the Pythagorean discovery that the earth was spherical, a discovery of which he cannot have been ignorant, and taught that it was in shape 'like a tambourine', resting on the air. The reason why it sloped toward the south was that the heat there made the air thinner and therefore less able to support it. In fact, the Atomists rejected the Pythagorean theory of the earth exactly as Anaxagoras had done, and it was only the fusion of Eastern and Western cosmology at Athens that finally established the new view. Though Aristotle's earth is in the centre of the universe, it never occurs to him to doubt its spherical shape.

§ 85. It is not worth while to follow in detail the application of the atomic theory to particular phenomena, and the atomic explanation of sensation and knowledge will be better kept till we come to Demokritos, to whom it was chiefly due. All we need say further here is that Leukippos has answered the question of Thales in the sense in which Thales had asked it, and no further advance was possible on these lines. Before that could take place it was necessary that attention should be directed to the kindred problems of knowledge and of conduct, and we shall see in the next book how that came about. The very completeness of the mechanical theory of the world which had now been given brought science to a standstill for a time, and it also provoked a revolt against cosmology. On one side that came from specialists in the particular sciences, especially medicine, who disliked the sweeping generalisations of the cosmologists, and maintained the right of each science to deal with its own province. The Hippokratean treatise on *Ancient Medicine* (by which is meant the art of medicine based on experience and observation, as contrasted with the new-fangled medical theories of the school of Empedokles and others) is the best evidence of this. On the other side, there was a revolt against science which proceeded from men whose chief interest was in practical life. How do you know these things are true, they said, and even if they are, what does it matter to us? Those two questions can only be dealt with by a theory of knowledge and a theory of conduct.

BOOK II

KNOWLEDGE AND CONDUCT

VII

The Sophists

LAW AND NATURE

§ 86. We have now to consider a period of breakdown and reconstruction. Science had done all it could to make the world intelligible, and the result was a view of reality in flat contradiction to the evidence of the senses. Apparently it was not this world science explained but another one altogether. What, then, are we to say about this world? Why should we regard the world of science as truer than it? After all, that world is a product of human thinking, and how can we tell that thought is not as misleading as sense is said to be? Science proceeds on the assumption that there is some fundamental reality (φύσις) which we can discover, but what guarantee have we for that? It is very plain that men's views of right and wrong, fair and foul, vary from people to people, and even from city to city, so there is no fundamental reality in them at any rate. In the same way the scientific schools only agree in one thing — namely, that all other schools are wrong. It is surely just as unlikely that any of these schools should possess the truth as that any of the the nations, Hellenic or barbarian, should have established among themselves the true law of nature. Such were the thoughts that must have kept suggesting themselves to cultivated men in the middle of the fifth century B.C.

It is very significant that the difficulties which were felt as to knowledge and conduct should both have been summed up in the same antithesis, that of nature (φύσις) and law (νόμος), though the latter term has to do primarily with conduct and the former with knowledge. This shows that the two problems were felt to be the same. The use of the term Law was evidently due to the great legislative activity of the preceding centuries. In early days the regularity of human life had been far more clearly apprehended than the even course of nature. Man lived in a charmed circle of law and custom, but the world around him still seemed lawless.

So much was this so that, when the regular course of nature began to be observed, no better name could be found for it than Right or Justice (δίκη), a word which properly meant the unchanging custom that guided human life. We have seen that Anaximander spoke of the encroachment of one element on another as 'injustice' (§ 6), and, according to Herakleitos, it is the Erinyes, the avenging handmaids of Right, that keep the sun from 'overstepping his measures' (§ 42). But a code of laws drawn up by a human lawgiver whose name was known, a Zaleukos, or a Charondas, or a Solon, could not be accepted in the old way as part of the everlasting order of things. It was clearly something 'made', and it might just as well have been made otherwise or not made at all. A generation that had seen laws in the making could hardly help asking itself whether the whole of customary morality had not after all been made in the same way. That is why we find the word which is properly applied to the legislator's activity (θέσις)[1] used synonymously with law (νόμος) in this connexion.

The best evidence of this state of feeling is the work of Herodotos. He must certainly have known Protagoras at Thourioi, and some have thought that they could detect the influence of Protagoras in his work. It may be so, but it is just as likely that he is the mouthpiece of a feeling which was widely spread at the time, and to which Protagoras gave expression in another form. In any case, it is quite wrong to regard him as a representative of old-fashioned morality and religion. He is utterly sceptical, and his respect for conventions is due to his scepticism, just like that of Protagoras. The strongest proof he can give of the madness of King Cambyses is that he laughed at the rites and customs of other nations as if his own were a bit less artificial. 'If we were to set before all men a choice, and bid them pick out the best uses (νόμοι) from all the uses there are, each people, after examining them all, would choose those of their own nation.' So 'it is not likely that any one but a madman would laugh at such things', and Pindar was right in saying that 'Law is king of all.'[2]

---

[1] Whence 'positive' as opposed to 'natural' law.
[2] Herod. iii. 38. The quotation from Pindar is the more significant that Pindar meant something quite different (see below, § 97). It was therefore a familiar 'text' that could be made to mean anything.

THE 'SOPHISTS'

§ 87. It is usual to speak of the men we have now to deal with as 'the Sophists', and so they called themselves and were called by others. For us, however, the name Sophist is apt to be misleading in more ways than one. It is misleading if it is used to indicate a contrast between these men and the thinkers and teachers of an earlier generation. Herodotus calls Pythagoras a Sophist (iv. 95). It is still more misleading if it makes us think of them as forming in any sense a sect or school, or even as teachers with identical aims and methods. There is the further difficulty that, by the fourth century B.C., the word had already begun to acquire the meaning it still bears in ordinary language. This seems to have originated with Isokrates, who was anxious to keep what he called 'philosophy' distinct from intellectual pursuits of another order. Plato, too, for reasons we shall have to consider, was anxious to distinguish the Sophist from the Philosopher, and in one of his later dialogues defines the former as a paid huntsman of rich and distinguished young men. Aristotle formulated all that, and defines the Sophist as one who makes money out of apparent wisdom.[1]

Now we must observe that the Sophists here referred to are primarily contemporaries of Isokrates, Plato, and Aristotle themselves, not the distinguished teachers of the fifth century who commonly go by the name, and we have no right to transfer the polemics of a later generation to that of Protagoras and Gorgias. Aristotle's definition of the Sophist must, therefore, be left out of account altogether, and we shall see that the people Isokrates calls Sophists are certainly not those the word most naturally suggests to a modern reader. Plato is a safe guide when he is dealing by name with the great Sophists of the fifth century; his general discussion in the dialogue entitled *The Sophist* has, we shall see, another bearing.

We do learn from Plato, however, that, even in the fifth century, there was a prejudice against the name which made it possible for it to acquire the unfavourable sense it had in the fourth. That prejudice took two forms, an aristocratic and a democratic. From the democratic point of view, indeed, there was no blame attaching to the title σοφιστής that did not equally attach to the word σοφός itself. To be 'too clever' was always an offence, and in the *Apology*

---

[1] Plato, *Soph.* 223 b; Arist. *Soph. El.* 165 a, 22.

it is just the charge of being a 'wise man' that Sokrates is most eager to rebut. From the aristocratic point of view, the name was open to another objection. Its very form suggested professionalism,[1] a thing the high-born Hellene shrank from instinctively. Above all, the fact that these distinguished men were foreigners made them unpopular at Athens. The Athenian public was full of prejudices, and that against 'the foreigner' was particularly well developed. It was in part the cause and in part the effect of the growing stringency with which the privilege of citizenship was guarded. An Athenian orator or comic poet had no more effective weapon than the charge of foreign extraction. We know something of such nationalism in our own day, and in democratic Athens it was a very potent force indeed. Such considerations as these explain why Plato represents Protagoras as wearing the name of Sophist with a certain bravado.[2]

This view is more or less common ground at the present day; but it can hardly be said that all its consequences have been fully realised. German writers in particular continue to be much influenced by a superficial analogy between the 'age of the Sophists' and the eighteenth century *Aufklärung*, with the result that the Sophists are represented either as subverters of religion and morality, or as champions of free thought, according to the personal predilections of the writer. The truth is rather that, so far as there is any parallel to the *Aufklärung* in the history of Greek thought at all, it occurs much earlier, and Xenophanes, not Protagoras, is its apostle. It is not to religion but to science that Protagoras and Gorgias take up a negative attitude, and we shall never understand them if we lose sight of that fundamental distinction. The 'age of the Sophists' is, above all, an age of reaction against science.

§ 88. It has been pointed out that the Sophists did not constitute a school, but it is true for all that that their teaching had something in common. They all aim chiefly at practical ends. Their profession is that they teach 'goodness' (ἀρετή), and that is explained to mean the power of directing states and families aright. In practice this was apt to work out in a curious way, especially in a democratic state like Athens. The Sophists quite naturally taught people who could pay them, and these were generally the well born and well-

---

[1] The σοφιστής makes a profession of 'being clever' or 'playing the wit' (τὸ σοφίζεσθαι) just as the κιθαριστής makes a profession of playing on the lyre.
[2] *Prot.* 317 b.

to-do, who were the natural prey of the democracy. To a large extent, then, what they taught was the art of succeeding in a democratic State when you do not yourself belong to the ruling democracy, and, in particular, the art of getting off when you are attacked in the courts of law. That is the questionable side of the Sophist's work, but it is hardly fair to make it a ground of accusation against the men themselves; it was the natural outcome of the political conditions of Athens at the time. There is no reason to doubt that Protagoras was perfectly sincere in his profession that he was a teacher of 'goodness': only the goodness demanded by his clients was apt to be of a rather odd kind, and in practice his teaching became more and more confined to the arts of rhetoric and disputation. He would never have been entrusted by Perikles with the highly responsible task of framing a code of laws for Thourioi unless he had really possessed considerable skill in politics and jurisprudence; but the young men he was called on to train were more likely to be engaged in conspiracies against the State than in legislation. That was not his fault, and it will help us to understand the Sophists much better if we bear in mind that, from the nature of the case, they were compelled to depend mainly for their livelihood on the men who afterwards made the oligarchic revolutions. In that sense only were they the products of democracy; what a sincere though moderate democrat really thought of them we may gather from what Anytos is made to say in Plato's *Meno* (91 c *sqq.*).

PROTAGORAS

§ 89. The earliest Sophist in the sense just explained was Protagoras of Abdera. In the dialogue called by his name, Plato has described his second visit to Athens. He had been there once before when Hippokrates, the Athenian youth who asks Sokrates for an introduction to him, was still a boy. This time there is a great gathering of Sophists from all parts of the Hellenic world in the house of Kallias, son of Hipponikos, who was known to have spent more money on Sophists than any man of his day. It is obvious that such a gathering would have been impossible at any time during the first stage of the Peloponnesian War. Alkibiades is quite a lad, though he has a beard coming (309 a). Protagoras is represented as much older than Sokrates, and indeed he says (317 c) there is no one in the company (which includes Hippias and

Prodikos) whose father he might not be, and also that he has been engaged in his profession for many years. All through he addresses his hearers as men who belong to a younger generation. In the *Hippias maior* (282 e) Hippias is made to say that Protagoras was 'far older' than he was. From the *Meno* we get further information. That dialogue is supposed to take place before the expedition of Cyrus (401 B.C.) in which Meno took part, and Protagoras is spoken of (91 e) as having died some considerable time before, when he was seventy years old and had been forty years in practice, in which time he had made more money than Pheidias and any other ten sculptors put together. Lastly, in the *Theaetetus*, a dialogue supposed to take place just before the trial of Sokrates, Protagoras is spoken of as one long dead.

Now all these statements are perfectly consistent with one another, and the total impression they make on us would not be affected by one or two minor anachronisms, if such there are.[1] They mean that Protagoras was born not later than 500 B.C., that his second visit to Athens cannot have been later than 432 B.C., and may have been some years earlier, and that he died in the early years of the Peloponnesian War. These dates are perfectly consistent with the well-attested fact that he legislated for Thourioi in 444/3 B.C.,[2] and they are quite inconsistent with the statement that he was prosecuted and condemned for impiety in the time of the Four Hundred (411 B.C.). Indeed, Plato represents Sokrates as saying things which make it impossible to believe Protagoras was ever prosecuted for impiety at all.[3] In the *Meno* a special point is made (91 e) of the fact that throughout his long life no one ever suggested that he had done any harm to his associates, and that his

---

[1] Though Protagoras is represented as putting up παρὰ Καλλίᾳ τοῦ Ἱππονίκου (311 a), that does not imply that Hipponikos was dead. In the *Republic* (328 b) Sokrates and the rest go εἰς Πολεμάρχου, though Kephalos is certainly living. The imperfect ἐχρῆτο (315 d) rather implies that Hipponikos was still living.

[2] The traditional date of Protagoras is based solely on this. Everyone connected with Thourioi is supposed to have 'flourished' in the year of its foundation, and to 'flourish' is to be forty years old. For that reason Empedokles, Herodotos, and Protagoras are all said to have been born in 484/3 B.C. It seems probable, however, that a lawgiver would be over forty.

[3] The statement that Protagoras was accused by Pythodoros, son of Polyzelos (Diog. Laert. ix. 54), sounds circumstantial, but the next words, 'but Aristotle says it was Euathlos', shows that this notice really refers to the celebrated 'Suit for his Fee' (Δίκη ὑπὲρ μισθοῦ). The story was (*ib.* ix. 55) that Euathlos was to pay the fee when he had won his first case. When Protagoras demanded it, he replied, 'I have not won a case yet.' The answer was that Protagoras would sue him, and then he would have to pay. 'If I win, because I have won; if you win, because you have won.'

good name remained unsullied down to the supposed date of the dialogue, several years after his death. Further, there is no reference to any accusation of Protagoras in the *Apology*, though such a reference would have been almost inevitable if it had ever taken place.[1] Sokrates has to go back to the trial of Anaxagoras to find a parallel to his own case. It is therefore safer to dismiss the story altogether.

The portrait Plato has drawn of Protagoras has been called a caricature, but there does not seem to be much ground for such a view. In the first place, we must observe that he does not speak of him in his own person. It is Sokrates that describes him, and he only applies to Protagoras the irony he habitually applied to himself. Such good-humoured raillery as there is refers mainly to the enthusiastic admirers of the great man. Indeed, we are made to feel that Sokrates has a genuine respect for Protagoras himself. It is true that in the *Theaetetus* he does caricature his teaching, but he immediately confesses that it is a caricature, and goes on to give a much more sympathetic account of it.

§ 90. There is considerable uncertainty about the number and titles of the works of Protagoras, which is due, no doubt, to the fact that titles, in the modern sense, were unknown in the fifth century.[2] The work Plato refers to as *The Truth* ('Aλήθεια) is probably identical with that elsewhere called *The Throwers* (Καταβάλλοντες, sc. λόγοι),[3] and was no doubt the most important. If we reject the story that Protagoras was accused of impiety, we must also, of course, reject that of the destruction of all copies of his work by public authority. In any case, it is absurd. The book is represented as widely read long after Protagoras died. In the *Theaetetus* of Plato (152 a) the lad from whom the dialogue takes its name says he has read it often, and in the *Helen* (10. 2) Isokrates says: 'Who does not know that Protagoras and the Sophists of that time have written elaborate works and left them to us?' And even

---

[1] It is worth while noting that the oldest form of the story appears to have made the accusation of Protagoras subsequent to that of Sokrates (cf. Timon, fr. 5 Diels). He was supposed to be a contemporary of Plato owing to the common confusion of Sokrates and Plato, and was accordingly made a disciple of Demokritos, who really belonged to a later generation.

[2] This statement refers primarily to prose works. Dramas had titles of a sort (*i.e.* they were called after the chorus or the protagonist), and Plato followed this custom in naming his dialogues.

[3] Metaphors from wrestling are regular in this connexion, and καταβάλλειν means 'to throw'. The phrase καταβάλλειν τὰς αἰσθήσεις became technical for attacks upon sensation as a source of knowledge.

if the Athenians had been so silly as to burn all the copies they could find at Athens, there must have been many others scattered through the Greek world from Abdera to Sicily, and these would not be at the mercy of the Athenian authorities. It is clear, then, that the book was extant and widely read when Plato quoted it, and that it would have been impossible for him to interpret the doctrine of Protagoras in a sense not really suggested by it.

§ 91. That doctrine is the famous one that 'Man is the measure of all things, of things that are that they are, and of things that are not that they are not.' The meaning of this dictum has been much canvassed, but the curious use of the word 'measure' has not been sufficiently remarked. We have become so accustomed to the phrase that it hardly strikes us as peculiar, and yet it is surely not the most obvious way of expressing any of the meanings that have been attributed to Protagoras. Why 'measure'? To understand this, we should probably start from the arithmetical meaning of the word. It is recorded that Protagoras attacked mathematics, and in particular the doctrine that the tangent touches the circle at a point. There must, he urged, be a stretch for which the straight line and the circle are in contact.[1] It is probable, then, that his use of the word 'measure' was due to the controversies about incommensurability which were so rife in the fifth century. The geometers tell us, he may have said, that the side and the diagonal of the square have no common measure, but in cases like that man is the measure, that is, they are commensurable for all practical purposes. Theories that set themselves in opposition to the commonsense of mankind may safely be ignored. We shall find that this is just the position Protagoras took up on other questions. In the great controversy about Law and Nature he is decidedly on the side of the former.

In this connexion it is interesting to note that tradition represents Protagoras as having met Zeno at Athens, which he may well have done, and there was a dialogue in which the two men were introduced discussing a question closely bound up with the problem of continuity. A quotation from it has been preserved, and its authenticity is guaranteed by a reference to it in Aristotle.[2] 'Tell me, Protagoras,' said Zeno, 'does a single grain of millet make a

[1] Arist. *Met.* B, 2. 998 a, 2.
[2] Simplicius, *Phys.* 1108, 18 (*R.P.* 131), Ar. *Phys.* 250 a, 20. That such dialogues existed is the presupposition of Plato's *Parmenides*. It professes to be one of them.

noise in falling or the ten-thousandth part of a grain?' And when he said it did not, Zeno asked him, 'Does a bushel of millet make a noise when it falls or not?' And, when he said it did, Zeno replied, 'What then? Is there not a ratio of a bushel of millet to one grain and the ten-thousandth part of a grain?' When he said there was, Zeno replied, 'Well, then, will not the ratios of the sounds to one another be the same? As the sounding objects are to one another, so will the sounds be to one another; and, if that is so, if the bushel of millet makes a noise, the single grain and the ten-thousandth part of a grain will make a noise.' This quotation proves at least that it was thought appropriate for Protagoras and Zeno to discuss questions of the kind, and so confirms the view that it really was the Eleatic dialectic which made men turn away from science. Moreover, Porphyry said he had come across a work of Protagoras containing arguments against those who introduced the doctrine that Being was one.[1]

§ 92. But who is the 'Man' who is thus 'the measure of all things'? Plato more than once explains the meaning of the doctrine to be that things are to me as they appear to me, and to you as they appear to you. It is possible that this may not be a verbal quotation, but it is hard to believe that Plato could have ventured on such an interpretation if there was no ground for it. It also seems to me that the modern view which makes Protagoras refer, not to the individual man, but to 'Man as such', attributes to him a distinction he would not have understood, and would not have accepted if he had. The good faith of Plato is further confirmed by the hint he gives us, when he does go on in the *Theaetetus* to develop an elaborate sensationalist theory from the dictum of Protagoras, that it was not so developed by Protagoras himself. He says it was something he kept back from the common herd and only revealed to his disciples 'in a mystery'. We could hardly be told more plainly that the theory in question was not to be found in the book of Protagoras itself.

Nor does Plato stand alone in his interpretation of this dictum. Demokritos, who was a younger fellow-citizen of Protagoras, understood it precisely in the same way. We learn from Plutarch that the Epicurean Kolotes had accused Demokritos of throwing human life into confusion by teaching that 'nothing was such rather than such' (οὐδὲν μᾶλλον τοῖον ἢ τοῖον). Plutarch (or rather his

[1] Eus. *P.E.* x. 3, 25 (Bernays, *Ges. Abh.* i. 121).

authority) replies that, so far from holding this view, Demokritos combated Protagoras who did hold it, and wrote many convincing arguments against him.[1] It is impossible to ignore that, and the testimony of Demokritos is not only of the highest value in itself, but is, of course, quite independent of Plato's.

The practical inference to be drawn from all this is that on every subject it is possible to make two opposite statements (λόγοι), both of which are 'true', though one may be 'weaker' and another 'stronger'. It is the business of the disputant to make the weaker statement the stronger (τὸν ἥττω λόγον κρείττω ποιεῖν), and that is an art which can be taught. It is important to notice that this is not in itself an immoral doctrine. Plato distinctly tells us that though, according to Protagoras, all beliefs are equally true, one belief may nevertheless be better than another, and he seems to have regarded as 'better' the beliefs which were most in accordance with those of the man in a normal condition of body and mind. People who have jaundice see all things yellow, and just so it is possible for a man to have his moral beliefs coloured by some abnormal condition of soul. The things that appear yellow to the jaundiced eye really are yellow to it, but that does not alter the fact that it would be better for the sick man if they appeared different to him. His belief would not be truer, but it would be better. In the same way, then, as it is the business of the doctor to bring his patient's body into such a condition that he may see normally, so it is the business of the Sophist to make the better statement, which may be the weaker in a given case, not only better but stronger.

§ 93. This explains further how it is that Plato represents Protagoras as a convinced champion of Law against all attempts to return to nature for guidance. He was a strong believer in organised society, and he held that institutions and conventions were what raised men above the brutes. That, at any rate, is the meaning of the myth Plato puts into his mouth in the dialogue called by his name. So far from being a revolutionary, he was the champion of traditional morality, not from old-fashioned prejudice, but from a strong belief in the value of social conventions. In this sense, he not only professed to teach 'goodness' himself, but he believed it was taught by the laws of the state and by public opinion, though not perhaps so well. He had a profound belief in the value of such teaching, and he considered that it begins in early

[1] Plut. adv. Col. 1108 f. sq. Cf. Sextus Empiricus, adv. Math. vii. 389.

childhood. The less he could admit anything to be truer than anything else, the more sure he felt that we must cleave to what is normal and generally recognised.

The attitude of Protagoras to religion is generally looked at in the light of the highly improbable story of his accusation for impiety. We still have a single sentence from his work *On the Gods*, and it is as follows: 'With regard to the gods, I cannot feel sure either that they are or that they are not, nor what they are like in figure; for there are many things that hinder sure knowledge, the obscurity of the subject and the shortness of human life.' There is surely nothing impious in these words from any point of view, and certainly there is none from the Greek. Speculative opinions on subjects like these were no part of Greek religion, which consisted entirely in worship and not in theological affirmations or negations.[1] And, in any case, the sentence quoted might just as well be the prelude to a recommendation to worship according to the use of one's native city (νόμῳ πόλεως) as to anything else, and such a recommendation would be in complete harmony with the other views of Protagoras. If we cannot attain sure knowledge about the gods by ourselves, we shall do well to accept the recognised worship. That is what we should expect the champion of Law against Nature to say.

HIPPIAS AND PRODIKOS

§ 94. The other Sophists mentioned as present in the house of Kallias are of no great importance for the history of philosophy, though they are of considerable interest as typical figures. Hippias of Elis is chiefly memorable for his efforts in the direction of universality. He was the enemy of all specialism, and appeared at Olympia gorgeously attired in a costume entirely of his own making down to the ring on his finger. He was prepared to lecture to anyone on anything, from astronomy to ancient history. Such a man had need of a good memory, and we know that he invented a system of mnemonics. There was a more serious side to his character, however. This was the age when men were still sanguine of squaring the circle by a geometrical construction. The lunules of Hippokrates of Chios belong to it, and Hippias, the universal genius, could not be behindhand here. He invented the curve still known

[1] Cf. § 140.

as the quadratrix (τετραγωνίζουσα), which would solve the problem if it could be mechanically described. Prodikos of Keos is
chiefly known nowadays for the somewhat jejune apologue of the
Choice of Herakles which Xenophon has preserved. We shall see
presently how important the personality of Herakles was at the
time. The chief work of Prodikos, however, seems to have been the
discrimination of synonyms, a business which may possibly have
been important in the infancy of grammar. Protagoras too contri-
buted something to grammar. He called attention to the arbitrary
character of certain grammatical genders, no doubt in illustration
of the reign of Law or convention, and his classification of sen-
tences into command, wish, etc. prepared the way for the distinction of the moods.

GORGIAS

§ 95. Gorgias of Leontinoi in Sicily came to Athens as ambassador from his native city in 427 B.C., when he was already
advanced in years. His influence, therefore, belongs to a later
generation than that of Protagoras, though he need not have been
younger than Hippias and Prodikos. He had, it seems, been a
disciple of Empedokles, and we learn incidentally from Plato's
Meno (76 c) that he continued to teach that philosopher's doctrine
of 'effluences' even in his later days, when he had retired to Larissa
in Thessaly. He is said to have lived to a great age, but no precise
date can be given for his death. It is evident from Plato's account
of him that he was not so much a teacher of politics, like Protagoras,
as a teacher of rhetoric. That is accounted for by the change in the
political situation brought about by the Peloponnesian War and
the death of Perikles. The relations between the democracy and the
well-to-do classes were becoming more and more strained, and the
importance of forensic rhetoric was accordingly increased. What
Gorgias did was to introduce to Athens the methods of persuasion
by means of artistic prose which had been elaborated during the
struggle of classes in Sicily. His influence on Athenian literature,
and through it on the development of European prose style in
general, was enormous. It does not concern us here, except
incidentally, but it is worth while to note that the terms 'figure'
(εἶδος, σχῆμα) and 'trope' (τρόπος), which he applied to the
rhetorical devices he taught, are apparently derived from Pytha-

gorean musical theory (§ 32), and mean primarily the arrangement of words in certain patterns.[1]

§ 96. Like Protagoras, Gorgias had been driven by the Eleatic dialectic to give up all belief in science. Protagoras, as we have seen, fell back on 'common sense', but Gorgias proceeded in a much more radical fashion. If Protagoras taught that everything was true, Gorgias maintained there was no truth at all. In his work entitled *On Nature or the non-existent* (Περὶ φύσεως ἢ τοῦ μὴ ὄντος)[2] he sought to prove (1) that there is nothing, (2) that, even if there is anything, we cannot know it, and (3) that, even if we could know it, we could not communicate our knowledge to anyone else. We have two apparently independent accounts of the arguments by which he established these positions; but, though they agree generally with one another, they are obviously paraphrases in the language of a later time. We can still see, however, that they were borrowed in the main from Zeno and Melissos, and that is a mark of their being in substance authentic. Isokrates, who had been a disciple of Gorgias, mentions his assertion that *Nothing is* in the *Helen* (10.3), and he couples his name with those of Zeno and Melissos, thus confirming in a general way the later accounts. The reasoning of Zeno and Melissos was of a kind that is apt to cut both ways, and that is what Gorgias showed. The argument given as peculiar to himself was to this effect. 'What is not' *is* not, that is to say, it *is* just as much as 'what is'. The difficulty here raised is one that was not cleared up till Plato wrote the *Sophist*. We shall consider it when we come to that.

§ 97. In the ethical sphere the counterpart of this nihilism would be the doctrine that there is no natural distinction between right and wrong. Plato, however, is very careful not to represent Gorgias as drawing this conclusion himself, and even his ardent disciple Polos shrinks from the extreme consequences of opposing natural to legal right. These are drawn by one Kallikles, who is introduced as an Athenian democratic statesman. We know nothing of him otherwise, but he impresses us as a real man of flesh and blood. He is still young in the dialogue, and he may very well have disappeared during the revolutionary period. It is not Plato's way to introduce fictitious characters, nor does he introduce

[1] Taylor, *Varia Socratica*, i. p. 206, *n*. 1. Cf. also the uses of εἶδος and εἰδύλλιον for poems.
[2] The title cannot be ancient in this form, as is shown by the use of ἢ to introduce an alternative.

living contemporaries, except where, as in the *Phaedo*, that is made necessary by historical considerations. In any case, we have abundant evidence that the doctrine upheld by Kallikles, namely, that Might is Right, was current at Athens towards the close of the fifth century. In the Melian dialogue, Thucydides has shown us how it might be used to justify the attitude of the imperial democracy to its subject allies, and the *Herakles* of Euripides is a study of the same problem.[1] Its theme is that the 'strong man' is not sufficient for himself, and is only safe so long as he uses his strength in the service of mankind. This conception of the 'strong man' (of which Herakles was the regular type) was not in itself an ignoble one. It had its ideal side, and Pindar sings how Herakles took the oxen of Geryones without paying for them in virtue of that higher law, which 'justifies even the most violent deed with a high hand', a passage duly quoted in Plato's *Gorgias* (484 b). Such theories are a natural reaction against that rooted jealousy of everything above the common which is apt to characterise democracy. In modern times Carlyle and Nietzsche represent the same point of view. The worship of the strong man or 'hero', who can rise superior to all petty moral conventions — in fact, of the 'superman' — seems to have been fostered in the fifth century B.C. by much the same influences as in the nineteenth century A.D. It is clear, then, that even the doctrine of Kallikles is not a complete ethical nihilism. Might really is Right. That is a very different thing from saying Right is Might.

In the *Republic* that is the doctrine maintained by Thrasymachos. According to him there is no Right at all, and what we call by that name is only 'the interest of the stronger' which he is able to force the weaker to accept as lawful and binding on themselves in virtue of his strength. It is important to observe that Thrasymachos belongs to the generation we are now considering; for readers of the *Republic* are often led to suppose, by an illusion we shall have to note more than once, that Plato is there dealing with the controversies of his own day. It is well to remember, then, that Thrasymachos was mentioned as a celebrated teacher of Rhetoric in the earliest comedy of Aristophanes, which was produced in 427 B.C., the year Plato was born and Gorgias came to Athens. It is not to be supposed that he was still living when the *Republic* was

[1] See my paper 'The Religious and Moral Ideas of Euripides', in the *Proceedings of the Classical Association of Scotland*, 1907–8, pp. 96 *sqq.*

written; he belonged to a generation that was past and gone. We can hardly imagine anyone maintaining such vigorous doctrine in Plato's day, but it was natural enough that it should find advocates in the second half of the fifth century. It is the real ethical counterpart to the cosmological nihilism of Gorgias.

Plato's final judgment on the Sophists (in the sense in which we have been using the word) is to be found in the *Laws* (889 e). It is that, by thus insisting on the opposition between Law and Nature, they tended to do away with the distinction between right and wrong. If that distinction is not rooted in nature, but depends solely on human laws and institutions, it is valid only so long as we choose to recognise it. On the other hand, if we appeal from human law to a supposed higher law, the law of Nature, all restraint is abolished. We are forbidden by Plato's own account of them to attribute immoral intentions of any kind to the great Sophists; but we can hardly dispute his estimate of the inevitable consequences of their teaching in a state of society such as existed at Athens in the closing decades of the fifth century. It is an impartial historical judgment; for, in Plato's day, there were no longer any Sophists in the proper sense of the word.

ECLECTICS AND REACTIONARIES

§ 98. Besides these men there were a good many others, also called 'Sophists' by their contemporaries, who attempted to carry on the traditions of the Ionian cosmological schools. They were not, certainly, men of the same distinction as Protagoras or Gorgias, but they have their place in history as the vehicles by which the ideas of Ionian science were conveyed to Sokrates and his circle. From this point of view the most important of them is Diogenes of Apollonia, whose date is roughly fixed for us by the statement of Theophrastos that he borrowed from Anaxagoras and Leukippos, which shows that he belonged to the latter part of the fifth century B.C.

We have considerable fragments of Diogenes, written in an Ionic prose similar to that of some of the Hippokratean writings. We find here the first explicit justification of the old Milesian doctrine that the primary substance must be one, an assumption which the rise of pluralism had made it necessary to defend. The action and reaction of things on one another, he says, can only be

explained in this way. We may also trace the influence of Anaxagoras in another matter. Diogenes not only said the primary
substance was a 'god', which was nothing new, but also identified
it with Mind (νοῦς). On the other hand, he follows Anaximenes in
holding that this primary substance is air, and in deriving all things
from it by rarefaction and condensation. It is possible to see the
influence of Herakleitos in the close connexion he established
between wisdom and the dryness of the air we breathe. 'Damp
hinders thought' was one of his dicta, and is burlesqued in the
Clouds (232) accordingly. In one respect only does Diogenes
appear to have shown some originality, and that was in his medical
work. His account of the veins was celebrated, and bears witness
to the influence of Empedokles.

Hippon of Samos is of less importance. He revived the doctrine
of Thales that water was the primary substance, and defended it
on physiological grounds. We now know from Menon's *Iatrika*
that he was a medical writer and that he was a native of Kroton.
He was, therefore, one of the men who brought Western medicine
to Ionia, and that accounts for the character of the arguments with
which he defended his thesis. It is probable that the reasoning
conjecturally attributed to Thales by Aristotle is really his. We
may be sure that Thales defended his theory on meteorological,
not physiological, grounds. That is just the difference between the
two periods.

Archelaos of Athens was a disciple of Anaxagoras, and the first
Athenian to interest himself in science or philosophy. He deserves
mention for this, since, with the exception of Sokrates and Plato —
a considerable exception certainly — there are hardly any other
Athenian philosphers. There is not the slightest reason to doubt
the statement that he had Sokrates for a disciple. The contemporary
tragic poet, Ion of Chios, said in his *Memoirs* that Sokrates came to
Samos in the company of Archelaos as a young man. We know that
Ion gave an account of the visit of Sophokles and Perikles on the
occasion of the blockade of Samos in 441/0, and this statement will
refer to the same occasion.[1] Sokrates would be about twenty-eight

---

[1] Ion, fr. 73 (Köpke). The title of Ion's work was Ἐπιδημίαι ('Visits'). There is
no inconsistency between his statement and that of Plato (*Crito*, 52 b) that
Sokrates never left Athens except on military service. This is a case of military
service like the others we shall have to consider directly. It is most unlikely that
Ion should have meant any other Sokrates in this connexion, as has been
suggested.

at the time. Aristoxenos, as usual, repeats scandals about Archelaos and Sokrates. We are not bound to believe them, but they would have been pointless unless Sokrates had been generally known to have associated with Archelaos. Aristoxenos says that he was seventeen years old when this association began, and that it lasted many years.[1] Though Plato does not mention Archelaos by name, he refers unmistakably to his doctrines as having occupied Sokrates in his early youth, and it is natural to suppose that the man who is mentioned as reading aloud the book of Anaxagoras was no other than his Athenian disciple.[2] It is, therefore, quite unjustifiable to discredit the statement that Sokrates was his follower. It rests on practically contemporary evidence, and Theophrastos accepted it.[3]

[1] Aristoxenos, fr. 25 (F.H.G. ii. 280).

[2] *Phaedo*, 96 b, 97 b, with my notes. The theory that the warm and the cold gave rise by 'putrefaction' (σηπεδών) to a milky slime (ἰλύς), by which the first animals were nourished, is that of Archelaos, and is mentioned first among the doctrines Sokrates considered.

[3] *Phys. Op.* fr. 4 (Diels).

VIII

The Life of Sokrates

§ 99. It is possible to construct a biography of Sokrates from the dialogues of Plato, and, on the face of it, they seem to present us with an intelligible and consistent account of the man and his ways. Xenophon has left us three or four works purporting to record actual conversations of Sokrates, whom he had known as a young man, but whom he saw for the last time just before he joined the expedition of Cyrus as a volunteer (401 B.C.). He tells us himself how he consulted Sokrates on the wisdom of that step, and was referred by him to the Delphic oracle. He was careful, however, not to ask the oracle whether he should join the expedition at all; he only inquired to which of the gods he should offer prayer and sacrifice so as to ensure a prosperous issue to the journey he had in mind. He tells us frankly that Sokrates rebuked him for this evasion, and that is really all we know about their intercourse. If there had been much more to tell, we may be pretty sure Xenophon would have told it; for he is by no means averse to talking about himself. At this time he was under thirty, and Sokrates had passed away before his return from Asia. Several of the Sokratic conversations he records are on subjects we know Xenophon was specially interested in, and the views put forward in them are just those he elsewhere expresses in his own name or through the mouth of Cyrus, the hero of his paedagogic romance. No one ever thinks, accordingly, of appealing to such works as *The Complete Householder* (the Οἰκονομικός) for evidence regarding 'the historical Sokrates'. There are two other writings, the *Apology* and the *Symposium*, which seem to have been suggested by the dialogues of Plato bearing the same names, and these are generally left out of account too. Since the eighteenth century, however, it has been customary to make an exception in favour of a single work, the *Memorabilia*, composed by the exiled Xenophon with the professed intention of showing that Sokrates was not irreligious, and that, so far from corrupting the young, he did them a great deal of good by his conversations. It is quite intelligible that the eighteenth century should have preferred the Sokrates of the *Memorabilia* to that of the Platonic dialogues; for he comes much nearer the idea then current of what a philosopher ought to be.[1] In other respects it is hard to see what there is to recommend him. It is recognised that Xenophon is far from being a trustworthy historian, and the *Cyropaedia* shows he had a turn for philosophical romance. It is certainly unsound methodically to isolate the *Memorabilia* from Xenophon's other Sokratic writings, unless very strong reasons indeed can be given for doing so. Above all, it is quite impossible to get anything like a complete picture of Sokrates from the *Memorabilia* alone, and so in practice every writer fills in the outline with as much of the Platonic Sokrates as happens to suit his preconceived ideas of the man.[2] Such a procedure is hopelessly arbitrary, and can only land us in unverifiable speculations. It would be far better to say at once that we cannot know anything about Sokrates, and that for us he must remain a mere *x*. Even so, however, the Platonic Sokrates is actual enough, and he is the only Sokrates we can hope to know well. If he is a fictitious character, he is nevertheless more important than most men of flesh and blood. The only sound method, therefore, is to describe his life and opinions without, in the first instance, using any other source. Only when we have done that can we profitably go on to consider how far the Sokrates we learn to know in this way will account for the slighter sketch of Xenophon. We shall also have to consider in what relation he stands to the caricature in the *Clouds* of Aristophanes.

THE PLATONIC SOKRATES

§ 100. Sokrates, son of Sophroniskos, of the deme Alopeke, was seventy years old, or a little more, when he was put to death (399

---

[1] The first writer to prefer the Sokrates of the *Memorabilia* to the Platonic Sokrates was apparently Brucker (1741). The only reason he gives is that Xenophon had only one master, from whom he inherited not only moral philosophy, but integrity of life, while Plato was taken up with a 'syncretism' of various doctrines. He quotes also an anecdote about Sokrates hearing the *Lysis* read, and observing, 'Good heavens! what lies the young man tells about me!' But Sokrates was dead before the *Lysis* was written.

[2] In particular the 'irony' of Sokrates comes entirely from Plato. The Sokrates of the *Memorabilia* has no doubts or difficulties of any kind.

B.C.).[1] He was born, then, about 470 B.C., some ten years after Salamis, and his early manhood was spent in the full glory of the Periklean age. His family traced its descent to Daidalos, which means apparently that it was of some antiquity, and Sophroniskos must have been able to leave some property; for we shall find Sokrates serving as a hoplite. His mother was a midwife, Phainarete by name, and she had another son, Patrokles, by another husband. It is worthy of note that the great Aristeides was of the same deme, and his son Lysimachos speaks of Sophroniskos in the *Laches* as a family friend. He says he never had any difference with him to the day of his death. It is evident, then, that Sophroniskos was a man of some position in his deme. Another fellow-demesman was the wealthy Kriton, who was just the same age as Sokrates, and remained deeply attached to him till the end.

Late in life Sokrates married Xanthippe, by whom he had three sons. When his father was put to death, the eldest of them, Lamprokles, was a lad; but the other two, Sophroniskos and Menexenos, were children. The last named, indeed, was only a baby in arms. There is no hint in Plato that Xanthippe was a shrew. Her name and those of her eldest and youngest sons suggest that she was a woman of good family.[2] In the *Phaedo* we are told that the friends of Sokrates found Xanthippe and her baby in the prison when the doors were opened. They must have passed the night there, and she was in an overwrought condition. Sokrates sent her home, but she returned later in the day with the other women of the family and spent some time with Sokrates in an inner room, where she received his final instructions in presence of the faithful Kriton.[3]

Sokrates was very far from handsome. He had a snub nose and strangely protruding eyes. His gait was peculiar, and Aristophanes likened it to the strut of some sort of waterfowl. In other places,

---

[1] *Apol.* 17 d; *Crito*, 52 e. We know the date of his death from Demetrios Phalereus and the Marmor Parium. I have not given detailed references to the passages of Plato on which this account is based. They are well known and easily found. I do not think I have said anything which is not stated in Plato or to be immediately inferred from what Plato says. If this account of Sokrates is a 'construction', it is Plato's, not mine.

[2] It is noteworthy that it is the *second* son who is called after the father of Sokrates.

[3] The scandal-monger Aristoxenos tried to fix a charge of bigamy on Sokrates. He said he was married at the same time to Xanthippe and to Myrto, the daughter of Aristeides. Aristeides died in 468 B.C., so Myrto must have been about as old as Sokrates or older.

his appearance is compared to that of a torpedo-fish, a Silenos, or a Satyr. He always went barefoot, save on special occasions, and he never went outside the town except on military service, and once to the Isthmian games.

He was odd too in other ways. It was well known that, even as a boy, he had a 'voice', which he called his 'divine sign', and which he regarded as something peculiar to himself, and probably unique. It came to him often, and sometimes on the most trivial occasions. The remarkable thing about it was that it never prompted him to do anything; it only opposed his doing something he was about to do.[1] Besides this, Sokrates was subject to ecstatic trances. He would stand still for hours together buried in thought, and quite forgetful of the outer world. His friends were accustomed to this and knew better than to disturb him when it happened. They simply left him alone till he came to himself. There was a celebrated occasion in the camp at Poteidaia, when Sokrates was not quite forty years old, on which he stood motionless from early morning on one day till sunrise on the next, buried in thought ($\phi\rho o\nu\tau\iota\zeta\omega\nu$ $\tau\iota$), as we are told in the *Symposium*. His comrades in arms were much astonished, and some of them brought their camp-beds into the open to see if he would really remain standing there all night. When the sun rose next morning, he said a prayer and went about his business.[2]

§ 101. A man of this temperament would naturally be influenced by the religious movement of his time, and Plato indicates clearly that he was. He was a firm believer in the immortality of the soul and in the life to come, doctrines which were strange and unfamiliar to the Athenians of his day. He even believed, though not without reservations, in Rebirth and Reminiscence. When asked his authority for these beliefs, he would refer, not only to inspired poets like Pindar, but to 'priests and priestesses who have been at pains to understand the acts they perform'.[3] In particular he professed to have been instructed by a wise woman of Mantineia named Diotima. To the very end of his life, he was deeply interested in what he called 'sayings of yore' or the 'ancient word',

---

[1] Xenophon makes a point of contradicting Plato as to this. He says the 'voice' gave both negative and positive warnings. Obviously, if a young man asked Sokrates whether to go on a military adventure or not, and the 'voice' gave no sign, that could be interpreted as positive advice to go. The pseudo-Platonic *Theages* throws much light on the subject.

[2] *Symp.* 220 c–d. The statement would be pointless if it were not true.

[3] *Meno*, 81 a.

and expressly attributed to Orpheus,[1] according to which the body is a tomb in which the soul is kept in custody. It cannot attain to perfect purity till it is released from the body by God, whose chattel it is, and comes to be alone by itself. Then, and not till then, can it dwell with God. The man who follows philosophy, which is the highest music, will therefore practise death even in his lifetime by accustoming his soul to concentrate upon itself, and so to attain such wisdom as may be possible in this world.

But, with all this, Sokrates was no mere visionary. He had a strong vein of shrewd common sense that kept him from committing himself to the often fantastic details of Orphic and Pythagorean religion, however powerfully these might appeal to his imagination. He calls the doctrine that the soul is imprisoned in the body, a 'high one and not easy to understand', and though he was certain that the souls of the righteous would be with God when they departed from the body, he could not feel equally sure that they would be with the saints. When he related eschatological myths in the Orphic style, as he often did, he used to warn his hearers that they were at best something like the truth. No man of sense would insist on their literal accuracy. Besides this, he had a healthy contempt for the common run of Orphic and other traffickers in pardons and indulgences, whom he accused of demoralising the nation by their gross descriptions of heavenly joys. That, however, was perfectly consistent with the belief that Orphicism contained, in however dim a form, a great truth not to be found in the ordinary religion of the state. The manner of its expression he compared to fables or riddles, of which not everyone can guess the true sense.

§ 102. The truth is that there were two well-marked sides to his character. He was indeed a visionary or 'enthusiast', in the Greek sense of that word, but he was also uncommonly shrewd. His critics called him 'sly', using a word (εἴρων), which is properly applied to foxes. The Scots word 'canny' (not always a term of praise) comes nearest in meaning to the Greek. He did not like to commit himself further than he could see clearly, and he was apt to depreciate both his own powers and other people's. That was not a mere pose; it was due to an instinctive shrinking from everything exaggerated and insincere. As has been indicated, it is only

[1] *Crat.* 400 c.

the opponents of Sokrates that charge him with 'irony' (εἰρωνεία), a word which undoubtedly suggested the idea of humbug; but Plato shows us over and over again the real trait in his character which this uncomplimentary description was aimed at, with the result that the word 'irony' has changed its meaning for us. To a very large extent, we gather, 'the accustomed irony' of Sokrates was nothing more or less than what we call a sense of humour which enabled him to see things in their proper proportions.

§ 103. His interest in religion of a mystic type would naturally lead Sokrates to seek light from the science of his time. The two things were very closely connected at this date, as we have seen when dealing with Empedokles. In the *Phaedo* (96 a *sqq.*) Plato makes Sokrates give an account of his intellectual development which must be intended to be historical, seeing that the questions described as occupying his mind are just those that were of interest at Athens when Sokrates was a young man, and at no other time or place.[1] He asked himself whether life had arisen from the putrefaction of the warm and the cold (a doctrine we know to have been that of Archelaos), and whether the earth is flat (as the Ionians taught) or round (as the Pythagoreans held). He was interested in the relation between sensation, belief, and knowledge (a problem raised by Alkmaion), and he considered whether 'what we think with' is air (the doctrine of Diogenes) or blood (that of Empedokles). In fact, he is represented as having been influenced by practically every theory represented at Athens in the middle of the fifth century. But none of these could give him satisfaction; for they threw no light on what he chiefly wanted to know, the cause of things, why things are what they are and become what they become. They explained everything mechanically, whereas Sokrates wished to be shown that everything is as it is because it is best for it to be so. The system of Anaxagoras, indeed, seemed more promising at

[1] For a detailed discussion of these see the notes in my edition of the *Phaedo*, *ad loc.* The main point is that Sokrates is represented as hesitating between Ionic doctrine, such as he would learn from Archelaos and Diogenes (cp. § 93), and Italic doctrines, some of which belong to the school of Empedokles, whilst others are Pythagorean. Sokrates may have learnt the latter directly or indirectly from Philolaos. Empedokles, who took part in the colonisation of Thourioi, probably visited Athens (for we know that Kritias adopted his theory of sensation) and it is not difficult to suppose that Philolaos came there too. Athens is the only place where the Ionic and Italic philosophies could come into sharp conflict like this, and the middle of the fifth century is the only time at which it could happen.

first; for it attributed the origin of the world to Mind. But this proved disappointing too; for Anaxagoras made no use of Mind except when he was at a loss for another explanation. Otherwise he spoke of 'airs' and 'aethers' just like the rest. Sokrates accordingly turned his back on all such speculations, and resolved to work out a new method for himself.

§ 104. According to Plato, Sokrates must have reached this point when he was quite young; for he makes him discuss his new theory with Parmenides and Zeno when they visited Athens shortly after the middle of the century (§ 63). It is also made clear that he came into contact with the great 'Sophists' of the day at a very early age. The first visit of Protagoras to Athens must have taken place before Perikles entrusted him with the important duty of legislating for Thourioi in 444 B.C., that is to say, it must have coincided very nearly with the visit of Parmenides and Zeno, and we have seen that tradition represents Zeno and Protagoras as engaged in controversy. On his second visit, several years later, Protagoras remembers the young Sokrates quite well. He is made to say that of all the people he meets he admires Sokrates most, certainly far more than anyone else of his age.[1] A very similar compliment is put into the mouth of Parmenides.[2] Plato clearly means us to understand that Sokrates had attracted the notice of the most distinguished men of the time when he was not more than about twenty-five.[3] He was also intimate with Hippias and Prodikos, and he used to say that he had attended one of the cheaper courses on synonyms given by the latter. Gorgias, on the other hand, did not visit Athens till Sokrates was over forty years old.

It is clear, however, that Zeno, 'the Eleatic Palamedes',[4] had more influence on Sokrates than anyone. As Aristotle said,[5] he was the real inventor of Dialectic, that is to say, the art of argument by question and answer. If the Periklean age had left any literature we should probably hear more about his work at Athens than we do, but the Athenians of the middle of the fifth century did not

[1] *Prot.* 361 e. Protagoras adds that he would not be surprised if Sokrates became distinguished for wisdom. Surely that is the remark of an old man to a very young one, not that of a man under sixty to a man over forty. Cp. § 89.
[2] *Parm.* 130 a. Cf. *ib.* 135 d.
[3] This is strikingly confirmed by the statement of Aristoxenos that Sokrates became a disciple of Archelaos at the age of seventeen (p. 124, *n.* 2).
[4] *Phaedr* 261 d.
[5] In his dialogue entitled the *Sophist* (*ap.* Diog. Laert. ix. 25).

write books. We have traces enough, however, of the impression he left. We are told in the *Parmenides* of young Athenians who had been his associates, and it is recorded that Perikles himself 'heard' him (§ 63). We shall see that the Eleatic philosophy was sedulously cultivated at Megara, where its dialectical side was still further developed. Dialectic is literally the art of conversation or discussion, and its procedure is governed by strict rules. The 'answerer' (ὁ ἀποκρινόμενος) is required to reply to the questioner (ὁ ἐρωτῶν) in the fewest possible words, and to answer the question exactly as it is put. He is not allowed to ask other questions or to boggle at the form of those put to him. Obviously this is a procedure which can be employed in the most fallacious manner, and in the *Euthydemus* we have a delightful sketch of its abuse. Even that, however, was of service in directing attention to the nature of the most common fallacies, and this helped in turn to indicate the direction in which the real difficulties were to be looked for. At any rate, it was the method that appealed most to Sokrates, and there can be little doubt he learnt it from Zeno. The influence of Zeno is also attested by the *Phaedo* (96 e), where Sokrates is represented as puzzled, not only by the problem of growth, which was that of Anaxagoras and Archelaos, but also, and even more, by that of the unit, which was the special object of Zeno's attention.

§ 105. If we bear in mind the extreme youth of Sokrates when he began to strike out a line for himself, and also how unusual it was for an Athenian to busy himself seriously with such matters, we shall not be surprised to find that he had enthusiastic admirers among the younger men. We see from the opening scene of the *Protagoras* how some of them looked up to him as a guide even then, and consulted him about their studies. One of these, Chairephon, was particulary enthusiastic, and actually asked the Delphic oracle whether there was anyone wiser than Sokrates. The Pythia of course replied that there was no one. That proved a turning-point in the life of Sokrates, but Plato is careful to let us know that he did not accept the oracular response as its face value. His humour (εἰρωνεία) did not fail him when he turned it on himself, and he at once set out to prove the god in the wrong. He would find someone wiser than himself, and use him to refute the oracle. So he went to one of the politicians, whose name he does not think it necessary to mention, and talked to him, with the result that he found him wise, indeed, in his own opinion and that of other people, but really quite ignorant. And he had the same experience with one set of people after another. The poets could give no intelligible account of their own works. Apparently it was by some sort of divine inspiration they succeeded; for they did not know how it was themselves. The craftsmen, indeed, did as a rule know something about their own trades, but unfortunately, on the strength of this bit of knowledge, they fancied they knew a great many other things of which they were quite ignorant, such, for instance, as how to govern an empire. At last he saw what the god meant. Neither Sokrates nor anyone else knew anything, but Sokrates was wiser than other men in one respect, namely, that he knew he was ignorant and other men did not know they were. From this time forward, he regarded himself as having a mission to his fellow-citizens. He had been set apart by God to convince them of their ignorance.

Now according to Plato all this happened before the beginning of the Peloponnesian War; for Sokrates is represented as resuming his mission after his return from Poteidaia.[1] We cannot, therefore, date the oracle later than about his thirty-fifth year, and it is obvious that he was already well known by that time. The inquiry of Chairephon would be inexplicable on any other supposition. Plato himself was not born yet, and of course what he tells us must be based on the statements of Sokrates himself, and no doubt of Chairephon. It does not require great literary tact to see that Sokrates only took the oracle half-seriously, and that what he did was to apply to it the same methods of interpretation that he usually applied to Orphic and other mythology. On the other hand, he clearly believed it quite possible that a higher power might make use of oracles, dreams, and the like to communicate with human beings. He was the least dogmatic of men on such subjects, and his own 'voice' and his visions seemed a case in point. What is quite certain is that he sincerely believed his mission to be imposed on him by God. He gave up everything for it, and that was the cause of his poverty in later life. He spoke of his service (λατρεία) to God, and called himself the fellow-slave (ὁμόδουλος) of Apollo's swans. That, according to Plato, was a genuine faith, and he was intensely in earnest about it.

§ 106. The mission of Sokrates was interrupted by the outbreak of the Peloponnesian War, in which he was called on to do his duty

----

[1] *Charm.* 153 a.

as a citizen-soldier. He fought at Poteidaia (432 B.C.), at Delion (424 B.C.), and at Amphipolis (422 B.C.), and Plato has been careful to leave a record of his bravery in the field.[1] In the *Symposium* (220 d *sq.*) he makes Alkibiades describe his conduct with enthusiasm. In one of the battles Alkibiades was wounded, and Sokrates saved his life by watching over him till the danger was past. The generals awarded the prize of valour to Alkibiades, but he himself maintained it ought to go to Sokrates. Again at Delion, when the Athenians had to retreat, Alkibiades tells how Sokrates retired along with Laches, and far surpassed him in presence of mind, so that they both came off unhurt. Laches is made to refer to the same incident in the dialogue called by his name (181 b), and he adds that, if everyone else had done his duty like Sokrates, the defeat would have been turned into a victory. Sokrates was then about forty-six.[2]

§ 107. As we shall see, he had by this time gathered round him a circle of associates (ἑταῖροι), but these must be carefully distinguished from the young men he influenced in the course of his public mission. It appears, in the first place, that he exercised a singular fascination over those who were devoting themselves to what was then the new calling of a professional soldier. That was only natural, and in the *Republic* Plato represents Sokrates as strongly impressed by the necessity for a professional army. Besides these there were, we are told, a number of young men of good family, who had no profession on which they could be cross-examined, and who took great pleasure in hearing the ignorance of others exposed. Some of them even thought they might get a better preparation for public life by listening to Sokrates than any professional Sophist could give them. It is certain that Kritias associated with Sokrates in this way, though he did not do so for long. We hear of others, such as the fellow-demesman of Sokrates, Aristeides, son of Lysimachos, who soon fell away. No doubt they wished to learn the art of success, whereas Sokrates insisted on the necessity of serious study for a politician, just as for any other craftsman. There were others who were really devoted to him,

[1] We have seen (§ 98) that he probably served at Samos in 441/0, but Plato has no occasion to mention that. It was before the time of most of the speakers in his dialogues. It is interesting to think that Sokrates fought against a force commanded by Melissos.

[2] It is important to notice the way Plato insists on the military reputation of Sokrates. It accounts for the interest taken in him by Meno, Xenophon and others at a later date. See my edition of the *Phaedo* (Introduction, p. xiv).

notably Alkibiades and Charmides. Charmides was Plato's uncle, and it was doubtless through him that Plato came to associate with Sokrates. Even these, however, are not to be regarded as his disciples, or even as his associates in the strict sense like Chairephon. In the *Apology* he speaks of them as 'those they say are my disciples'.[1]

§ 108. In speaking of his relations with these young men Sokrates habitually used the language of love, tempered, of course, by his usual sly humour. To understand this, we must remember that at Thebes and Elis and in the Dorian States attachments of this kind were a recognised institution. They had their origin in the romantic relation of knight, squire and page in the Greek Middle Ages, and they were believed to have great value for military purposes.[2] In the *Laws* (636 b *sq.*) the Athenian Stranger, that is to say Plato, criticises the institutions of Sparta and Crete on the very ground that they were favourable to the abuse of such relationships.[3] In the Ionian States generally, on the other hand, they were considered disgraceful,[4] and, though the Dorian custom had made its way into Athens before the time of Solon, its abuse was condemned both by law and by public opinion.[5] Plato makes it abundantly clear, however, that it was the fashion in aristocratic circles to ape this feature of Spartan life among others. If we may trust the extremely vivid account of the matter he puts into the mouth of Alkibiades — and it is surely incredible that he invented it — it was Alkibiades himself that first posed as the ἐρώμενος of Sokrates, though it is also made quite clear that it was only a pose. The personal chastity of Sokrates is assumed as the foundation of the whole story, and we have therefore no right to interpret his language in a gross sense. What really surprises a modern reader is the matter-of-fact way in which the abuse of such relationships is spoken of. It will help us to understand that, if we remember that at Megara, only a few miles from Athens, no disgrace attached to it. In these circumstances, we can hardly look for the same reticence

[1] *Apol.* 33 a. In his *Bousiris* (11. 5) Isokrates represents the matter exactly as Plato makes Sokrates represent it himself. He criticises Polykrates (Cf. § 116, *infra*) for making Alkibiades a disciple (μαθητής) of Sokrates, whereas no one ever knew of him being educated (παιδευόμενον) by Sokrates.

[2] See Bethe in *Rhein. Mus.* lxii. (1907), pp. 438 *sqq.*

[3] Addressing a Spartan and a Cretan, he says: καὶ τούτων τὰς ὑμετέρας πόλεις πρώτας ἄν τις αἰτιῷτο (636 b).

[4] Plato, *Symp.* 182 b.

[5] Plato, *Phaedr.* 231 e: εἰ τοίνυν τὸν νόμον τὸν καθεστηκότα δέδοικας, μὴ πυθομένων τῶν ἀνθρώπων ὄνειδός σοι γένηται κτλ. Aischines *Against Timarchos, passim.*

on the subject as is commonly observed at the present day, though Plato's condemnation is unequivocal.

The thing appealed to Sokrates on another side, however, and here we may note once more his accustomed humour. He had a way of speaking of the birth of thoughts in the soul in language derived from his mother's calling. He professed, of course, that he himself was incapable of giving birth to wisdom, but he claimed to be an excellent man-midwife, well skilled in the art of bringing new thoughts to the birth. Besides that, just as midwives are the best matchmakers, he claimed to have a peculiar gift for discerning who the best teacher for a young man would be. That is all playful, to be sure, but we must never forget that Sokrates was a mystic as well as a humorist, and the mystics have always found the language of love more adequate than any other to express their peculiar experience. The love of a fair body is only the earthly type of something far higher. It leads on to the love of a fair soul, to the love of fair studies and fair ways of life, and at last it brings us into the very presence of the 'forms' of beauty, righteousness, and holiness in that supercelestial region where they have their dwelling-place.[1] When thus regarded as the objects of love, these 'forms' are seen to be the realities of which the things in this world are but shadows, and from which they derive such imperfect being as they have. There can be no doubt Plato means us to believe that Sokrates had actually attained to this beatific vision. It is not for nothing that he is represented as having one of his trances just before the conversation recorded in the *Symposium*. That must be intended to throw light on that other trance of twenty-four hours in the camp at Poteidaia more than a dozen years before. The man who saved the life of Alkibiades by his fearless devotion in the battle was fresh from the contemplation of a far higher beauty than his.

§ 109. Plato has left us more than one description of the effect the discourses of Sokrates had on young men. It will be well to quote the words he puts into the mouth of Meno, a reluctant admirer, and Alkibiades, an enthusiastic one. Meno says (*Meno*, 79 e):

> Before I met you I was told you did nothing but confuse yourself and make other people confused. And now I really think you are just

[1] *Phaedr.* 247 c *sqq.* I cannot believe that this is a description of Plato's own experience. It is strictly in keeping with all we know about the temperament of Sokrates.

bewitching me and casting spells and enchantments over me, so that I am full of confusion. I think, if I may be allowed the jest, you have a strong resemblance, not only in figure but in other respects, to the torpedo-fish. It benumbs anyone who comes near it and touches it, and that is just what you have done to me. Both my soul and my lips are literally benumbed, and I don't know what answer to give you. I have made speeches over and over again about goodness, and before large companies, with complete success as I fancied, but now I can't even tell what it is. I think it extremely prudent on your part never to take a voyage or leave your own country. If you were to do these things as a stranger in a foreign land, you would probably be taken up for a sorcerer.

And Alkibiades, who, with all his faults, or because of them, was very dear to Sokrates, says this (*Symp.* 215 a):

I shall endeavour to praise Sokrates as well as I can by means of images. Very likely he will think it is to make fun of him, but my image is chosen for its truth and not its absurdity. I say he is just like the figures of Silenos we see in the statuaries' shops, those they make with pipes or flutes in their hands, and when you open them you find they have images of the gods inside them. And I say too that he is like the satyr Marsyas. That you are like these in appearance, Sokrates, I fancy you won't deny yourself, and now let me tell you how you are like them in other ways. You're a wanton, aren't you? If you don't admit it, I shall call witnesses. Ay, and aren't you a piper? A far more wonderful one than he was! He only charmed men by his instruments; ... you beat him because you produce the very same effect by words alone without any instrument. When we hear anyone else speak, even a very good speaker, none of us care a bit; but when anyone hears you or anyone else repeating your words, even if the speaker is an indifferent one, and whether it is a woman or a man or a lad that hears him, we are all confounced and inspired. My friends, unless I was afraid you would think me quite drunk, I would tell you on my oath the effect his words have had on me and still have. When I listen to him my heart leaps even more wildly than those of people in a Korybantic ecstasy, and his words make the tears gush from my eyes. And I see many others affected in the same way. When I used to hear Perikles and other good speakers, I thought they spoke very well, but I had none of these feelings. My soul was not troubled or angry at the idea that it was in a state like a slave's. But I have often been put into such a condition by this Marsyas here, that I thought life not worth living so long as I remained as I was. And I am quite sure that if I were to consent to lend him my ears now, I couldn't hold out, but should feel just the same. He forces me to confess that, though I myself fall far short in many a thing, I neglect myself and busy myself about the affairs of Athens. So I stop my ears and run away from him as if from the Sirens, to prevent myself becoming rooted to the spot and growing old by his side. Why, he is the only human being that has ever made me feel ashamed in his presence, a feeling of which I might be supposed incapable. I know very well I can give no reason for not doing what he tells me to, but, when I have left him, I find my popularity too much for me. So I act like a runaway slave and a fugitive, and whenever I see him, I am ashamed of the admissions I have made. Many a time I feel that I should be glad to see him wiped out of existence altogether, and yet, if that were to happen, I know I should be far more distressed than relieved. In fact I don't know what to make of him.

Of course Plato himself was too young to hear Alkibiades talk like that, but he had the opportunities enough of knowing about his relations to Sokrates. It is at least plain that he believed Sokrates to have been capable of exerting this fascination over Alkibiades as late as 416 B.C., when the banquet described in the *Symposium* is supposed to take place. It is natural, too, to regard the passage as evidence of the effect produced by the discourses of Sokrates on Plato himself in his youth.[1]

§ 110. In 423 B.C. Aristophanes produced the *Clouds*, in which Sokrates, then about forty-seven years old, was the central figure. It will be necessary to say something later as to the picture there drawn of him; here we have only to do with what Plato says about it. It is true that, in the *Apology*, he makes Sokrates attribute much of the popular prejudice against him to the *Clouds*. He had been represented as walking on air and talking a lot of nonsense about the things in the heavens and those beneath the earth, and that, he says, suggested the notion that he was irreligious. It may very well have done so at the time of his trial, when old memories of the *Clouds* would occur to the judges in confirmation of the charges Sokrates had then to face, but we gather also from Plato that no one took it very seriously at the time, least of all Sokrates and his circle. In the *Symposium*, Sokrates and Aristophanes are represented as the best of friends six or seven years after the production of the *Clouds*, and Alkibiades does not hesitate to quote a burlesque description of the gait of Sokrates from that very play. We are to understand, then, that at the time no offence was taken, and we need not suppose any was meant. It was only in the light of subsequent events that the *Clouds* was resented, and even so the matter is quite lightly treated in the *Apology*.

---

[1] It is not easy to imagine such discourses as we find in Xenophon's *Memroabilia* producing such effects as these.

§ 111. But more difficult times were at hand. We have seen that Sokrates did his duty as a soldier, but he never held any office. The 'voice' would not allow him to take part in politics. In 406 b.c., however, it fell to his lot to be a member of the Council of Five Hundred, and it so happened that it was the turn of the fifty representatives of the tribe Antiochis, to which his deme belonged, to act as the executive committee of the Council at the time the generals were tried for failing to recover the bodies of the dead after the naval battle of the Arginoussai. The conduct of the trial showed that the democracy was getting into an ugly temper. It was proposed to judge all the generals together instead of taking the case of each separately. That was against the law, and Sokrates, who presided, refused, in spite of the popular clamour, to put the question to the meeting. The generals were ultimately condemned by an illegal procedure, but the action of Sokrates made a deep impression, and he referred to it with justifiable pride at his trial. A little later, during the illegal rule of the Thirty, he had the opportunity of showing that he could not be intimidated by the other side either. The Thirty sent for him along with four others and gave them orders to arrest Leon of Salamis that he might be put to death. The four others carried out the order, but Sokrates simply went home. Plato makes him say that he would probably have suffered for this if the Thirty had not been overthrown shortly after. From this we may infer — and we shall see that the point is of consequence — that Sokrates did not feel called upon to leave Athens with the democrats, though his devoted disciple, Chairephon, did so.

ARISTOPHANES AND XENOPHON

§ 112. Let us now consider how far this account of Sokrates is confirmed or otherwise by Aristophanes and Xenophon. In the first place, we must observe that Plato represents the life of Sokrates as sharply divided into two periods by the response of the oracle. In the earlier, he was chiefly occupied with the religious and scientific movements of his time, and with his new theory of the participation of sensible things in the 'forms'; in the latter, his mission to his fellow-citizens is his chief, and almost his sole interest, though in the month that elapsed between his condemnation and his death he naturally recurred to the themes that had busied his youth. It is further to be noticed that the testimony of

Aristophanes refers to the first of these periods, and that of Xenophon to the second. The *Clouds* was produced in 423 B.C., the year between the battles of Delion and of Amphipolis, in both of which Sokrates fought. His mission, though begun, was interrupted, and Aristophanes would be thinking mainly of the earlier Sokrates. Chronology is vital in dealing with this question, and we must never allow ourselves to forget that Sokrates was only forty-seven when Aristophanes produced the *Clouds*, and that Plato and Xenophon were babies. We must, therefore, compare the caricature of Aristophanes only with what Plato tells us of the youth of Sokrates, and not with what he tells us of the later period.

§ 113. That the *Clouds* is a caricature is obvious, and it must be interpreted accordingly. There are two canons for the interpretation of comedy which are often neglected. In the first place, the very occurrence of a statement in a comedy affords a presumption that it is not a mere statement of fact. Statements of fact are not funny. On the other hand, every such statement must have some sort of foundation in fact; for absolute fictions about real people are not funny either. What we have to ask, then, is what Sokrates must have been in the earlier period of his life to make the caricature of the *Clouds* possible. In the first place, he must have been a student of natural science, and he must have been interested at one time or other in the things in the heavens (τὰ μετέωρα) and the things beneath the earth (τὰ ὑπὸ γῆς). Plato makes Sokrates declare that these were the chief studies of his youth. Aristophanes represents Sokrates as an adherent of a system which is recognisable as that of Diogenes of Apollonia, and that is just why the chorus consists of clouds. We know that Diogenes had revived the theory of Anaximenes that everything is condensed or rarefied 'air', and the clouds are one of the first results of the condensation of air. Just so Plato makes Sokrates say that he had studied, among other questions, whether 'what we think with' was air (the doctrine of Diogenes) or blood (the doctrine of Empedokles), and Aristophanes represents him as swinging in a basket in order to get pure dry air for his thought. Aristophanes also knows of the spiritual midwifery of Sokrates, for he has a jest about the miscarriage of a thought. On the other hand, he represents him as a spiritualistic medium, and he calls the inmates of the *Phrontisterion* 'souls', a word which to the ordinary Athenian would only suggest ghosts. He also ridicules them for going barefoot and unwashed, and speaks of them as 'semi-corpses'. All that, and more of the same kind, has a sufficient foundation in what Plato tells us of the Sokratic doctrine of the soul and the 'practice of death'. The only thing that strikes us at first as inconsistent with everything we can gather from Plato is that Sokrates teaches his pupils to make the weaker argument the stronger. That is not true even of Protagoras in the sense suggested, while the introduction of the Righteous and the Wicked Logos (possibly a later addition) seems even wider of the mark. And yet, if we look closer, we shall find there are sufficient indications of features in the teachings of the Platonic Sokrates to account for such a distortion on the part of a not too scrupulous comic poet. We know from Plato that the new method of Sokrates consisted precisely in the consideration of things from the point of view of propositions (λόγοι) rather than from that of facts (ἔργα), and Aristophanes would not be able, and certainly would not care, to distinguish that from the 'art of λόγοι', which seemed so dangerous to conservative Athenians. As for the suggestion that it was used for the purpose of establishing immoral conclusions, we need only suppose that discussions like that described in the *Hippias minor* had got talked about, as they certainly would. It would seem obvious to the plain man that anyone who maintained the voluntary wrongdoer to be better than the involuntary must be engaged in the subversion of morality. I submit, then, that if the Sokrates of this date was much what Plato represents him to have been, the caricature of the *Clouds* is quite intelligible; if he was not, it is surely pointless.

§ 114. But, above all, Aristophanes confirms Plato in the most explicit way by drawing a clear distinction between certain 'disciples' (μαθηταί), as he calls them, of Sokrates, of whom Chairephon was the chief, and who were his permanent associates (ἑταῖροι) in a scientific school, and the young men who frequented his society or were sent to him by their parents in order to learn how to succeed in life. What Plato tells us about Lysimachos and Aristeides[1] is enough to justify the burlesque figures of Strepsiades and Pheidippides. But the machinery of the *Phrontisterion* implies that there was something much more serious. It is usually said, indeed, that Aristophanes is taking Sokrates as a type of the Sophists of the day, but that view is untenable. In the first place, the Old Comedy does not deal in types but personalities, and when

---

[1] *Laches*, 178 a *sqq.*; *Theaet.* 151 a.

Aristophanes does introduce a type, as in the *Birds*, he gives him a fictitious name. But apart from that, the Sophists of the day had no permanent associates. They were here to-day and gone to-morrow, and they only gave short courses of lectures to audiences that were perpetually changing. Besides, they were the last people in the world to trouble themselves with scientific inquiries such as Aristophanes is obviously making fun of. The *Phrontisterion*, in fact, is a burlesque of an organised scientific school of a type which was well known in Ionia and Italy, but had not hitherto existed at Athens, unless, indeed, Archelaos had established one. If Sokrates did not, in fact, preside over such a society, are we to suppose that Aristophanes himself invented the idea of a scientific school, or that he knew of those in other cities by hearsay and transferred them in imagination to Athens? It is surely very hard to see what the point of that could be, and we must conclude, I think, that he expected his audience to know what an institution of the kind was like. If he has voluntarily or involuntarily confused Sokrates with anyone, it is not with Sophists like Protagoras and Gorgias or their followers, but with Anaxagoras and Archelaos; and, if the latter did found a regular school, Sokrates would naturally succeed him as its head. That, in fact seems to me the most probable account of the matter. We have seen that Sokrates was a disciple of Archelaos for a number of years.[1]

§ 115. When we come to Xenophon, we must remember, in the first place, that he was very young, and Sokrates already an old man, when he knew him, and that he left Athens never to return about three years before Sokrates was put to death. In the second place, we must remember that the *Memorabilia* is an *apologia*, and must be judged by the canons of criticism applicable to such writings. The chief of these is that most weight is to be attached to statements not directly connected with the main purpose of the work; above all, when they seem to involve admissions in any degree inconsistent with that. Now what Xenophon wished to prove is that Sokrates was unjustly accused of being irreligious, and that his conversations, so far from corrupting the young, did them a great deal of good. One of the chief arguments for the soundness of his religious attitude is that he refused to busy himself with natural science and dissuaded others from studying it. What Plato tells us of the disappointment of Sokrates with

[1] See p. 124, *n.* 2.

Anaxagoras, and his renunciation of physical speculations at an early age, is enough to explain what Xenophon says, and yet he feels at once that he has gone too far. In fact he gives his point away completely by adding twice over: 'Yet he himself was not unversed in these subjects' — subjects of which he gives a list, and which correspond exactly to the most highly developed mathematics and astronomy of the time.[1] Further, he knew that what Aristophanes burlesqued as the *Phrontisterion* was a reality; for he makes Sokrates tell the Sophist Antiphon, who was trying to rob him of his disciples — a very significant touch — that he does in fact study the writings of the older philosophers with his friends. 'I spend my time with them,' he says, 'unrolling the treasures of the men of old, which they have written down in books and left behind them.'[2] Admissions like these are far more important than the philistine words put into the mouth of Sokrates about scientific study. No one who talked like that could have attracted Pythagoreans like Kebes and Simmias from Thebes to listen to him, as Xenophon also says he did.[3]

It would be possible to find a good many more admissions of this sort in Xenophon, but it is not clear to me how far the *Memorabilia* can be regarded as independent testimony at all. In fact, it seems hardly possible to doubt that Xenophon got the greater part of his information about Sokrates from the dialogues of Plato. Otherwise, it would be very significant that he has heard of the importance of 'hypothesis' in the dialectic of Sokrates.[4] I do not feel able to rely on such things as first-hand evidence, however, and therefore I make no use of them. Those who treat the *Memorabilia* as a historical work are bound, on the other hand, to admit a good many things that are hard to explain on the assumption that Sokrates was the sort of man Xenophon wishes us to think he was. In fact, Xenophon's defence of Sokrates is too successful. He would never have been put to death if he had been like that.

§ 116. The conclusion we are, in my opinion, forced to is that, while it is quite impossible to regard the Sokrates of Aristophanes and the Sokrates of Xenophon as the same person, there is no difficulty in regarding both as distorted images of the Sokrates we know from Plato. The first is legitimately distorted for comic effect;

[1] *Mem.* iv. 7. 3–5.   [2] *Mem.* i. 6. 14.
[3] *Mem.* iii. 11. 17.   [4] *Mem.* iv. 6. 13.

the latter, not so legitimately, for apologetic reasons. To avoid misunderstanding, I should say that I do not regard the dialogues of Plato as records of actual conversations, though I think it probable that there are such embedded in them. I also admit fully that the Platonic Sokrates is Sokrates as Plato saw him, and that his image may to some extent be transfigured by the memory of his martyrdom. The extent to which that has happened we cannot, of course, determine, but I do not believe it has seriously falsified the picture. Like Shakespeare, Plato had a marvellous gift of suppressing his own personality when engaged in dramatic composition. That is why his personality is so elusive, and why that of Sokrates has so often been substituted for it. We shall return to this when we come to Plato himself, but first I must warn the reader that there is another view of the evidence, according to which the Sokrates of Plato and that of Aristophanes and that of Xenophon are all alike pure fiction, so that we really know nothing at all about the man. One of the most recent writers on the subject[1] doubts whether there is even a grain of truth in the story of the campaigns of Sokrates, and denies that he had any relations of any kind with Alkibiades. According to him, that was a malicious invention of the Sophist Polykrates,[2] who wrote a pamphlet against Sokrates before 390 B.C. Plato did not stoop to contradict this commonplace pamphleteer, and besides, the idea of bringing the two men together appealed to him as an interesting one, so he simply wrote a romance round it. Now, however incredible such theories may appear, they are really far sounder than anything we can get by picking and choosing whatever we please out of Plato, and using it to embroider Xenophon's bald tale. It seems to me that we have to choose between the Platonic Sokrates and the thoroughgoing nihilism of the view just indicated. It is really impossible to preserve Xenophon's Sokrates, even if he were worth preserving, and, if we disbelieve the testimony of Plato on the most vital points, it is impossible to assign any reason for accepting it on

---

[1] A. Gercke in Gercke-Norden, *Einleitung*, vol. ii. p. 366 *sq.*

[2] This statement is based on a passage in the *Bousiris* of Isokrates (11. 5), which is supposed to mean that there was not the slightest ground for the assertion that Alkibiades was a disciple of Sokrates. As I have pointed out (p. 138 *n.* 1) Plato makes Sokrates himself say exactly the same thing. It is nowhere suggested in Plato that Alkibiades was a μαθητής, or that Sokrates 'educated' him. It may be added that the *Protagoras* is almost certainly earlier than the pamphlet of Polykrates, and that the relation between Sokrates and Alkibiades is presupposed in it.

others. The Platonic Sokrates would remain, indeed, as one of the greatest characters in fiction, but some people would find it very hard to read Plato with patience, if they supposed him capable of a mystification such as this hypothesis credits him with.

IX

The Philosophy of Sokrates

THE ASSOCIATES OF SOKRATES

§ 117. We know pretty accurately who composed the inner Sokratic circle at the end. In the *Phaedo* (59 b) we have a list of fourteen associates (ἑταῖροι) who were present at the death of Sokrates, and to these we must add the narrator, Phaidon of Elis, who afterwards founded a school of his own. Of these men nine were Athenians, Apollodoros, Kritoboulos and his father Kriton, Hermogenes son of Hipponikos, Epigenes, Aischines, Antisthenes, Ktesippos of Paiania, and Menexenos. Xenophon also gives us a list of true Sokratics (*Mem.* i. 2, 48). It includes Chairephon, who is absent from Plato's list because, as we know from the *Apology*, he had died a short time before. Kriton and Kritoboulos are also mentioned, but not the other Athenians. Apollodoros and Epigenes, however, occur in other parts of the *Memorabilia*, and it is from Hermogenes that Xenophon professes to have got his information about the trial of Sokrates.

The most striking thing about the list, however, is that it includes the names of certain foreigners who are known to have belonged to Italic schools of philosophy, and who are represented as coming to Athens for the express purpose of seeing Sokrates before his death. The three Thebans, Simmias, Kebes and Phaidondas, were Pythagoreans and disciples of the exiled Philolaos. In the *Crito* (45 b) we learn that Simmias had brought a considerable sum of money with him to assist Sokrates in escaping. Xenophon also mentions these three in his list of true Sokratics, and in another place (iii. 11, 17) he lets us know that Sokrates had attracted them from Thebes, and that they never left his side. In the *Phaedo* (58 d) the Pythagoreans of Phleious are represented as equally enthusiastic. Echekrates says that they are like their guest Phaidon in loving above all things to speak of Sokrates and to hear about him. Eukleides and Terpsion are interesting in a similar way. They were Eleatics and lived at Megara. The Academic tradition preserved by Cicero makes Eukleides the successor of Parmenides and Zeno, and we are told that he 'handled' the doctrines of Parmenides. The close relation between the Eleatics of Megara and Sokrates is further illustrated in the *Theaetetus*, where we are told (143 a) that Eukleides took notes of the discourses of Sokrates, and it was with him that some of the Sokratics, including Plato, took refuge after their Master's death. Besides these men, Aristippos of Kyrene and Kleombrotos were expected, but did not arrive in time. It is evident that the condemnation of Sokrates had deeply moved all the philosophical schools of Hellas.

§ 118. Now Plato unquestionably represents the Pythagoreans as sharing a common philosophy with Sokrates, and even as looking up to him as its most authoritative exponent. It is Sokrates who instructs them in certain old doctrines that the contemporary Pythagoreans had allowed to drop, and who refutes the theory held both at Thebes and Phleious that the soul is an attunement of the body. The Eleatic Eukleides is said not only to have taken notes of his discourses, but to have had the accuracy of these notes confirmed by Sokrates himself when he visited Athens. In fact Plato makes all these men regard Sokrates as their Master, and it is impossible to suppose he could misrepresent their attitude seriously at a time when most of them were still living and in close intercourse with himself. The suggestion seems to be that, after the departure of Philolaos for Italy, Sokrates became to all intents and purposes the head of the Pythagoreans who remained behind. On one point he is made to express surprise that Simmias and Kebes had not been instructed by Philolaos (61 d), and Echekrates of Phleious is shaken in his belief that the soul is an attunement as soon as he is told that Sokrates does not share it (88 d). He also accepts the main doctrine of Sokrates as soon as he hears it (102 a).

Plato's account is, I think, confirmed by what we are told of Aristoxenos. We know that he was acquainted with the last generation of the Pythagoreans at Phleious, and that he maintained the doctrine of Philolaos that the soul was an attunement even after he had become a follower of Aristotle. We have seen too (§ 70) that he and his friend Dikaiarchos made a great point of denying that Pythagoras had ever practised any of the ascetic abstinences and purificatory rites generally attributed to him. Now Aristoxenos is the source of a great deal of scandalous gossip about Sokrates and

Plato. He came from Taras and Dikaiarchos from Messene, and Aristoxenos professed to have got his information about Sokrates from his father Spintharos, who had known him personally. Why should a Tarentine be anxious to blacken the character of Sokrates? The answer suggests itself that the friends of Philolaos were annoyed because Sokrates had corrupted their doctrine of the nature of the soul and had revived the mystical side of Pythagoreanism, which they believed they had got rid of once for all (§§ 70, 75). It is at any rate a fact that they laid special stress on the very doctrine of the soul which Plato represents Sokrates as refuting. From their point of view, he would be just another Hippasos.

THE FORMS[1]

§ 119. In the *Phaedo* the doctrine Sokrates and the Pythagoreans are represented as holding in common is that of 'intelligible forms' (νοητὰ εἴδη), which we have seen reason for believing to be Pythagorean in origin (§ 32). Further, Sokrates is described as making an important original contribution to the theory which, in fact, completely transforms it. Modern writers generally treat this as fiction, and ascribe the doctrine of forms to Plato under the name of 'the Ideal Theory' or 'the Theory of Ideas'. The chief ground for this ascription is that it is not to be found in the most distinctively Sokratic of the dialogues, and it is generally said that it makes its first appearance in the *Phaedo*. That, however, is a circular argument; for the sole ground on which certain dialogues have been singled out as specially Sokratic is just that the theory in question is not supposed to occur in them. There is surely no reason for thinking that Sokrates would drag it into all his conversations, and in fact it would have been inappropriate for him to refer to it except in talking with people who would be likely to understand. Nothing, then, can be inferred from his silence on the subject in most of the dialogues, especially as that silence is not unbroken. By a curious minor epicycle in the argument we are warned indeed that, when the doctrine does appear to be referred to in a Sokratic dialogue proper, we are not to understand the words in the sense they afterwards acquired, but this is surely

---

[1] I have purposely avoided the word 'idea'. It inevitably suggests to us that the 'forms' (εἴδη, ἰδέαι) are concepts (νοήματα), whether our own or God's, and this makes a right interpretation of the doctrine impossible.

arbitrary in the highest degree.[1] It is much more to the point to observe that the theory of forms in the sense in which it is maintained in the *Phaedo* and *Republic* is wholly absent from what we may fairly regard as the most distinctively Platonic of the dialogues, those, namely, in which Sokrates is no longer the chief speaker. In that sense it is never even mentioned in any dialogue later than the *Parmenides* (in which it is apparently refuted), with the single exception of the *Timaeus* (51 c), where the speaker is a Pythagorean. On the other hand, nothing can well be more explicit than the way Plato ascribes the doctrine to Sokrates. In the *Phaedo* it is spoken of (100 b) as 'nothing new', but just what Sokrates is always talking about. In the *Parmenides* (130 b) Sokrates is asked by the founder of Eleaticism whether he had thought of the theory himself, and replies in the affirmative. That is supposed to happen at least twenty years before Plato was born. Again in the *Phaedo* (76 b), Simmias is made to say that he doubts whether 'this time to-morrow', when Sokrates has passed away, there will be anyone left who is able to give an adequate account of the forms. If that is fiction, it is at least deliberate, and I can only ask, as I have asked before,[2] whether any philosopher ever propounded a new theory of his own by representing it as perfectly familiar to a number of distinguished living contemporaries some years before he had thought of it himself.

§ 120. The theory which is simply taken for granted in the first part of the *Phaedo*, not only by Simmias and Kebes, but also by Echekrates at Phleious, to whom the conversation is reported, is as follows. There is a sharp distinction between the objects of thought and the objects of sense. Only the former can be said to *be*; the latter are only *becoming*. It is made clear that the origin of this theory is to be looked for in the study of mathematics, and the distinction between being (οὐσία) and becoming (γένεσις) must be interpreted accordingly. We know what we mean by equal, but we have never seen equal sticks or stones. The sensible things we call

---

[1] In the *Euthyphro*, for instance, Sokrates demands that Piety should be referred to μίαν τινὰ ἰδέαν (5 d), and asks for ἐκεῖνο τὸ εἶδος ᾧ πάντα τὰ ὅσια ὅσια ἐστίν (6 c). He also speaks of this as a παράδειγμα (6 e). In the *Meno* (72 c) he demands to know the form (εἶδος) of Goodness. In the *Cratylus* (389 b) we have the highly technical phrase αὐτὸ ὅ ἐστι κερκίς. I entirely agree with Professor Shorey (*Unity of Plato's Thought*, Chicago, 1903) in holding that it is futile to look for any variation or development of thought in Plato's dialogues down to the *Republic*, though at that point I must part company with him, as will be seen.

[2] *E. Gr. Ph.*[2] p. 355.

equal are all 'striving' or 'tending' to be such as the equal, but they fall far short of it. Still, they are tending towards it, and that is why they are said to be becoming. Sensible equality is, as it were, equality 'in the making'; but, however near it may come to true equality, it never reaches it. The connexion of this with the difficulties raised by Zeno is obvious. The problem of an indefinite approximation which never reaches its goal was that of the age.[1]

As we have seen, this theory on its mathematical side is essentially Pythagorean. Where it differs from anything we can reasonably attribute to the Pythagoreans is in the systematic inclusion of what we should call moral and aesthetic forms on an equality with the mathematical. We have never seen anything that is 'just beautiful' (αὐτὸ ὅ ἐστι καλόν) or 'just good' (αὐτὸ ὅ ἐστιν ἀγαθόν) any more than we have seen anything 'just equal' (αὐτὸ τὸ ἴσον). This tends to emphasise that aspect of the forms in which they are regarded as patterns or exemplars (παραδείγματα), the 'upper limits' to which the manifold and imperfect things of sense tend to approximate as far as possible. It may sound a little strange to say that an isosceles right-angled triangle would be a triangular number if it could, but such a way of speaking becomes quite natural when we introduce moral and aesthetic forms. This is what Aristotle appears to mean when he makes the preoccupation of Sokrates with ethical matters play so important a part in the development of the theory. The Pythagoreans, he tells us, had only determined a few things numerically, such as opportunity, justice, and marriage, and they had been influenced by superficial analogies;[2] it was Sokrates that suggested a systematic search for the universal in other fields than mathematics.[3] It will be observed further that we do not hear in the *Phaedo* of any attempt to connect the forms with numbers, and this suggests that the persons whom Aristotle refers to as those 'who first said there were forms', and distinguishes from Plato on that very ground,[4] are no other than the persons who call themselves 'we' in the *Phaedo*. I do not, however, quote that as external evidence; for I think we shall see reason to believe that everything Aristotle tells us about Sokrates comes

---

[1] We may illustrate the relation of γένεσις to οὐσία by the evaluation of π to any number of decimal places.
[2] *Met.* M. 3. 1078 b, 21; A. 5. 987 a, 22.
[3] *Met.* A. 6. 987 b, 1.
[4] *Met.* M. 4. 1078 b, 11.

from the Platonic dialogues, and especially from the *Phaedo* itself.[1]

§ 121. The account given by Sokrates in the *Phaedo* of the process by which we come to know the forms is apt to be insufficiently appreciated because it is expressed in the mythical language of the doctrine of Reminiscence, which we are expressly warned in the *Meno* (86 b, 6) not to take too literally. The question really is, how we come to have a standard which enables us to pronounce the things of sense to be imperfect. We certainly do not start with such a standard in our possession; it is only our experience of sensible things that gives rise to our apprehension of it. On the other hand, our apprehension of the standard when it does arise cannot be produced by the sensible things, since it is something that goes beyond any or all of them. Now when we apprehend a thing, and this apprehension gives rise at the same time to the thought of another thing which the first thing is either like or unlike, we call that being 'reminded' or put in mind of the one thing by the other (73 c). The sticks and stones we call equal are like the equal, and those we call unequal are unlike it, but both alike give rise to the thought of what is 'just equal' (αὐτὸ τὸ ἴσον). It follows that, as we are put in mind of it both by things that are like it and things that are unlike it, our knowledge of the equal must be independent of sense altogether. And the same is true of 'the beautiful itself' and 'the good itself'.

Aristotle expresses this in his own way by saying there are two things that may fairly be attributed to Sokrates, universal definitions and inductive reasoning. In the *Prior Analytics* (67 a, 21) he definitely associates the doctrine of the *Meno* that learning is Reminiscence with what he calls the 'recognition' of the universal in a particular case. 'In no case,' he says, 'do we find that we have a previous knowledge of the particulars, but we get the knowledge of the particulars in the process of induction by recognising them as it were (ὥσπερ ἀναγνωρίζοντας).' There is no doubt, then, what Aristotle means by saying that Sokrates may be credited with the

[1] It must be remembered that Sokrates had been dead for over thirty years when Aristotle first came to Athens at the age of eighteen. His summary and highly ambiguous statements must, therefore, be interpreted, if possible, in the light of the other evidence. To use them for the purpose of rebutting it appears to me methodically indefensible. That is to employ hearsay and inference to discredit first-hand testimony, and we must have some rules of evidence in historical as well as in judicial inquiries. I believe that, if we allow for Aristotle's personal way of looking at things, his statements can be interpreted so as not to do violence to the record; but, if not, that is a question which concerns the interpreter of Aristotle, not the interpreter of Sokrates.

introduction of inductive reasonings, and it is exactly the process
described in the *Phaedo*. It is also correct to say, as he does, that the
universal which we come to recognise in this way is 'the What is
it?' (τὸ τί ἐστι); for in the *Phaedo* (78 d) Sokrates describes the
sort of reality possessed by the forms as 'that of the being of which
we give an account in our questions and answers', that is, in the
dialectic process. It will be observed that there is nothing here
about abstracting the common attributes of a class and setting it up
as a class-concept. That is a modern gloss on Aristotle's words,
and his reference to the *Meno* shows he was quite aware of the real
meaning of the doctrine of Reminiscence. There is nothing to
suggest, then, that what he says on this point is derived from any
other source than Plato's dialogues. He has expressed the thing
in his own way, no doubt, and it may be a question whether it does
full justice to the doctrine of Sokrates, but that is another matter.
If he was to express it in his own language, he could hardly say
anything else, and, after all, his own theory of induction is much
more like the doctrine of Reminiscence than the travesty of it given
in some text-books. It should be added that, when Aristotle says
certain things may 'fairly' (δικαίως) be attributed to Sokrates, he is
thinking, as he often does, of earlier philosophers as contributing
certain elements to his own system, and that he is contrasting
Sokrates in this respect with the Pythagoreans. He is not thinking
of any distinction between the 'historical' and the 'Platonic' Sokrates, and there is no evidence that he ever made such a distinction.

§ 122. Now it is with the soul by means of reasoning (λογισμός)
that we apprehend the forms, while particulars are apprehended
through the body by sensation. Indeed, the body and its senses are
only a hindrance to the acquisition of true wisdom, and the more
we can make ourselves independent of them, the nearer we shall
come to the knowledge of reality and truth. We have seen that the
things of sense cannot be said to have being (οὐσία) at all, but
only becoming (γένεσις), and that they are merely likenesses or
images of the eternal and immutable standards or patterns
(παραδείγματα) we are forced to postulate. Of these alone can
there be knowledge; our apprehension of the things of sense is
only 'imagination' (εἰκασία)[1] or at best belief (δόξα, πίστις). If we

---

[1] *Rep.* 534 a. There is an untranslatable play on words here; for εἰκασία is
properly 'guess work' (from εἰκάζεσθαι), but it also suggests the apprehension of
images (εἰκόνες).

would have true knowledge, we must seek to rid ourselves of the body, so far as that is possible in this life; for it is only when the soul has departed from the body that it can have knowledge in its purity. Yet even in this life, by the practice of dying daily, we may so far mortify the flesh that for a brief space we may behold the eternal realities in a vision, and so being 'out of the body' obtain a foretaste of immortality. Such is the teaching of the first part of the *Phaedo*, and there can be no doubt that it points to an almost complete severance of the world of sense from the world of thought.

§ 123. But then, by one of those dramatic surprises so characteristic of Plato's dialogues, when we have been raised to this pitch of spiritual elevation, we are brought to the ground once more, and made to feel that, however beautiful and edifying the doctrine may be, it does not really satisfy us. It is Plato's way to mark the importance of the different sections of an argument by the length and elaboration of the digressions that precede them. In the present case he uses every resource of his art to make us feel that we are coming to something fundamental. In the first place, there is a long and ominous silence (84 c), broken at length by a whispered conversation between Simmias and Kebes. Sokrates sees they are not convinced, and he urges them to state their difficulties; for, as he allows, the doctrine is open to many objections if we discuss it seriously. Then follows (84 e) the magnificent passage in which he compares himself to the dying swan who sings in praise of their common master Apollo, the lord of Delphoi and of Delos, who had played so mysterious a part in the life of Sokrates himself, and was also the chief god of the Pythagoreans. Simmias replies (85 c) that Sokrates no doubt feels with him that certain knowledge is impossible on such subjects, but that we must test and try all theories, and, in default of some divine doctrine (θεῖος λόγος), make the best of the human one that approves itself most. The particular difficulty he feels is just the theory, of which we have seen the great historical importance, that the soul is an attunement (ἁρμονία) of the body, and cannot therefore be immortal (85 e). Kebes has a different theory, of which we do not hear elsewhere, but which seems to be Herakleitean in origin, namely, that the soul is the organising principle of the body which it weaves as a garment. The body is always being worn out and woven afresh, and thus the soul may properly be said to outlast many bodies. That does not prove, however, that one of these bodies may not be the last, and that the soul may not perish before it (88 b). We are told (88 c) that the effect of these words was to produce a feeling of profound dejection in the company. They felt as if they could never trust themselves to believe any doctrine again, since this one had been so easily overthrown. The narrative is even interrupted, and we are taken back to Phleious, where Echekrates says the same effect has been produced on him. Then comes the warming of Sokrates against 'misology', or hatred of theories. It is just like misanthropy, which arises from ignorance of the art of dealing with men. Just as the man who knows the world knows that very good men and very bad men are equally rare, so the man who knows the art of dealing with theories will not expect too much of philosophical doctrines, but neither will he lose faith (89 d *sq.*). The impression intended to be left on us by all these digressions is certainly that the doctrine of forms as expounded in the earlier part of the dialogue is somehow inadequate, and we are prepared to find that it will be considerably modified in the sequel. We are also intended to understand that the later Pythagorean view of the soul is a serious obstacle to a sound theory.

§ 124. This doctrine is disposed of without much difficulty, chiefly by the consideration that, if the soul is an attunement and goodness is an attunement, we have to assume an attunement of an attunement, so that one tuning will be more tuned than another. The theory of Kebes, however, raises a far more fundamental question, namely, that of the cause of coming into being and ceasing to be (γένεσις καὶ φθορά). To say that becoming is an image or likeness of being explains nothing at all. It really amounts to saying that there is a world of sense which is a vain show, standing in no intelligible relation to reality. Unless we can overcome this separation between appearance and reality in some way, we cannot say anything at all, and least of all that the soul is immortal. What we want is not merely a theory of being (οὐσία), but also a theory of becoming (γένεσις). It is at this point that Sokrates gives the sketch of his intellectual development already referred to (§ 103); and, if words mean anything, it must be implied that we are now coming to his personal contribution to the doctrine. He speaks of this (97 b, 100 d) with characteristic irony as a 'silly and muddled' theory, and calls it a makeshift or *pis-aller* (δεύτερος πλοῦς, 99 d), but we must not be deceived by this way of speaking. It is also the hypothesis from which we will not suffer himself to be dislodged

by anyone, and he believes it to be capable of showing the cause of
coming into being and ceasing to be in the world of sensible
experience, a thing the earlier form of the doctrine could give no
intelligible account of.

§ 125. Sokrates tells us, then, that when he could find no satisfaction in the science of his time, and in particular no answer to the
question of the cause of becoming and ceasing to be (γένεσις καὶ
φθορά), he resolved to adopt a new method of inquiry. He would
no longer consider the question from the point of view of the
things (ἐν τοῖς ἔργοις) but from that of the judgements we make
about them and the propositions in which these are expressed
(ἐν τοῖς λόγοις). He is represented both in the *Meno* and in the
Phaedo as much impressed by the efficacy of the mathematicians'
method of 'hypothesis', which Zeno had made matter of common
knowledge at Athens by this time. To understand its meaning, we
must leave out of account for the present the special use of the
term 'hypothesis' in Aristotelian Logic, and also the popular
etymology alluded to by Plato in the *Republic* (511 b) which regards
the primary meaning of the word as foundation or basis, a sense in
which it is not used. If we do this, we shall be struck at once by the
fact that the corresponding verb (ὑποτίθεσθαι) has two chief
significations, firstly that of setting before oneself or others a task
to be done, and secondly that of setting before oneself or others a
subject to be treated, in a speech, for instance, or a drama. This
usage is as old as Homer,[1] and by a natural extension the verb is
freely used in Ionic of suggesting a course of action. That way of
speaking accounts for Euclid's use of the word 'given', and also of
perfect imperatives like 'let there be given' (δεδόσθω). The original
idea is that of a piece of work given out to be done, and the proposition accordingly ends up with a statement that it has been done
(Q.E.F. ὅπερ ἔδει ποιῆσαι or Q.E.D. ὅπερ ἔδει δεῖξαι).

The procedure is as follows. It is assumed that the proposition
stated in the 'hypothesis' is true (or that the required construction
has been performed), and then the consequences (τὰ συμβαίνοντα)
of that assumption are deduced till we come to a proposition we
know to be true (or a construction we are able to perform). If,
however, we come to a proposition which is absurd (or to a con-

---

[1] See Liddell and Scott, *s.v.* ὑποτίθημι, ii. 2. The materials for a correct account of the term ὑπόθεσις are also to be found in Liddell and Scott, *s.v.*, but they
require rearrangement. The article should be read in the order iii, iv, i. 2, ii. 2, ii. 1.

HYPOTHESIS 133

struction which is impossible), the hypothesis is 'destroyed' (ἀναιρεῖται, *tollitur*). The regular terminology accordingly is, 'if A is B, what must follow?' (τί χρὴ συμβαίνειν;), and that explains why the conjunction 'if' has come to be regarded as the mark of a hypothesis. Plato's *Parmenides* is the *locus classicus* for all this, but the method is older. In the Hippokratean treatise on *Ancient Medicine*, the fundamental doctrines of Empedokles and others are called hypotheses, and the key to this way of speaking is also to be found in Plato's *Parmenides*. There the doctrine of Parmenides is referred to as the hypothesis *If it is one*, and that of his opponents as the hypothesis *If there are many*.[1] In the same way the hypothesis of Empedokles might be stated in the form *If there are four*. This is a result of the Eleatic dialectic. It is not implied in the least that Parmenides or Empedokles regarded their theories as 'merely hypothetical'. That is a far later use of the word. It is only meant that their method of exposition was to trace out the consequences of their fundamental postulates. We can see for ourselves that this is what Parmenides does in his poem. Zeno systematised the procedure, and it was doubtless from Zeno Sokrates learnt it.

Like all dialectical methods, this procedure is subject to strict rules. We first take a statement which appears to have a high degree of probability, and we set down as true whatever agrees with that and as false whatever does not. It is not allowable for the answerer to raise any questions about the hypothesis itself till this has been done, and until it is seen whether the consequences of the hypothesis involve anything absurd. If they do not, and there is still any doubt about the hypothesis, the answerer may question it, but not till then. The deduction of consequences must be kept quite separate from the question of the truth of the hypothesis. If that is not admitted even then, we may go on to show that it is a consequence of some higher hypothesis which we assume in the same way, till at last we come to some hypothesis which is adequate in the sense that the answerer accepts it (101 d). It will be seen that there is no question of demonstrating this ultimate hypothesis; it only holds good because it is accepted by the other party to the discussion. The whole fabric depends on the agreement of the two parties to the debate.

[1] *Parm.* 128 d, 5. The reading of the best MSS. and Proclus is αὐτῶν ἡ ὑπόθεσις εἰ πολλά ἐστιν.

§ 126. In the present case, the hypothesis Sokrates starts from is the distinction of the sensible from the intelligible, which is of course allowed to be true by his Pythagorean interlocutor without any hesitation (100 c). Assuming, then, that there is a form of the beautiful, we have next to ask what makes us call a particular thing beautiful. It is no answer to say it has a bright colour or anything else of the kind; that throws no light on the meaning of the statement, 'This is beautiful.' On the one hand, this is, of course, the problem of predication, the question of what is involved in saying 'A is B', but that is not quite the form it takes in the *Phaedo*. We are discussing coming into being and ceasing to be (γένεσις καὶ φθορά), or, in other words, we are asking how there can be a world of becoming alongside of the world of being which alone is the object of knowledge. The question is better formulated, then, if we say 'What makes a thing beautiful?' The 'simple-minded answer' Sokrates gives to this is: *If there is anything beautiful besides Beauty itself, Beauty makes it beautiful*, and this is explained to mean that it is the 'presence' (παρουσία) of the form in it that makes anything beautiful or whatever else we say it is. The predicate of a proposition is always a form, and a particular sensible thing is nothing else but the common meeting-place of a number of predicates, each of which is an intelligible form, and in that sense there is no longer a separation between the world of thought and the world of sense. On the other hand, none of the forms we predicate of a thing is present in it completely, and this relation is expressed by saying that the thing 'partakes in' the forms that are present in it. Apart from these, it has no independent reality; and, if we know all the forms in which anything participates, there is nothing more to know about it. The doctrine is most distinctly stated in the *Republic* (476 a), where we are told that each of the forms is one, but by reason of their communion (κοινωνία) with actions and bodies and with one another, they appear everywhere, and each seems to be many.[1] It is in that sense that Sokrates — the Sokrates of the *Phaedo* and the *Republic* — does not separate the forms from the world of sensible particulars,[2] and it is just because he denies all reality to the sensible particulars

---

[1] The κοινωνία of the forms with one another *in the sensible world* is quite different from their κοινωνία with one another *in the intelligible world* which Plato taught. That is just where Plato differs from Sokrates, as we shall see.

[2] Ar. *Met.* M. 4. 1078 b, 30. ἀλλ' ὁ μὲν Σωκράτης τὰ καθόλου οὐ χωριστὰ ἐποίει οὐδὲ τοὺς ὁρισμούς.

except what they derive from the partial presence of the forms in them. The Pythagorean doctrine of imitation left the sensible and intelligible as two separate worlds; the doctrine of participation makes the sensible identical with the intelligible, except that in sensible things the forms appear to us as a manifold instead of in their unity, and that they are only imperfectly embodied in the particulars. We should not be entitled to predicate the form of the thing unless the form were really in it.

§ 127. We may say, then, that the problem of Sokrates was to show how it was possible for the things of sense to be real, and he answers it by saying that they are real in so far as they partake in reality or as reality is present in them. He is conscious that these are metaphorical expressions, and so is the formula he substitutes in the latter part of the dialogue, namely, that the form 'occupies' or 'takes possession of' ($\kappa \alpha \tau \acute{\epsilon} \chi \epsilon \iota$) particular things. That way of putting the matter is adopted in the course of the final argument for the immortality of the soul, which, though not an object of sense, is nevertheless a particular thing and not a form. The proof is briefly that, from its very nature, the soul partakes in the form of life or is 'occupied' by it, and it is shown that a thing which is necessarily and of its own nature occupied by a given form will not admit the form opposite to that. If attacked by it it will either withdraw or perish. The soul cannot perish, however, so it will necessarily withdraw. For reasons which will be obvious, Sokrates himself is not altogether satisfied with this argument, and Plato found it necessary to defend the belief in immortality in quite another way. The real result of the *Phaedo* is not this, but simply that no particular thing can become anything except by partaking in, or being occupied by, the form of what it becomes, nor cease to be anything except by ceasing to partake in the form.[1] Such is the doctrine Plato attributed to Sokrates, and it is as clearly distinguished from his own as from that of the Pythagoreans.

§ 128. But though the Pythagorean separation ($\chi \omega \rho \iota \sigma \mu \acute{o} s$) of the things of sense from the things of thought has been overcome, it still remains true that there is a gulf between the confused manifold of sense and what is called in the *Phaedrus* (247 c) the 'colourless, shapeless, intangible reality' beheld by thought alone. This gulf the soul is ever seeking to bridge over, and its striving

---

[1] This is how Aristotle formulates the theory of the *Phaedo* in *Gen. Corr.* B. 6. 335 b, 10. He does not attribute it to Plato, but to 'Sokrates in the *Phaedo*'.

can only be described in the language of passionate love. That is involved in the very name of philosophy itself, and is brought home to us by calling philosophers 'lovers of wisdom' (ἐρασταὶ φρονήσεως), where the verbal variation is meant to remind us of the original meaning of the name. No one who is wholly dull and stupid feels this craving, nor does he who is already wise, as God is. Love is the child of Poverty and Resource. Now the soul itself and its strivings can only be adquately described in mythical language; for they belong to the middle region which is not yet wholly intelligible. The objects of its yearning are not mythical at all. The inspired lover is seeking the intelligible just as much and more than the mathematician, and I can see no ground for holding that even in the *Phaedrus*, the forms are regarded as supernatural 'things' of any kind. The 'supercelestial region' is clearly identified with that of pure thought, and the forms the mind beholds in it — Righteousness itself, Soberness itself, Knowledge itself — do not lend themselves in any way to crude pictorial fancies. It is true that our relation to this supreme reality can only be expressed in the language of feeling, but it is not by feeling we apprehend it when and in so far as we can do so. It is expressly said to be visible to mind alone (μόνῳ θεατὴ νῷ). There is no suggestion of a different way of knowing to which we may have recourse when reason and intelligence fail us. To put the matter in another way, allegory and myth are not employed to express something above reason, but to adumbrate what is below reason, so far as that can be done at all. It has its place half-way up the scale and not at the top; for it is only the poverty Love inherits from his mother that gives rise to these passionate yearnings. When they are satisfied, there is no more room for striving and longing. I suspect that all true mysticism is of this nature, and that to set feeling above reason as a means of knowing is only a perversion of it. However that may be, I am firmly convinced that the mystical side of the doctrine of forms is due to Sokrates and not to Plato. We know certain facts about him, such as his 'voice' and his trances, which prove him to have possessed the mystic temperament, and we know certain facts which explain the manner in which he conceives the mystic love. On the other hand, we have seen that there was another side to his nature which would safeguard him from the spurious kind of mysticism. I entirely agree with the demand[1] for a psychological

---

[1] See Professor Stewart's *Myths of Plato*, which is far the best treatment of

explanation of the two sides of the doctrine of forms, but the soul in which that is most easily to be found appears to me to be the soul of Sokrates, son of Sophroniskos. It is certainly in the *Symposium* that we have the most vivid picture of his personality, and there the 'enthusiasm' and the 'irony' are in perfect unison.

§ 129. Nevertheless the Sokrates of the *Phaedo* does not succeed in reaching the goal he has set before himself. He had turned away from the science of his time just because it could not show how everything is as it is because it is best for it to be so; and, though coming into being and ceasing to be have been explained in a sense, we cannot be said to be much nearer the fulfilment of that demand. That is because we have assumed certain forms which serve to explain the world of experience; but we have not gone on to examine this hypothesis itself in the light of a higher one, and therefore we cannot say why there should be a world of experience at all. Sokrates is represented as quite conscious of this in the *Republic*. There he is made to say (505 d *sqq.*) that we must look at all the other forms in the light of the Form of the Good, which is no mere hypothesis, but the true starting-point of knowledge. He confesses, however, that he can only describe it in a parable, and it is never referred to again in Plato's dialogues. The passage in the *Republic* stands quite by itself. We can see dimly what the Good must be if we liken it to the Sun, which is the cause both of growth and of vision in the sensible world, though it is neither growth nor vision itself. In the same way the Good must be the cause of knowledge and being in the intelligible world, though it is neither of these, but far beyond both of them in glory and power.[1] It is very significant that Sokrates is made to regard this purely negative characterisation of the Good as marking a failure to apprehend its true nature; it was left for thinkers of a later age to find satisfaction in it as a positive doctrine. That Sokrates really did speak of it in some such way as this appears to be proved by the fact that Eukleides of Megara identified the Good with the Eleatic One.

this part of the subject. It will be obvious that I am obliged to differ from it in some important respects, but that does not impair my appreciation of the work.

[1] This language has led some to identify the form of the Good with God, but that is certainly wrong. God is a soul and not a form, and in the *Timaeus* (which, as we shall see, represents a highly developed form of Pythagoreanism) the Good is above God. The difficulties raised by this doctrine led in later days to the conception of a highest and unknowable God and a secondary creative God (the Demiurge), but there is no trace of this till Hellenistic times. The Demiurge of the *Timaeus* is the highest God there is.

That seems to be how he reconciled his Eleaticism with his position as an 'associate' of Sokrates. The Pythagoreans would have little or no difficulty in accepting the doctrine of the *Phaedo*, but an Eleatic could not be expected to acquiesce in a plurality of forms. If Sokrates hinted at the ultimate unity of all the forms in the Good, we can understand what Eukleides meant; otherwise it would be very hard to follow him. Even so, there is a rift here in the doctrine of the Sokratic society, and we shall see how important that became in the next generation.

<h2 style="text-align:center">GOODNESS</h2>

§ 130. The theory of goodness Plato attributes to Sokrates is only intelligible in the light of the theory of knowledge and reality we have been considering. It is made clear, in the first place, that he was led to formulate it because he was dissatisfied with the teaching of the 'Sophists', and we must try to understand exactly where he differed from them. No doctrine is more closely associated with the name of Sokrates or better attested than that of the identity of goodness and knowledge, with its corollary that no one is voluntarily bad. No one who really knows what is good and what is bad can possibly choose the bad, and badness is, therefore, in the last resort, a form of ignorance. That Sokrates held this doctrine is more universally admitted than any other fact whatsoever about him.

That being so, it is not a little remarkable that, in a considerable number of his dialogues, Plato represents Sokrates as arguing against the doctrine, at least in its most obvious sense. He is made to say, for instance, that goodness cannot be knowledge; for, if it were, the great statesmen of Athens would certainly have taught their own goodness to their sons, whereas most of these were complete failures. Nor can it be said that the 'Sophists' really teach it; for then these same statesmen would have had their sons taught goodness just as they had them taught riding and music. In fact, goodness appears to be something that comes by chance or divine favour (θεία μοίρα) to some people and not to others. Those who have it can give no account of it; they cannot even tell what it is, and are therefore quite unable to impart it. They are like the poets who compose under the influence of inspiration of some kind, and cannot even give an intelligent interpretation of their own works. The connexion of this with what we are told about the mission of Sokrates in the *Apology* is obvious.

Nevertheless, the contradiction between these statements and the doctrine that goodness is knowledge is puzzling at first sight. It has been said, of course, that in these dialogues Plato is feeling his way to a more advanced doctrine than that of 'the historical Sokrates', but this line of interpretation breaks down as usual. It is perfectly certain that the arguments about statesmen and their sons was actually used by Sokrates himself, and we gather from the *Meno* and from Xenophon that it was one of the things that annoyed Anytos. As for Plato, he still maintains the doctrine that goodness is knowledge, and that no one is voluntarily bad, in his very latest work, the *Laws* (860 d).

§ 131. It will help us to understand this difficulty if we remember that the identification of goodness and knowledge was not really a doctrine peculiar to Sokrates, but was implied in the general belief of his time that goodness could be taught. The question between Sokrates and his contemporaries was not that, but the much more fundamental one of what goodness was identical with knowledge and therefore teachable. The Sophists were not wrong in holding that goodness could be taught; they were wrong in so far as the goodness they professed to teach was just that which, not being knowledge, could not be taught, and in so far as they ignored altogether that higher kind of goodness which alone was knowledge and therefore alone teachable. If we attribute this distinction to Sokrates we shall find no real contradictions in the dialogues dealing with the subject.

Nor are we without external evidence in support of this view. In the *Helen* of Isokrates (10. 1) we read that there are certain people who pride themselves on setting up a paradox and arguing tolerably in favour of it. 'Some have grown old in denying that it is possible to say what is false, or to contradict, or to make two opposite statements about the same thing.' That, no doubt, is meant for Antisthenes. 'Others argue in detail that justice and courage and wisdom are the same thing, and deny that any of these things come by nature, saying that there is one knowledge of them all.' That, I take it, refers to Sokrates. 'Lastly, there are those who spend their time in contentions (περὶ τὰς ἔριδας διατρίβουσι).' Plato uses that phrase too, and we shall have to discuss its application later. A little further on (10. 5) Isokrates makes light of the distinction between knowledge (ἐπιστήμη) and belief (δόξα), asserting that it is better to have a reasonable belief about useful things than a precise knowledge of what is useless. Similarly in his pamphlet *Against the Sophists*, he speaks (13. 1) of those who spend their time in disputations, and who profess to teach the young their duties and how to attain happiness (13. 3). Here too knowledge and belief are contrasted, and finally Isokrates denies that righteousness and morality can be learnt.

It is very difficult to believe that any of these references can be intended for Plato, as is often supposed. Isokrates was older than Plato, and both the *Helen* and the tract *Against the Sophists* are dated with probability some time before 390 B.C., when Isokrates opened his school, and therefore some time before Plato came forward as a teacher. It is plain too that Isokrates is concerned with the educational theories of his immediate predecessors, and it is not very likely he should go out of his way to attack a younger contemporary whom he had no reason at that date to regard as a rival. On the other hand, the question of Sokrates was very actual indeed at the time; for the Sophist Polykrates had just published his pamphlet against him, with the object of showing he was rightly put to death for the bad influence of the education he gave. We know too from the *Bousiris* that Isokrates had busied himself with this pamphlet. He must, then, have wished to make his attitude to Sokrates quite clear, while there was no reason for him to trouble about Plato yet awhile. But, if that is so, we may safely attribute the distinction between belief (δόξα) and knowledge (ἐπιστήμη) to Sokrates himself, and also the doctrine that goodness is one and that the knowledge of it is one, and that means in turn that there is no difficulty in attributing to Sokrates himself the whole theory of goodness expounded in Plato's earlier dialogues down to and including the *Meno*, and even, in substance, that set forth in the *Republic*.

§ 132. We are left in no doubt as to what 'goodness' (ἀρετή) meant in the language of the time. The Sophists, we have seen, professed to teach the goodness of the man and the citizen, and that was explained as the art of managing states and families rightly. It was, in fact, what we call efficiency. To the Greeks goodness was always something positive; it meant a habit of soul that enabled the possessor of it to do something, and not merely, as it is apt to mean with us, one that leads him to abstain from doing any particular harm. No Greek would have called a man good on purely negative grounds like that; he must be good for something. So far neither Sokrates nor Plato nor Aristotle would have the least quarrel with the current view. We have seen, however (§ 88), that the political condition of Athens was such in those days that the word tended to acquire a peculiar colour. That comes out better than anywhere else in the passage of Thucydides where he tells us that Antiphon, the chief contriver of the Revolution of the Four Hundred, was second to no other Athenian in 'goodness' (ἀρετή). That was, in practice, the only sort of goodness the Sophists had the opportunity of teaching; for it was the only sort demanded by those who could pay for it. It amounted to little more than skill in the arts of party intrigue.

The goodness Sokrates identified with knowledge was naturally of a different order, but he always admitted the relative value of 'true belief' (ἀληθὴς δόξα) for practical purposes. In the *Meno* he says (97 b) that if you want to go to Larissa a true belief about the way will take you there as well as knowledge. There is nothing astonishing in such an admission in view of the account we have given of his theory of knowledge. As we have seen, he was very far from denying the relative value of ordinary experience. Its objects are the same as those of knowledge, though they are imperfect and confused. He never meant to say that the great statesmen of Athens did no good at all, or to deny all value to the works of the poets. If the statesmen of the past had no goodness of their own, there would be nothing surprising in their failure to impart goodness to their sons. The weak point of such goodness, however, is that it is not based on any rational ground (λόγος) and cannot therefore be counted on. It is mainly an affair of temperament and happy chance. It is only, we are told in the *Meno* (98 a), when it has been chained fast by a reasoned knowledge of its cause (αἰτίας λογισμῷ) that we can be sure of its not running away like the Statues of Daidalos. Then, and then only, do we have goodness which is also knowledge and can therefore be taught.

It will be observed that this theory of goodness and the good is the exact counterpart of the theory of knowledge and reality which Plato ascribes to Sokrates, and this is another indication of the correctness of that ascription. Just as we cannot explain the cause (αἰτία) of things in the world of coming into being or ceasing to be

unless we regard them as participating or ceasing to participate in
an intelligible 'form', so we cannot have true goodness unless each
act is referred by reasoning (λογισμός) to its true cause (αἰτία).
Everyday goodness is just like the world of sensible experience in
that it is inconstant and variable; true goodness must be constant
and invariable. According to the *Phaedo* (82 a) Sokrates distinguished the two as 'philosophic goodness' (φιλοσοφικὴ ἀρετή) and
'popular goodness' (δημοτικὴ ἀρετή), or the 'goodness of the
citizen' (πολιτικὴ ἀρετή). The former depends on intellect (νοῦς),
the latter on habit (ἔθος). It is the former alone that is teachable;
for it alone is knowledge, and nothing can be taught but knowledge. The latter is only good at all in so far as it participates
in the former. Apart from that, it is a shifting and uncertain
thing.

§ 133. But though goodness in the full sense of the word is
knowledge, it is not an art, that is to say, an external accomplishment that may be acquired by anyone, and which he may exercise
or not at his pleasure. Plato has given us at full length two very
similar arguments on this point, and they bear every mark of being
genuinely Sokratic. In particular their constant reference to the
practice of artificers is highly characteristic. The best known is the
argument with Polemarchos in the *Republic*, which is less likely to
be misunderstood if read in the light of the other, which occurs in
the *Hippias minor*. In the *Republic* (332 e *sqq.*) the argument is
directed to showing that, if goodness is an art (a view for which
Polemarchos and not Sokrates is responsible) the honest man will
be the best thief, just as the doctor will be the most successful
murderer. The argument of the *Hippias minor* is that wisdom is
required as much or more to tell lies as to tell the truth, and that it
is better to do wrong voluntarily than involuntarily. The point is
the same in both cases. An art or capacity (δύναμις) is always 'of
opposites'. The man who can make a good use of it is also the man
who can make a bad one, and therefore something more must be
implied in goodness than this. That too was forced on Sokrates by
the practice of the Sophists. Gorgias disclaims all responsibility
for the use his pupils may make of the art of Rhetoric which they
learn from him. We have no more right, he says (456 d) to blame
the teacher of rhetoric for the misdeeds of his pupils than we should
have to blame the teacher of boxing if his pupil used his art to
injure his neighbours. The question involved in the argument

with Polemarchos is really the same. Is it possible to regard goodness as a purely neutral accomplishment of this kind, or is it
something that belongs to the very nature of the soul that possesses
it, so that it is really impossible for the good man to do evil or to
injure anyone?

§ 134. Another question that was much discussed at this time
was that of the unity of goodness, and to Sokrates this question
was closely bound up with the other. The professional teaching of
goodness was apt to suggest that you could learn one branch of it
and not another. You might, for instance, learn courage without
learning honesty, or *vice versa*. If the different forms of goodness
are so many 'arts' or external accomplishments, they will stand in
no necessary connexion with one another, and we cannot say that
goodness is one. Sokrates approaches this question from the point
of view of the different kinds of goodness. The *Laches*, for example,
starts from courage, and the *Charmides* from soberness. In both
cases the particular virtue under discussion is identified with
knowledge, but the identification is not made by Sokrates. On the
contrary, his argument is entirely directed to showing that, if we
identify any particular form of goodness with knowledge, it is
impossible to maintain any distinction between it and any other
form of goodness. From that point of view they all become merged
in one.

Both these doctrines, that of the unity of goodness, and that
which refuses to identify goodness with an art, are supported by
another line of argument of which Sokrates is fond. A good example of this too is to be found in the argument with Polemarchos
in the *Republic* (332 c). It is that, if you identify any form of goodness with an art, it is impossible to discover any use for it. The
whole field is already covered by the particular arts appropriate to
each department, and there is no room for the 'virtue'. One might
suppose that honesty or justice was a virtue useful in partnerships,
but we should all prefer a good player to an honest man as our
partner in a game of skill or as an accompanist to our singing. If
goodness is looked at in this way, it will have no special function
to perform; there is no room for it alongside of the other arts. It
may be harmful, since it is a capacity of opposites, and it is in any
case superfluous.

§ 135. What, then, is the knowledge with which true goodness
is to be identified? In the first place it is knowledge of what is good

for the human soul. It is at this point we see most clearly how the theory of conduct taught by Sokrates, like his theory of knowledge, was influenced by Pythagorean doctrine. The Pythagoreans had already regarded the health of the soul as something analogous to the health of the body, and for them this was much more than a metaphor. We have seen (§ 75) how they arrived at their fundamental notion of an attunement (ἁρμονία) or blend (κρᾶσις), and it was this that dominated all medical theory so far as it fell under Pythagorean influence. It was partly the necessity of explaining goodness in this way that made Sokrates reject the later Pythagorean view that the soul itself was an attunement (§ 124), and he preferred to work out the idea from the point of view of what was probably an earlier Pythagorean doctrine, that of the parts of the soul. In the *Gorgias* (504 a *sqq.*) Sokrates says that goodness is due to the presence of arrangement (τάξις) and order (κόσμος) in the soul, and that this can only be produced by knowledge, not by experience or routine. In the *Republic* the same theory is worked out in the most elaborate fashion. It is shown that there are three parts of the soul, the philosophical or reasoning part (φιλόσοφον, λογιστικόν), temper (θυμός), and desire (ἐπιθυμία). The special virtues of each of these are wisdom, courage, and soberness, while justice or righteousness is the principle that keeps them all in their proper place. It is shown how each of these virtues is represented in the different classes of a well-ordered State, and we learn from a consideration of that how the inner polity of the soul should be ordered. We see that wisdom should command, while temper assists in the execution of these commands, and how the desires should be confined to their proper task of supplying the necessary material basis for the rest, and how all this is to be secured by justice, which assigns to each its proper part and sees that it keeps to it. It is shown further how inferior types of State arise from the usurped supremacy of one or other of the subaltern parts of the soul, and how there are inferior types of character corresponding to each of these and arising from the same cause. No doubt the elaboration of this idea which we find in the *Republic* owes much to the artistic genius of Plato, but it appears to me quite certain that the leading idea is Sokratic, and indeed Pythagorean. Plato's own view of the soul was so different that he would not naturally fall into this way of expressing himself, though he might quite well use it for purposes of more or less popular exposition. As we shall see, it is improbable that he had a definite original philosophy of his own by the time the *Republic* was written.[1]

§ 136. This account of the Sokratic philosophy is in brief that to which Plato gave currency within fifteen years or so of his master's death. It is, I submit, an intelligible and consistent whole, and it is quite different from anything Aristotle ever ascribes to Plato himself. If Plato had originally taught this system, and if the doctrine Aristotle ascribed to him was only a development of his later years, we may be sure that we should have heard something about this remarkable change of opinion. As it is, there is no hint anywhere in Aristotle that Plato ever taught anything else than what he regards as the genuine Platonic doctrine. It is impossible, of course, to decide the matter finally till we have seen what Plato's own philosophy was, but there are two considerations I should like to urge before leaving the subject. In the first place, it is surely worth while to try the experiment of taking Plato's dialogues in their natural sense. That is the 'hypothesis' on which this work proceeds, and it can only be destroyed if we come to consequences that are impossible or untrue. In the second place, I would urge that the burden of proof does not lie with those who adopt this hypothesis, but with those who deny it. We cannot be forced to regard the Sokrates of Plato as a fiction unless some really cogent argument can be produced for doing so, and I am not aware that this has ever been done. It is not maintained, of course, that Plato is ever a mere reporter. He is clearly a dramatic artist, and arranges his material artistically. But he knew Sokrates well, and he wrote for people who knew Sokrates well, and the dialogues made use of in this sketch were probably all written before he came forward as a teacher of philosophy himself. If Plato's Sokrates is not meant for the real Sokrates, I find it very hard to imagine what he can be meant for.

[1] I have not thought it necessary to give the argument of the *Republic* in detail as there are so many excellent accounts of it in existence already.

X

The Trial and Death of Socrates

THE CONDEMNATION

§ 137. In 399 B.C. Sokrates was brought to trial by Anytos, the democratic leader, Meletos, a 'youthful and unknown' tragic poet, 'with lanky hair, a scanty beard, and a hooked nose',[1] and Lykon, an even more obscure rhetorician. The indictment stated that he was guilty of not worshipping ($νομίζων$)[2] the gods the State worshipped but introducing other new divinities, and further that he was guilty of corrupting the young by teaching them accordingly. In the *Apology*, Plato gives us what profess to be the speeches delivered by Sokrates at his trial. It is not to be supposed that even here he is a mere reporter. It was usual for speeches to be carefully revised and adapted for publication, and no doubt Plato meant to do for Sokrates what other accused persons either did for themselves or more often had done for them by a professional speechwriter. On the other hand it seems incredible that he should have misrepresented the attitude of Sokrates before the court or the general line of his defence. It is perfectly true, no doubt, that the *Apology* is not a defence at all, but that makes it all the more characteristic of the man. Sokrates treats the accusation with contempt, and even goes out of his way to import things into the case that were hardly of a nature to conciliate the judges. That does not prove the *Apology* to be pure fiction, as it has been supposed to do.[3] Far from it.

§ 138. The actual conduct of the prosecution was entrusted to Meletos, who bungled it, according to Plato. By a skilful cross-examination Sokrates got him to admit that he believed him to be

---

[1] *Euthyphro*, 2 b.

[2] The least inadequate translation of $νομίζειν$ in its legal sense is 'worship'. The world does not refer primarily to 'religious opinions', but to the observance of certain current 'uses' ($νόμοι$), though Plato makes Sokrates take advantage of the secondary sense 'think' in order to confuse Meletos (*Apol.* 26 c).

[3] See the Introduction to Schanz's edition of the *Apology* with German notes.

an out-and-out atheist, which was of course inconsistent with the indictment. In any case Sokrates did not stoop to defend himself against either the one charge or the other, though he showed himself more sensitive to the accusation of corrupting the youth, and offered to allow the fathers and elder brothers of his associates to give evidence on the point. He was found guilty, however, in spite of the failure of Meletos to make anything of the principal count in the indictment, which he does not seem to have understood himself. The majority was a considerable one, though Sokrates says he had expected it to be larger. He knew therefore that there was something else against him besides the trumpery charge of introducing new divinities, which he did not for a moment treat seriously.

The penalty proposed by the accusers was death, but there is no reason to suppose Anytos really wished it to be carried out. By a very ingenious provision of the Athenian law, it was ordained that in cases of a certain class the condemned man should be allowed to propose an alternative sentence. The idea was that an adequate punishment would probably be arrived at in this way; for the judges were bound to choose between the two penalties proposed, and could not suggest another themselves. It was, therefore, the interest of the condemned man to propose something the judges would be likely to accept. There can be no doubt that if Sokrates had proposed exile or imprisonment till he had paid a reasonable fine, everyone would have been satisfied, but he refused to do anything of the sort. That, he said, would amount to an acknowledgment of his guilt. If he had really to propose what he thought he deserved, he would assess the penalty at free quarters in the Prytaneion at the public expense, an honour sometimes voted to Olympic victors and public benefactors. Ultimately, however, he proposed a fine of one mina, an inconsiderable sum, which his friends induced him to raise to thirty, offering to become surety for the payment. Plato was one of these friends, and this is the only act of his he has seen fit to put on public record.

§ 139. The judges were apparently incensed by this way of treating the court; for they condemned Sokrates to death by a larger majority than that by which they had found him guilty. He then delivered a short address to those judges who had voted for his acquittal. He said that, even if death were the end of all things, it was no more an evil than a dreamless sleep, and few waking days are better than a night of that. He also hinted pretty plainly that, in his own belief, the soul was immortal, and that a good man had nothing to fear in the next life. And so he bade his judges farewell. 'It is now time to depart, for me to die and for you to live. Which of us is going to meet the better lot, none knows but God.'[1]

THE ALLEGED OFFENCE

§ 140. We have now to ask why Sokrates was charged with irreligion and why he was put to death. We must at once put aside the idea that it was for not believing the stories told about the gods. It is not likely that any educated man believed these, and un-educated people probably knew very little about them.[2] There was no church and no priesthood, and therefore the conception of religious orthodoxy did not exist. So far as mythology was con-cerned, you might take any liberty. No one appears to have found fault with Aischylos for his *Prometheus*, though, judged by modern standards, it is flat blasphemy. He did get into trouble for inad-vertently revealing some Eleusinian formula, and the contrast is instructive. If it had been required of anyone that he should treat the stories about the gods respectfully, Aristophanes would not have survived Sokrates. He does not scruple to make fun of Zeus himself, and he represents Dionysos as a vulgar poltroon in a comedy which was actually part of the service of that very god and was presided over by his priest. In the *Phaedrus* (229 e *sqq.*) Sokrates is described as totally indifferent to the truth or falsehood of mythology, though he has the good taste to prefer the stories in their traditional form to the versions produced by the 'homely wit' of rationalist historians. One thing he does indeed feel strongly, namely, that it is dangerous to repeat stories that ascribe untruth-fulness and wickedness and strife to the gods, and in the *Euthyphro* (6 a) he does suggest that it is possibly for this that he is regarded as an innovator in religion. The suggestion is certainly not serious, however, and even Euthyphro is not shocked, though he himself

[1] It has actually been inferred from the *Apology* that 'the historical Sokrates' had no fixed belief in immortality, and this has been used to discredit the *Phaedo*. I can only ask anyone who holds this view to read the passage aloud and see what effect it makes upon him. Of course Sokrates was addressing what was practically a public meeting, and he knew that few of his hearers held such beliefs, so there is some necessary reserve, but that is all.
[2] Arist. *Poet.* 1451 b, 25.

believes these stories and others stranger still. The truth is that belief in narratives of any kind formed no part of ancient religion; anyone might reject or accept such things as he pleased. Mythology was looked on as a creation of the poets, and 'poets tell many falsehoods'. No one could be prosecuted for what we call religious opinions.[1]

§ 141. Nor is it credible that the divine 'voice' should have had anything to do with the prosecution. It is true that Euthyphro is represented as jumping at once to the conclusion that it had; for that is the sort of thing he himself is interested in. At the same time, he makes it quite clear that, in his opinion, Sokrates need have no fear of a charge like that, though he must expect to be laughed at.[2] In the *Apology* Plato makes Sokrates himself say that the divine voice is presumably what Meletos has caricatured and made the ground of the charge in his indictment, but the way he says it makes it quite clear that Meletos meant nothing of the sort and had said nothing about the 'voice'.[3] The Athenians might and did think Sokrates eccentric because of his voice and his trances, and, as Euthyphro says, such things are 'easily misrepresented'[4] and are apt to make people jealous. But the belief in 'possession' (κατοκωχή) was much too firmly established, and cases of it were much too familiar, to allow of a charge of irreligion being based on anything of the kind.[5] The accepted view was that such things were a sort of disease which could be treated by 'purifications', but even madness and epilepsy were supposed to make the sufferer 'holy' (ἱερός). From the point of view of the ordinary Athenian, the irreligion would be on the side of anyone who treated the 'voice' disrespectfully.

§ 142. It must also be remembered that the charge of introducing new divinities was no novelty; for it had been definitely formulated by Aristophanes a generation earlier. In the *Clouds* Sokrates announces that Zeus has been dethroned and Vortex reigned in his stead. He offers prayer to the Clouds and swears by

---

[1] Cf. p. 76, *n.* 2.   [2] *Euthyphro*, 3 b *sq.*

[3] *Apology*, 31 d. Professor Taylor's interpretation of the words ὃ δὴ καὶ . . . ἐν τῇ γραῇ . . . ἐγράψατο (*Varia Socratica*, i. p. 14) seems to me the only sound one. Sokrates says he supposes (δὴ) that Meletos meant the divine voice when he spoke of δαιμόνια *in the indictment*. It is clear, then, that Meletos said nothing about it *in his speech*.

[4] The word εὐδιάβογα means no more.

[5] The 'voice' would no doubt strike the average δεισιδαίμων as an ordinary case of ἐγγαστριμυθία.

Respiration, Chaos, and Air. It will be remembered that Diogenes of Apollonia held Air to be a 'god'. That being so, it is surely very significant that Aristophanes does not make the most distant allusion to the 'voice', though he must have known all about it, and it would lend itself admirably to comic treatment. The omission is the more striking, as there is an allusion to the trances of Sokrates (150). Xenophon is even more instructive. He says he got his information about the trial from Hermogenes, and we may be sure the religious Xenophon would be anxious to discover all he could about the meaning of this charge. He does not appear, however, to have got any definite explanation of it; for he only gives it as his personal opinion that it must have been the 'voice' on which the accusers chiefly relied, and it seems most probable that he is only repeating this from Plato's *Apology* and *Euthyphro*. At any rate, in his own *Apology*, he makes Sokrates speak about the 'voice' very much as Plato does, and he makes him say, just like Euthyphro, that the Athenians are jealous of it as an exceptional divine favour. In fact, everyone speculates about the meaning of the charge, and the one fact that stands out clearly is that no one — not even the prosecutor — seems to know it. It surely follows that the charge of introducing new divinities, though stated in the indictment, was neither explained nor justified at the trial. Such things were possible in an Athenian dikastery, which was more like a public meeting than a court of justice. There was no judge to rule the prosecution irrelevant to the indictment.

THE REAL OFFENCE

§ 143. But, if that is the true account of the matter, it follows further that this accusation was a mere pretext. That would explain why Meletos falls so easily into the trap laid for him by Sokrates, and substitutes the charge of atheism for that of introducing strange divinities. It will also make the conduct of the judges more intelligible. We know that a number of them, after voting for the acquittal of Sokrates on the charge brought against him, turned round and voted for the death sentence. That is partly to be explained, no doubt, by the attitude Sokrates took up in his second speech, but this will not explain it altogether. Death is surely an extreme penalty for contempt of court, and those judges must have believed Sokrates to be guilty of something. Everything becomes clear if we suppose that the real ground of the accusation could not for some reason be stated in the indictment, and that some of the judges thought it unfair to condemn a man for an offence with which he was not formally charged, even though they might believe him guilty of it. The defiant attitude of Sokrates would account for their change of mind in that case.

Now we know that Sokrates had refused to obey the illegal orders of the Thirty, but we also know that he did not leave Athens. He was therefore suspect of *incivisme*, but the amnesty made it impossible to charge him with a strictly political offence. Plato indicates in the clearest possible manner that Sokrates really owed his death to his political attitude. There are two passages in which he is represented as criticising the democratic leaders of the fifth century, including Perikles, in a very severe manner. One of these is in the *Gorgias*, and there Kallikles, who is a democratic states-man, bluntly tells him (521 c) that, if he refuses to flatter the democracy instead of trying to make them see the error of their ways, he is in danger of being dragged into court by some sorry wretch, and then anything may happen to him. The other passage is in the *Meno*, where Anytos himself is brought on the stage to give a similar warning. That is surely meant to be significant. Anytos is not the chief interlocutor, and is apparently introduced solely for this purpose. After listening impatiently to the criticisms of Sokrates on the heroes of the democracy, he says (94 e), 'I think, Sokrates, you are rather ready to abuse people. I should advise you, if there was any chance of your taking my advice, to be care-ful. Even in other cities, I fancy it is easier to do people a mischief than a good turn, and most decidedly it is so in this one.' These are very broad hints, and Plato set them down deliberately some time after the event. They can only mean that the real offence of Sokrates was his criticism of the democracy and its leaders. No one in Plato ever gives him a hint that he had better be careful not to talk about unauthorised divinities, as he frequently does, and still less does anyone suggest that the 'voice' is a thing he would be wise in keeping to himself.

§ 144. From this point of view one of the most important things in the *Apology* is the statement of Sokrates (39 d) that his country-men will not be able to rid themselves of criticism even if they put him to death. There are many who will take up the task of ex-posing them, and they will be more merciless inasmuch as they are

younger. That is, to all intents and purposes, a plea of guilty to
what the hints of Kallikles and Anytos suggest was the real ground
of the accusation, namely, that Sokrates had fostered in young
men that antidemocratic spirit which had led to the oligarchical
revolutions. About half a century later Aischines put the matter
quite bluntly. He says (i. 173) that the Athenians 'put the Sophist
Sokrates to death because he was believed to have educated Kritias',
and less than ten years after his trial the Sophist Polykrates
charged him, as we saw, with having educated Alkibiades. In fact,
it looks as if Polykrates simply wrote the speech Anytos would have
delivered at the trial, if the amnesty had not stood in the way. That
the point was actually made by Meletos, a less responsible person,
is strongly suggested by the allusion Sokrates makes in the *Apology*
(33 a) 'to those they say are my disciples'. Xenophon also in the
Memorabilia (i. 2, 12 *sqq.*) makes a point of saying that Kritias and
Alkibiades were not really disciples of Sokrates.

§ 145. It is only fair to say that, from his own point of view,
Anytos was not altogether wrong. Xenophon, indeed, attributes
merely personal motives to him. He says in his *Apology* (29) that
he was angry with Sokrates for telling him he ought to give his son
a liberal education instead of bringing him up to his own business
as a tanner. It is impossible to say what truth there may be in that,
but in any case there were other reasons why Anytos should desire
to remove Sokrates from Athens. He had undoubtedly been an
uncompromising opponent of the Periklean democracy, the radical
vice of which, according to him, was that it denied the need for
expert knowledge in politics. It would take the advice of experts on
questions of shipbuilding or fortification; but when a vital point
of right or wrong in national policy had to be decided, anyone who
chose to get up and speak was supposed to be as good a judge as
anyone else. According to Plato, he went so far as to deny the title
of statesman to the democratic leaders of his time, including
Perikles. In the *Republic* we have an account of the democratic
State, which is certainly meant to be a description of Athens in the
fifth century, not of the humdrum *bourgeois* democracy of Plato's
own time, and the description is by no means flattering. Of course
the young men who followed Sokrates about would be far less
impressed by his positive teaching than by this destructive criticism of existing institutions. They would be prejudiced against
democracy to start with, and they would relish his attacks on it

keenly. It is a fact that many of them became vulgar oligarchs and
not statesmen. That is the tragedy of the situation. Sokrates was
not responsible for it, but it existed all the same. Now Anytos and
his friends were busily engaged in organising the restored democracy, and they could not afford to leave their work at the mercy of
reaction. They had every reason to believe that the teaching of
Sokrates was of a kind to imperil the constitution, and it is not
surprising that they took steps accordingly. It must be remembered
that they had probably no desire to see Sokrates put to death, but
it was natural they should wish to drive him into exile. In those
circumstances we can easily understand why some of the friends
of Sokrates thought it prudent to leave Athens for a time after his
death. Even Plato went, though, as we shall see, he had held aloof
from the oligarchical revolution in which his kinsmen were
implicated, and though he had intended to enter public life under
the restored democracy. Fortunately he found something better to
do.

THE PRETEXT

§ 146. Even assuming, however, that the charge of irreligion
was a mere pretext, it must have been a colourable one; for the
accusers ran the risk of being heavily fined if they did not secure a
fifth of the votes. We must ask, then, whether there was anything
that might be made to appear a justification of the charge, and on
which a statesman like Anytos might rely to produce the right kind
of prejudice against Sokrates. If we ask that question, we come at
once upon the fact that in the very same year as Sokrates was tried
Andokides appeared once more before the judges to explain his
connexion with the mutilation of the images of Hermes and the
profanations of the mysteries sixteen years before. We find also
that Anytos spoke in his favour, no doubt because his revelations
had been of service to the democratic party. We shall never know
the truth about this old scandal, but the speech of Andokides is a
precious document for the state of public feeling about it, not only
at the time, but under the restored democracy. It is certain that,
for the ordinary Athenian, the mutilation of the images was closely
bound up with the profanation of the mysteries, and that both
were supposed to be somehow directed towards the overthrow of
the democracy. No doubt this was a mistake. The mutilation had
probably nothing to do with the profanations of the mysteries, and

the latter were obviously distorted in the popular imagination. It does not seem credible that some of the most gifted and enlightened men in Athens should have found it amusing to parody Eleusinian ritual, not once only or in a single place, though even that would be silly enough, but systematically and in a number of private houses. On the other hand, the evidence that certain proceedings took place which were capable of being represented in that light is far too strong to be rejected, and conveys to a modern reader the idea that there may have been something resembling meetings of masonic lodges, exaggerated by public rumour into blasphemous mummeries of the most sacred rites.

Now many of the judges must have known quite well that some of the most intimate associates of Sokrates were implicated in this business. There is no doubt, for instance, about Axiochos of Skambonidai, the uncle of Alkibiades and of Adeimantos son of Leukolophides.[1] All three were denounced by Agariste, the wife of Alkmeonides, a high-born dame who had been the wife of one Damon before she married her kinsman.[2] This may very well be the same Damon whom Sokrates refers to as an authority on music. If that is correct, it is interesting to notice that one of the accused was called Taureas, and that is the name of the master of the *palaistra* in which Kritias introduced Charmides to Sokrates.[3] Further, if we remember that the banquet described in the *Symposium* is supposed to take place the very year the scandals occurred, it is suspicious that we find the names of Akoumenos, Eryximachos, and Phaidros among the persons inculpated.[4] Akoumenos was a celebrated physician, and he has an unusual name. We do not know of anyone else who bore it. He was not present at the banquet, though his son Eryximachos, who was also a physician, is one of the speakers there. Phaidros is not an uncommon name, and we cannot be sure that Phaidros of Myrrhinous is meant. We are, however, told that he was an 'associate' ($\dot{\epsilon}\tau a\hat{\iota}\rho o s$) of Eryximachos,[5] and it is at the very least a remarkable coincidence that all three names should occur. In any case, we know that public interest in this old business had just been revived, and that of itself

---

[1] The record of the public sale of his confiscated goods still exists on inscriptions, where his name is given in full, Ἀξίοχος Ἀλκιβιάδου Σκαμβωνίδης (Dittenberger, *Sylloge*[2], 39, 41, 42, 45).
[2] Andok. i. 16.
[3] *Ib.* i. 47; Plato, *Charm.* 153 a.
[4] Andok. i. 15, 18, 35.   [5] Plato, *Phaedr.* 268 a.

would be sufficient to create the atmosphere of prejudice required. Memories of the *Clouds* would do the rest.

For reasons I have given, I do not think it likely that Sokrates was explicitly charged with this or any other particular offence against religion, but it was in everyone's mind, and there were circumstances enough in his life to connect him with it. It was certainly believed at Athens that he had taken part in religious rites of a strange kind; for Aristophanes could count on his audience understanding his allusions to them. Aischines wrote a dialogue in which Sokrates is represented as conversing with the Pythagorean Telauges. Plato represents him as full of Orphic ideas, though, as I have said, there is always a certain reservation which does not allow us to suppose he accepted them implicitly. I do not think it likely that his Pythagorean friends had much to do with this; for, to all appearance, they had ceased to 'practise', and they had dropped the Orphic theory of the soul, which was just the thing that appealed most to Sokrates.[1] In fact, it is Sokrates who is represented as trying to bring them back to an earlier form of Pythagorean belief. All this can hardly be fictitious. What motive could Plato have had for inventing it? By his time Orphicism had hopelessly degenerated, so far as we can see, and it is not probable that it ever attracted him. In the youth of Sokrates things may well have been different. We know that the doctrine had been able to inspire a Pindar about the time Sokrates was born.

THE DEATH OF SOKRATES

§ 147. Sokrates was not put to death at once. It was the festival of the Delian Apollo, and the ship the Athenians sent to Delos every year had just been solemnly garlanded the day before the trial. Now it was the law that the city should be kept free from the pollution of death at the hands of the public authority till the ship had gone to Delos and returned, and that sometimes took a long time. So Sokrates had to spend a month in prison before his sentence could be carried out, and he passed that time in discussions with his friends, some of whom came from other parts of Hellas to bid him farewell. It would have been quite easy for him

---

[1] It will be seen where I am obliged to differ from my colleague Professor Taylor's conclusions in *Varia Socratica*, and I need not insist further on that. My agreement with him on other points will also be obvious.

to escape at any time during this month, and his friends were ready to bear any expense that might be needful. But, as we have seen, Sokrates was a firm supporter of law, and he would not stoop to the inconsistency of making an exception in his own case. However unjust the sentence might be, it had been legally pronounced, and a good citizen could only submit. He owed everything to the laws of his country, and it was not for him to call them in question.

In the *Phaedo* Plato has given an account of the last hours of Sokrates on earth. It would be difficult to match this narrative in the whole range of European literature, and it cannot be paraphrased. The last words of it are: 'Such, Echekrates, was the end of our associate (ἑταῖρος), a man, as we should say, the best and also the wisest and most righteous of his time.'

XI

Demokritos

§ 148. A quite independent attempt at reconstruction was made by Demokritos. Like his contemporary Sokrates he faced the difficulties about knowledge raised by his fellow-citizen Protagoras and others, and like him he paid great attention to the problem of conduct, which had also been forced to the front by the Sophists. Unlike Sokrates, however, he was a voluminous author, and we can still see from his fragments that he was one of the great writers of antiquity. For us, however, it is almost as if he had written nothing, and we really know less of him than we do of Sokrates. That is because he wrote at Abdera, and his works were never really well known at Athens, where they would have had a chance of being preserved, like those of Anaxagoras and others, in the library of the Academy. It is not clear that Plato knew anything about Demokritos; for the few passages in the *Timaeus* and elsewhere in which he seems to be reproducing him are easily explained by the Pythagorean influences that affected them both. Aristotle, on the other hand, knows Demokritos well; for he too was an Ionian from the North.

It is certain, nevertheless, that the Demokritean corpus (which included the works of Leukippos and others as well as those of Demokritos) continued to exist; for the school maintained itself at Abdera and Teos down to Hellenistic times. It was therefore possible for Thrasyllos in the reign of Tiberius to produce an edition of the works of Demokritos arranged in tetralogies just like his edition of Plato's dialogues. Even that did not suffice to preserve them. The Epicureans, who ought to have studied the man to whom they owed so much, were averse to study of any kind, and probably did not care to multiply copies of a writer whose works would have been a standing testimony to the lack of originality that marked their own system.

§ 149. We know extremely little about the life of Demokritos.

He belonged like Protagoras to Abdera in Thrace, a city which hardly deserves its proverbial reputation for dullness, seeing it could produce two such men.[1] As to the date of his birth, we have only conjecture to guide us. In one of his chief works he stated that it was written 730 years after the fall of Troy, but we do not know when he supposed that to have taken place. There were several eras in use at the time and later. He also said somewhere that he had been a young man in the old age of Anaxagoras, and from this it was inferred that he was born in 460 B.C. That seems rather too early, however; for it is based on the assumption that he was forty years old when he met Anaxagoras, and the expression 'young man' suggests something less than that. Further, we have to find room for Leukippos between him and Zeno. If Demokritos died, as we are told, at the age of ninety or a hundred, he was in any case still living when Plato founded the Academy. Even on purely chronological grounds, then, it is wrong to class Demokritos with the predecessors of Sokrates, and it obscures the fact that, like Sokrates, he tried to answer his distinguished fellow-citizen Protagoras.[2]

§ 150. Demokritos was a disciple of Leukippos, and we have contemporary evidence, that of Glaukos of Rhegion, that he also had Pythagoreans for his teachers. A later member of the school, Apollodoros of Kyzikos, says he learnt from Philolaos, and it seems quite likely. That accounts for his geometrical knowledge, and also, we shall see, for other features in his system. We know, too, that Demokritos spoke of the doctrines of Parmenides and Zeno in his works. These he would come to know through Leukippos. He mentioned Anaxagoras, as we have seen, and he appears to have said that his theory of the sun and moon was not original. That may refer to the explanation of eclipses, which was generally attributed at Athens, and no doubt in Ionia, to Anaxagoras, though Demokritos would, of course, know it to be Pythagorean.

He is said to have visited Egypt, but there is some reason for believing that the fragment in which this is mentioned (fr. 298 b)

---

[1] It has been plausibly suggested that the reputation of the Abderites may have arisen from some satirical remark of Demokritos himself. The other side of the same thing may be represented by the view of Demokritos as 'the laughing philosopher', which appears for the first time in Horace.
[2] As has been pointed out above (p. 112, *n*. 2), the stories which make Protagoras a disciple of Demokritos are based on the illusion that Protagoras was a contemporary of Plato.

is a forgery. There is another (fr. 116) in which he says: 'I went to Athens and no one knew me.' If he said that, he meant no doubt that he had failed to make such an impression as his more brilliant fellow-citizen Protagoras had done. On the other hand, Demetrios of Phaleron said Demokritos never visited Athens at all, so this fragment may be a forgery too. In any case, most of his time must have been spent in study, teaching and writing at Abdera. He was not a wandering Sophist of the modern type, but the head of a regular school.

The real greatness of Demokritos does not lie in the theory of atoms and the void, which he seems to have expounded much as he had received it from Leukippos. Still less does it lie in his cosmological system, which is mainly derived from Anaxagoras. He belongs to another generation altogether than these men, and he is not specially concerned in finding an answer to Parmenides. The question he had to deal with was that of his own day. The possibility of science had been denied and the whole problem of knowledge raised by Protagoras, and that had to be met. Further, the problem of conduct had become a pressing one. The originality of Demokritos lay, then, precisely in the same directions as that of Sokrates.

THEORY OF KNOWLEDGE

§ 151. Demokritos followed Leukippos in giving a purely mechanical account of sensation, and it is probable that he is the author of the detailed atomist doctrine on this subject. As the soul is composed of atoms like everything else, sensation must consist in the impact of atoms from without on the atoms of the soul, and the organs of sense must be simply 'passages' (πόροι) through which these atoms are introduced. It follows that the objects of vision are not strictly the things we suppose ourselves to see, but the 'images' (δείκελα, εἴδωλα) that bodies are constantly shedding. The image in the pupil of the eye was regarded as the essential thing in vision. It is not, however, an exact likeness of the body from which it comes; for it is subject to distortion by the intervening air. That is why we see things in a blurred and indistinct way at a distance, and why, if the distance is very great, we cannot see them at all. If there were no air, but only the void, between us and the objects of vision, this would not be so; 'we could see an ant crawling on the sky.' Differences of colour are due to the smoothness or roughness of the images to the touch. Hearing is explained in a similar way. Sound is a stream of atoms which flow from the sounding body and cause motion in the air between it and the ear. They therefore reach the ear along with those portions of the air that resemble them. The differences of taste are due to differences in the figures (εἴδη, σχήματα) of the atoms which come in contact with the organs of that sense, and smell was similarly explained, though not in the same detail. In the same way, touch, regarded as the sense by which we feel hot and cold, wet and dry, and the like, is affected according to the shape and size of the atoms impinging upon it.

Aristotle says Demokritos reduced all the senses to that of touch, and that is quite true if we understand by touch the sense that perceives such qualities as shape, size and weight. This, however, must be carefully distinguished from the special sense of touch which has just been described. To understand this point, we must go on to consider the doctrine of 'trueborn' and 'bastard' knowledge.

§ 152. It is here that Demokritos comes sharply into conflict with Protagoras, who had declared all sensations to be equally true for the sentient subject. Demokritos, on the contrary, regards all the sensations of the special senses as false, inasmuch as they have no real counterpart outside the sentient subject. In this he is of course true to the Eleatic tradition on which the atomic theory rests. Parmenides had said expressly that taste, colours, sound, and the like were only 'names' (ὀνόματα), and it is quite likely Leukippos said something of the same sort, though there is no reason to believe he had elaborated a theory on the subject. Coming after Protagoras as he did, Demokritos was bound to be explicit on the point. His doctrine has fortunately been preserved to us in his own words. 'By use (νόμῳ),' he said (fr. 125), 'there is sweet, by use there is bitter; by use there is warm and by use there is cold; by use there is colour. But in sooth (ἐτεῇ) there are atoms and the void.' In fact, our sensations represent nothing external, though they are caused by something outside us, the true nature of which cannot be apprehended by the special senses. That is why the same thing is sometimes felt as sweet and sometimes as bitter. 'By the senses,' Demokritos said (fr. 9), 'we in truth know nothing sure, but only something that changes according to the disposition of the body and of the things that enter into it or resist it.' We cannot know reality in this way; for 'truth is in the depths' (fr. 117). It will be seen that this doctrine has much in common with the modern distinction between the primary and secondary qualities of matter.

§ 153. Demokritos, then, rejects sensation as a source of knowledge just as the Pythagoreans and Sokrates did; but, like them, he saves the possibility of science by affirming that there is a source of knowledge other than the special senses. 'There are', he says (fr. 11), 'two forms of knowledge (γνώμη), the trueborn (γνησίη) and the bastard (σκοτίη). To the bastard belong all these; sight, hearing, smell, taste, touch. The trueborn is quite apart from these.' That is the answer of Demokritos to Protagoras. He had said that honey, for instance, was both bitter and sweet, sweet to me and bitter to you. In reality it was 'no more such than such' (οὐδὲν μᾶλλον τοῖον ἢ τοῖον). Sextus Empiricus and Plutarch tell us expressly that Demokritos argued against Protagoras, and the fact is therefore beyond question.

At the same time, it must not be overlooked that Demokritos gave a purely mechanical explanation of this trueborn knowledge just as he had done of the bastard. He held, in fact, that the atoms outside us could affect the atoms of our soul directly without the intervention of the organs of sense. The atoms of the soul were not confined to any particular parts of the body, but permeated it in every direction, and there was nothing to prevent them from having immediate contact with the external atoms, and so coming to know them as they really are. The 'true-born knowledge' is, after all, of the same nature as the 'bastard', and Demokritos refused, like Sokrates, to make an absolute separation between sense and thought. 'Poor Mind,' he makes the senses say (fr. 125), 'it is from us thou hast got the proofs to throw us with. Thy throw is a fall.'[1] The 'true-born' knowledge is, after all, not thought, but a sort of inner sense, and its objects are like the 'common sensibles' of Aristotle.

§ 154. As might be expected from a follower of the Pythagoreans and Zeno, Demokritos busied himself with the problem of continuity. In one remarkable passage (fr. 155) he states it in this form: 'If a cone is cut by a plane parallel to its base, what are we to think of the surfaces of the two sections? Are they equal or unequal? If they are unequal, they will make the cone uneven; for

[1] Cp. p. 113, n. 2.

it will have many step-like incisions and roughnesses. If they are equal, then the sections will be equal, and the cone will have the properties of a cylinder, which is composed of equal, not unequal, circles. Which is most absurd.' From a remark of Archimedes[1] it appears that Demokritos went on to say that the volume of the cone was a third of that of the cylinder on the same base and of the same height, a proposition first demonstrated by Eudoxos. It is clear, then, that he was engaged on problems such as those which ultimately gave rise to the infinitesimal method of Archimedes himself. Once more we see how important the work of Zeno was as an intellectual ferment.

THEORY OF CONDUCT

§ 155. The views of Demokritos on conduct would be even more interesting than his theory of knowledge if we could recover them completely. It is very difficult, however, to be sure which of the moral precepts attributed to him are genuine. There is no doubt that the treatise on *Cheerfulness* ($\Pi\epsilon\rho\grave{\iota}$ $\epsilon\vartheta\vartheta\upsilon\mu\acute{\iota}\eta s$) was his. It was freely used by Seneca and Plutarch, and some important fragments of it have survived.

It started (fr. 4) from the principle that pleasure and pain ($\tau\acute{\epsilon}\rho\psi\iota s$ and $\grave{\alpha}\tau\epsilon\rho\psi\acute{\iota}\eta$) are what determine happiness. This means primarily that happiness is not to be sought for in external goods. 'Happiness dwelleth not in herds nor in gold; the soul is the dwelling-place of the *daimon*' (fr. 171). To understand this, we must remember that the word $\delta\alpha\acute{\iota}\mu\omega\nu$, which properly meant a man's guardian spirit, had come to be used almost as the equivalent of 'fortune'. It is, as has been said, the individual aspect of $\tau\acute{\upsilon}\chi\eta$, and the Greek word we translate by 'happiness' ($\epsilon\vartheta\delta\alpha\iota\mu\upsilon\nu\acute{\iota}\alpha$) is based on this usage. On one side of it, then, the doctrine of happiness taught by Demokritos is closely related to that of Sokrates, though it lays more stress on pleasure and pain. 'The best thing for a man is to pass his life so as to have as much joy and as little trouble as may be' (fr. 189).

This is not, however, vulgar hedonism. The pleasures of sense are just as little true pleasures as sensations are true knowledge. 'The good and the true are the same for all men, but the pleasant is different for different people' (fr. 69). Further, the pleasures of

---

[1] Cf. Diels, *Vors.*[3] ii. p. 90 *n*.

sense are of too short duration to fill a life, and they easily turn
into their opposite. We can only be sure of having an excess of
pleasure over pain if we do not seek our pleasure in what is
'mortal' (fr. 189).

What we have to strive after is 'well-being' (εὐεστώ) or 'cheerfulness' (εὐθυμίη), and that is a state of the soul. To attain it, we must
be capable of weighing, judging, and distinguishing the value of
different pleasures. Just like Sokrates, Demokritos laid down that
'ignorance of the better' (fr. 83) was the cause of failure. Men put
the blame on fortune, but that is only an 'image' they have
invented to excuse their own ignorance (fr. 119). The great
principle which should guide us is that of 'symmetry' or 'harmony'.
That is, no doubt, Pythagorean. If we apply this test to pleasures,
we may attain to 'calm', calm of body, which is health, and calm of
soul, which is cheerfulness. That is to be found chiefly in the goods
of the soul. 'He who chooses the goods of the soul chooses the
more divine; he who chooses the goods of the "tabernacle" (*i.e.* the
body)[1] chooses the human' (fr. 37).

§ 156. For our present purpose it is not necessary to discuss the
cosmology of Demokritos in detail. It is thoroughly retrograde and
proves, if proof were needed, that his real interests lay in another
direction. He had inherited the theory of atoms and the void from
Leukippos, who was the real man of genius in this field, and he
was content for the rest to adopt the crude Ionic cosmology as
Leukippos had done. Yet he must have known the more scientific
system of Philolaos. The knowledge of the earth's spherical shape
was widely spread by the days of Demokritos, and Sokrates is
represented in the *Phaedo* (108 e) as taking it for granted. For
Demokritos the earth was still a disc. He also followed Anaxagoras
in holding that the earth was supported on the air 'like the lid of a
trough', another view which Sokrates rejects with emphasis. On
the other hand, Demokritos appears to have made valuable con-
tributions to natural science. Unfortunately our information is far
too scanty to permit even an approximate reconstruction of his
system. The loss of the complete edition of his works by Thrasyllos
is perhaps the most deplorable of our many losses of this kind. It is
probable that they were left to perish because Demokritos came to

---

[1] This use of σκῆνος for the body (found also in S. Paul, 2 Cor. v. 1) is
probably Pythagorean, and connected with the representation of human life as a
πανήγυρις or 'fair'. Our bodies are our temporary 'booths'.

share in the discredit that attached itself to the Epicureans. What we have of him has been preserved mainly because he was a great coiner of telling phrases, and these have found their way into anthologies. That is not the sort of material we require for the interpretation of a philosophic system, and it is very doubtful whether we know some of his deepest thoughts at all. At the same time, we cannot help feeling that it is mainly for their literary merit that we regret the loss of his works. He seems to stand apart from the main current of Greek philosophy, and it is to that we must now return. From our point of view, the only important fact about Demokritos is that he, too, saw the need of an answer to Protagoras.

BOOK III

PLATO

XII

Plato and the Academy

§ 157. If the *Epistles* are genuine — and some of the greatest scholars and historians hold they are — we know more of the life of Plato than of any other ancient philosopher.[1] Even apart from the *Epistles*, we know a good deal. Besides what we may infer from the dialogues, we have one or two statements resting on the authority of Hermodoros, who was a member of the Academy in Plato's time, and these give us certain fixed points to start from. The later *Lives* are almost entirely mythical. It is conceivable that they may contain one or two stray facts derived from older sources now lost, but their general character is such that it is safer to neglect them in the first instance. The *Epistles*, on the other hand, are free from this mythology, which is the more remarkable as Plato's own nephew, Speusippos, already credited him with a miraculous birth. If, then, the *Epistles* are forgeries, they are at least the work of a sober and well-informed writer, whose use of the Attic dialect proves him to have been Plato's contemporary. It would have been impossible to find anyone fifty years later who could handle the language as he does.[2] Even the oldest and most successful of the spurious dialogues betray themselves at every turn. We may, indeed, go so far as to say that the supposed forger of the *Epistles* must have been a man of almost unparalleled literary skill, or he could not have reproduced so many of the little

---

[1] The genuineness of the *Epistles* has been maintained by scholars like Bentley and Cobet, and by historians like Grote and E. Meyer. In practice most accounts of Plato really depend on them, though that is disguised by the custom of referring instead to Plutarch's *Life of Dion*. Plutarch, however, is obviously dependent on the *Epistles* for most, if not all, of what he tells us; so this is an illegitimate evasion. I should add that the *First Epistle* stands by itself. In my judgement, it has got into its present place by mistake. It is a genuine fourth-century letter, but I do not think the writer, whoever he was, meant to pass for Plato at all. I do not think either that he was Dion or meant to pass for Dion.

[2] After the rise of Atticism it might have been just possible, but we know the *Epistles* existed before that.

peculiarities that marked Plato's style at the very time of his life to which the *Epistles* profess to belong, though with just those shades of difference we should expect to find in letters as contrasted with more elaborate literary work. I believe that all the letters of any importance are Plato's, and I shall therefore make use of them. As, however, there are still eminent scholars who are not convinced, I shall warn the reader when I have occasion to do so.

§ 158. Plato was born in 428/7 B.C., more than a year after Perikles died and just before Gorgias came to Athens for the first time. We learn from a poem quoted in the *Republic* (368 a) and addressed to his brothers, Adeimantos and Glaukon, that his father, Ariston, was a man of distinction. He must have died when Plato was a child; for his wife, Periktione, afterwards married Pyrilampes, whose son by her, Antiphon, was in his youth an associate of Pythodoros son of Isolochos, who had been a disciple of Zeno. Adeimantos and Glaukon must have been older than Plato. The idea that they were younger is based on a misunderstanding of the *Republic*. It is assumed that Plato could not talk as he does there except to younger brothers, and it is forgotten, as usual, that Sokrates, not Plato, is the speaker. In the *Apology* (34 a) Sokrates says Adeimantos should have been called to give evidence whether Plato had got any harm from associating with him, and this implies that Adeimantos was so much older as to stand *in loco parentis* to his brother. Further, we learn from the poem quoted in the *Republic* that both Glaukon and Adeimantos had won distinction in the battle of Megara. It is natural, in the absence of further qualifications, to suppose that the battle of 424 B.C. is meant, though we cannot be quite certain. In any case, if both the brothers won distinction in the same battle, they cannot have differed widely in age. It may be added that it would not have been in accordance with Plato's usual practice to introduce his brothers in the *Republic* if they had been still living when that dialogue was written. Xenophon (*Mem.* iii. 6, 1) tells a story of how Glaukon was restrained by Sokrates from speaking in the Assembly before he had reached the legal age of twenty. Sokrates did that by asking him a series of questions about Athenian finance and the national defences, and it is impossible to read these questions without feeling that Xenophon conceived the incident to have taken place some time before the occupation of Dekeleia in 413 B.C. It is true that he says Sokrates was interested in Glaukon because of Charmides and Plato, but that may be a slip. Charmides was at least twenty years older than Plato, who would, perhaps, be too young to attract the attention of Sokrates much before 413 B.C. The slip, however, if it is one, is explicable enough in a writer so careless of chronology as Xenophon, and cannot outweigh the other presumptions. As to Charmides, we know that Sokrates made his acquaintance four or five years before Plato was born, so the mention of his name is quite appropriate.

The family of Plato's mother, Periktione, was also highly distinguished, and traced its descent to Dropides, the friend and kinsman of Solon. She herself was the cousin of Kritias and the sister of Charmides, son of Glaukon, and the fact that Glaukon bore the name of his maternal grandfather affords a further presumption that he was the second son. As we are told in the *Charmides* (158 a) that Pyrilampes was the maternal uncle of Charmides, we must assume that Periktione was his niece, and that he married her when she was left a widow by the death of Ariston. That would be in accordance with Athenian usage. The last we hear of Pyrilampes is that he was wounded in the battle of Delion, but Periktione reached a great age; for it appears from *Epistle* xiii. (361 e) that she was still living in 366/5, though her death was expected.[1] The importance of all this is that it enables us to identify the Glaukon and Adeimantos of the *Parmenides* with those of the *Republic*, and also to fix the supposed date of the latter dialogue before the departure of Polemarchos for Thourioi instead of after his return. That explains how Kephalos is still alive, and how Lysias, though present, does not take any part in the conversation. We shall see that a good deal depends on this.

Plato was undoubtedly proud of his illustrious kinsmen, and he introduces them over and over again in his writings. The opening scene of the *Charmides* is a glorification of the whole connexion. It recalls the praises bestowed on the house of Dropides by Solon and Anakreon, the youthful beauty and modesty of Charmides, and the fair stature of Pyrilampes, who was accounted the tallest and handsomest man in Asia when he went on an embassy to the King. The elder Kritias plays an important part in the *Timaeus*

---

[1] This has been used as an argument against the genuineness of *Epistle* xiii., but it involves no impossibility, even if Adeimantos and Glaukon fought at Megara in 424 B.C. Athenian girls married very young, and it was a long-lived family. See the genealogical table in the Appendix.

and in the dialogue called by his name.[1] Plato's reticence about himself stands in striking contrast to the way he celebrates the older members of his family, especially as their memory was by no means popular at the time he wrote. I have called attention elsewhere[2] to the dramatic skill with which he keeps the shadow of the Revolutions from falling on his picture. His dialogues are not only a memorial to Sokrates, but also to the happier days of his own family. Plato must have felt the events of the end of the fifth century keenly, but he is so careful to avoid anachronisms in these dialogues that no one could ever guess from them that they were written after Kritias and Charmides had met with a dishonoured end.

§ 159. The statement that Plato only made the acquaintance of Sokrates when he was twenty does not rest on the authority of Hermodoros, and is quite incredible. The nephew of Charmides must have known Sokrates ever since he could remember. It does not follow, however, that he was one of the inner circle of disciples, and it is not very likely. It seems rather to have been the death of Sokrates that converted him to philosophy. That, at any rate, is the impression left by *Epistle* vii. There we are told quite distinctly (324 b) that he had looked forward to a political career. Kritias and Charmides — for they are no doubt meant — suggested that he should enter public life under the Thirty, but he was disgusted by their excesses, which made the former constitution seem like gold by comparison (324 d). In particular, he was shocked by the treatment of Sokrates in the affair of Leon of Salamis (§ 111). When the democracy was restored, Plato thought once more of a political career, but the trial and death of Sokrates convinced him that this was impossible in the Athens of his time. He could do nothing, he says (325 d), without joining a party, and neither of the existing parties could satisfy him. It was just as well. Athenian politics at this time were of no serious importance, and, as he says in another letter (v. 322 a), 'Plato was born late in the day for his country.' He did, however, find an opening in politics later, and on a much wider stage.

§ 160. It has become a commonplace to say that Plato's birth and connexions would incline him from the first to the oligarchic side, but nothing can be more untrue. The traditions of the family were rather what we should call 'Whiggish', as is shown by the

---

[1] See p. 275, *n.* 1.   [2] See my edition of the *Phaedo*, Introduction, § IX.

stress laid on its connexion with Solon. Even at the time of the
brief domination of the Four Hundred, Kritias was an opponent
of the oligarchical extremists. Charmides became an oligarch at
a later date, when he had been ruined by the war, but he did not at
first take any part in politics. According to Xenophon it was
Sokrates that urged him to overcome his natural shyness and enter
public life (*Mem.* iii. 7). Moreover, Plato's stepfather and grand-
uncle, Pyrilampes, was a friend of Perikles and a convinced
democrat. It was not for nothing that he called his son Demos. It
appears also from the *Republic* that Glaukon and Edeimantos were
intimate with the family of Kephalos, the wealthy stranger whom
Perikles had persuaded to settle in Peiraieus. They were friends of
his son Polemarchos, who afterwards met his death at the hands of
the Thirty. In fact, so far as we can see, Plato's early upbringing
would predispose him in favour of the Periklean régime. He says
in the *Seventh Epistle* (325 b) that he was at first impressed by the
moderation of the restored democracy, and such a thought would
not be likely to occur to one brought up in the oligarchic camp.
We can understand, then, why Plato's own judgment of democracy,
as we have it in the *Statesman* and the *Laws*, is not nearly so harsh
as that he puts into the mouth of Sokrates.

§ 161. Plato tells us in the *Phaedo* (59 b) that he was ill at the
time Sokrates was put to death, and was therefore unable to be
present. He had been in court at the trial, as we know from the
Apology (38 b), and had offered with others to become surety for
the payment of a fine, if the court would accept that penalty. After
the death of Sokrates, Hermodoros said that he retired to Megara
with some of the other Sokratics. We have seen (§ 145) that they
may well have been in some danger. Eukleides would of course
receive them gladly, but we have no indication of the length of their
stay with him. The later *Lives* attribute extensive travels to Plato,
most of which are plainly apocryphal. It is probable, though by no
means certain, that he visited Egypt. In the *Laws* (656 e) he speaks
as if he had seen the monuments, and he shows some knowledge of
Egyptian methods of education (819 b). In any case, it was not to
study mathematics he went there; for we know that his opinion of
Egyptian science (747 c) was by no means so favourable as that he
expresses of Egyptian art. If he was in Egypt, it is likely that he
also went to Kyrene to visit the mathematician Theodoros, who
was a friend of Sokrates, but he may equally well have made his

acquaintance at Athens, where he was teaching just before the
death of Sokrates. All this, however, is extremely doubtful, and the
earliest definite fact we know is that he visited Italy and Sicily for
the first time when he was forty years old (*Ep.* vii. 324 a). It is
likely that he wished to make the acquaintance of the distinguished
Pythagoreans who were becoming powerful once more in these
parts, and it was probably through them that he made the acquaintance of Dion, who was then about twenty. That brought him to
the court of Dionysios I. at Syracuse, where he was disgusted by
the luxurious life he had to lead. The story goes that his freedom
of speech offended Dionysios, who handed him over to the Spartan
ambassador Pollis, who sold him as a slave at Aigina. His life was
even in danger, but he was ransomed by a man of Kyrene named
Annikeris. If this story is true, it is strange that it is not mentioned
in the *Seventh Epistle*. Perhaps Plato may have thought it irrelevant
in what is really a narrative of his relations with Dion and the
younger Dionysios. A forger would hardly have omitted it, if the
story had been current, but Plato himself might conceivably do so.
In any case, he was back at Athens before long.

§ 162. At this time Plato was just over forty, and Sokrates had
been dead twelve years. One good reason for holding he did not
spend these years in continuous travel, as the later accounts
suggest, is that he must have written a very considerable number
of his dialogues already. Without deciding anything as to the order
in which they were composed, we are able to say with some
confidence that the *Euthyphro, Apology, Crito, Charmides, Laches,
Lysis, Euthydemus, Protagoras, Gorgias*, and *Meno* at least were all
composed before Plato was forty.[1] That is about one dialogue a
year, assuming that he wrote none of them before the death of
Sokrates. If we remember that the great tragedians often brought
out four plays in one year, that will not seem an excessive rate of
production, and I have little doubt that the *Symposium* and *Phaedo*
were also written by this date, and the *Republic* at least well
advanced. In any case, it seems clear that all these works must
have been completed before the foundation of the Academy, and
I think we may take it that the *Phaedrus* is not very much later.
In all these dialogues the dramatic interest seems to outweigh
every other, except in some portions of the *Republic*. Plato's

---

[1] I have ventured to assume the results of the stylistic researches inaugurated
by Lewis Campbell in 1867. It would take too long to discuss them here.

dramatic power, though often acknowledged in words, is seldom done justice to. He had a marvellous gift of assuming the most diverse personalities, and this gift is seen at its best in the *Symposium*, which is certainly not one of the earliest dialogues, but goes with the *Phaedo* and the *Republic*. I cannot imagine that the man who could speak at will in the character of Protagoras or Gorgias, or Aristophanes or Alkibiades, without revealing anything of his own personality, should simultaneously, either voluntarily or involuntarily, have used Sokrates as a mask for himself. I do not therefore think it possible to learn much of Plato's own inmost thoughts from any of these dialogues, and I believe we have a perfectly serious statement to that effect in the *Second Epistle*. There he says (314 c): 'There is no writing of Plato, nor will there ever be. What go by the name really belong to Sokrates turned young and handsome.' The dialogues, in fact, profess to be pictures of a generation that had passed away, and that I believe them in the main to be. I do not think it likely that Plato had as yet anything that could rightly be called a philosophy of his own. He seems to have been one of those men whose purely intellectual development was late and continued into old age. At first the artistic interest was paramount; the purely philosophical does not gain the upper hand till his artistic gift declined. It is only in certain parts of the *Republic* and the *Phaedrus* that I can detect anything so far that seems to be Platonic rather than Sokratic, and I attribute that exception to the fact that Plato was about to open the Academy. The higher education of the Guardians seems to be a programme of the studies that were to be pursued there; and, as we shall see, Plato is not quite at his ease in making Sokrates speak of one of them, namely, solid geometry. Sokrates had proposed to take astronomy immediately after plane geometry, but he corrects himself and interpolates geometry of three dimensions, to which Glaukon objects that this has not yet been invented. It had been invented by Plato's time, and by a friend of his own. The awkwardness he evidently feels in introducing it is to my mind very instructive. If he had already attributed to Sokrates all manner of scientific interests that were really foreign to him, why should he boggle at solid geometry?

FOUNDATION OF THE ACADEMY

§ 163. The foundation of the Academy by Plato soon after his return to Athens was not only the most important event in his life, but also in the history of European science. The idea was no doubt suggested to him in the first place by the school of Eukleides at Megara, and by what he had seen of the Pythagorean societies in southern Italy. The name Academy is derived from a gymnasium outside the walls of Athens, which had been laid out as a public park by Kimon. Here Plato had a house and garden, and this remained for long the seat of the school, though it moved into the town after the siege of Athens by Sulla in 86 B.C., and continued to exist there till it was disestablished and disendowed by Justinian in 529 A.D. Like all societies of the kind, it was organised as a religious guild. It had its chapel, dedicated to the Muses, and its sacrifices at stated times. The members lived for the most part a common life.

From the first the Academy attracted a large number of young men, many of whom became distinguished afterwards. It is to be observed that they came from almost every part of the Hellenic world. That is one of the things that distinguish the fourth century from the fifth. In the fifth century, the youth of Athens got their higher education from a number of distinguished foreigners who paid flying visits from time to time; in the fourth, the youth of all Hellas came to Athens to sit at the feet of two Athenian citizens, Isokrates and Plato. Athens had, in fact, become 'the school of Hellas'. It is of interest to note further that a goodly number of these youths came from the North, and especially from the Greek colonies in Thrace and on the Black Sea. That may have been due in some measure to the existence of a mathematical school at Kyzikos, of which Eudoxos was the head. At any rate, Eudoxos transferred himself and his school bodily to the Academy, which is all the more remarkable as he did not by any means see eye to eye with Plato on mathematical and astronomical subjects. It can hardly be an accident that Ionia proper is so poorly represented in the Academy, so far as we know who composed it. The Ionians had rejected Pythagorean science, partly no doubt because it was mixed up with mysticism. The School of Demokritos continued to exist at Teos down to Hellenistic times. In Plato, Euthydemos and Dionysodoros come from Chios, and Euboulides, the adversary of Aristotle, was a Milesian. That is all we can say of Ionia till the time when Epicurus of Samos once more brought the old Ionic tradition to Athens, where it had been unrepresented since the days of Archelaos.

It is of the utmost importance to remember that Plato's real teaching was given in the Academy, and that even his later dialogues only contain what he thought fit to give to a wider public in order to define his attitude to other schools of philosophy. This fact, which is often overlooked, accounts for a great deal of the difficulty we feel in passing from Plato to Aristotle. We seem to be in a different world altogether, and that is natural; for we have neither Plato's lectures nor (except in fragments) the published works of Aristotle, and we are thus comparing two quite different things. If we only had Plato's lecture on *The Good* and the *Protreptikos* of Aristotle, we should get a very different impression. As it is, we may fairly assume that Plato's lectures had far more resemblance to Aristotle's than to his own dialogues.

§ 164. It will help us considerably to understand the purpose of the Academy if we first consider what Plato meant by the word 'philosophy'. In Ionia it had been used of a more or less scientific curiosity which led men to visit strange lands and note their usages. It may have been applied also to the researches (ἱστορίη) of the Milesians, but there is no evidence of that. It was in all probability Pythagoras that first gave it the deeper meaning of science 'touched with emotion', and it was certainly in the Pythagorean community that it came to be regarded as a 'way of life'. For Sokrates too, according to Plato, philosophy had been above all things a life. At Athens, however, the word was current in a vaguer and shallower sense, derived probably from the Ionian usage. It had, in fact, a range of meaning something like that of our word 'culture'. The great teacher of philosophy in this sense was Isokrates, the only Athenian of the time whose influence was at all comparable to Plato's. Much that has been written about the attitude of these two men to one another is extremely fanciful, but the main facts are clear enough. It will be well to state them briefly here, for it is really necessary to understand Isokrates if we are to estimate Plato aright.

PLATO AND ISOKRATES

§ 165. One thing was common to both men, and that was an intense belief that the only remedy for the ills of Hellas was enlightenment, though they differed enormously as to the kind of enlightenment required. There is a striking passage at the end of the *Phaedrus*, where Sokrates is made to contrast Isokrates with mere professional advocates like Lysias. He says:

> Isokrates is still young, but I am ready to tell you what I presage for him. . . . I think that, so far as natural gifts go, he is capable of higher things than the speeches of Lysias, and that his character is more nobly tempered. It would be no wonder, then, as he grows older, if, even in composing speeches, which is the task he is now engaged on, he should make all who have ever taken up speech-writing seem children compared to him. If, however, that should not satisfy him, it would be no wonder if a divine impulse should lead him to higher things still; for, my dear Phaidros, there really is philosophy in the man (279 a).

It is important not to overlook the dramatic setting here. It is Sokrates, not Plato, who pays Isokrates this handsome compliment, and, of course, Sokrates cannot speak otherwise than prophetically of anything but the forensic speeches of which Isokrates was afterwards ashamed. On the other hand, Plato would not have been likely to put into the mouth of Sokrates a prophecy that had not in some measure been fulfilled. I take it, then, that this is a perfectly sincere compliment, and that the tradition which represents Plato and Isokrates as friends is much more likely to be right than modern speculations about a feud between them. They differed, indeed, on fundamentals, but they had a good many opinions in common, especially about politics. Plato must have understood and sympathised with the ideals of Isokrates regarding Greek union against Persia, while Isokrates would appreciate the Sicilian projects of Plato, which we shall have to consider later, though he doubtless thought it very absurd of him to begin the training of a prince with mathematics. The main point is, however, that both Isokrates and Plato were convinced that the future of Hellas depended on the revival of monarchy, a conviction which the course of history showed to be well founded.

§ 166. Where Plato and Isokrates differed was in their conception of education. Isokrates was what we call a humanist, and the rivalry between him and Plato was really the first chapter in the long struggle between humanism and science. It must be remembered, however, that Greek humanism was of necessity a far shallower thing than what we call by the name. In the first place, modern humanism has gained immeasurably from having to deal

with the langugage and literature of other peoples, and especially
with those of classical antiquity. An exclusive preoccupation with
the literature of one's own country always tends to shallowness.
That is why even Roman humanism, as we know it in Cicero, for
instance, is a far deeper thing than the contemporary Greek
rhetoric. It has Greek antiquity as well as Roman behind it, and
that gave it strength. The humanism of the Renaissance, again,
was saturated with the results and spirit of Greek science, and so
prepared the way for the scientific discoveries of the sixteenth and
seventeenth centuries, while Greek humanism inherited from the
Sophists of the fifth century a rooted distrust of science and scientific methods. The humanism of Isokrates had, therefore, hardly
any real content, and tended to become little more than the art of
expressing commonplaces in a perfect form.

§ 167. At the same time, the form invented by Isokrates really
was perfect in its way, and he has, directly or indirectly, influenced
every writer of prose down to the present day. Even commonplace
thinking may have its value, and it is a very good test of that to
express it in an artistic way. If one has to utter one's thoughts in
accordance with a prescribed scheme, they will at least gain in
lucidity and coherence, so far as they are reasonable at all. Thoughts
that are wholly unreasonable do not admit of artistic expression.
In this way Isokrates was quite entitled to claim that his teaching
was of service to his pupils, and he certainly did a great deal to
make Hellenism a possibility, in spite of the fact that his own
political thinking is unduly coloured by the rhetorical antithesis of
Hellenes and barbarians, a division of mankind which Plato
regarded as unscientific (*Polit.* 262 d). At any rate, whatever we
may think of Isokrates, there can be no doubt that Plato recognised
his merits, and it is curious to note how, the more he came to
diverge from him on matters of greater importance, the more he
fell under the fascination of his style. It is just in these later dialogues where the scientific spirit is most dominant that the influence
of Isokrates may be traced most clearly. In every other respect
such a work as the *Sophist* is wide as the poles asunder from anything Isokrates was capable of understanding, and yet it is in that
very dialogue that Plato for the first time troubles to avoid *hiatus*,
and even adopts some specially Isokratean devices for doing so. It
seems as if, when he felt his own gift of artistic writing beginning
to fail, he was glad to reinforce it in this way.

§ 168. To Plato philosophy was, of course, something quite different from what it was to Isokrates. If we look at the dialogues he was writing about the time he founded the Academy, and especially the *Symposium*, the *Republic*, and the *Phaedrus*, we shall see, I think, that he regarded it chiefly in two lights. In the first place, it is the conversion of a soul, and in the second place it is the service of mankind. We shall take the latter point first, because it is impossible to understand Plato's object in founding the Academy till it has been made clear. No one has insisted more than he has on the necessity of disinterested scientific study, freed from all merely utilitarian preoccupations, but at the same time no one has maintained more firmly that such study is only justified in the last resort by the service it can render to human life. The Sokratic demand that the man who knows shall rule had, he tells us (*Ep.* vii. 326 a), taken the more precise form that the only hope for mankind is that kings should turn philosophers or that philosophers should become kings. That ideal never left him, and, though he ceased to hope for its realisation, he was always ready to welcome any approach to it. In default of the philosopher king much might be effected by the co-operation of a philosopher and a tyrant, especially if the latter was young and impressionable. He reaffirms this conviction in the *Laws* (709 e), though he had already been disappointed in one attempt to work upon that plan. The Academy was first and foremost, then, an institution for training rulers and legislators, and it was extremely successful in its task. It was, in fact, made a charge against it that it produced tyrants, which is true enough, and much to its credit, if the facts are rightly estimated. It also produced its fair share of tyrannicides.

Isokrates boasts that his training was more practical than that of his rivals, but most of his pupils turned out rhetorical historians or rhetorical tragedians, while Plato trained statesmen and men of science. We shall see later that the Academy was often applied to for legislators by new communities. There is not the slightest improbability in the story that Epameinondas, who had been an associate of the Pythagorean Lysis, asked Plato himself to frame a code of laws for Megalopolis, though we are told that Plato declined.

THE METHODS OF THE ACADEMY

§ 169. Two methods are specially associated with Plato's name, that of Analysis and that of Division. The former, indeed, is said to have been invented by Plato, who 'delivered it' to Leodamas, and it is significant that in Book XIII. of Euclid, which is in a pre-eminent sense the work of the Academy, analytical proofs are given for the first time in addition to those in the usual form. It can hardly be supposed, however, that analysis is no older than Plato. The proof called apagogic (*reductio ad absurdum*) is an application of the analytic method, and it was certainly used by the Pythagoreans. Moreover, Plato himself represents Parmenides as teaching it to Sokrates, while in the *Meno* and *Phaedo*, as we have seen (§ 121), Sokrates himself explains it. It follows that what Plato did was at most to formulate the method more clearly, and very probably to show the necessity of supplementing analysis by synthesis, in order to secure that all the intermediate steps discovered by the analysis are reciprocal.[1] The chain of consequences must be reversible if the proof is to be complete. Each analysis given in Euclid is immediately followed by the corresponding synthesis. This was revived by Galileo in the seventeenth century as a substitute for the prevailing Aristotelian methods.[2]

§ 170. The other Platonic method is that of Division (διαίρεσις), which even the comic poets knew to be characteristic of the Academy. As analysis aims at explanation or proof, so division is the instrument of classification or definition. The method is this. The thing to be defined or classified is first referred to its genus, and then, by a series of dichotomies, the genus is divided into species and sub-species. At each division we ask to which of the species it gives us the thing to be defined belongs, and that is divided once more, the 'left-hand' species being left undivided as irrelevant to our purpose. The definition is found by adding together all the species 'on the right-hand side'. The examples of this method which Plato gives in the *Sophist* and *Statesman* are only to be understood as more or less popular and playful applications of it, but just for that reason they serve to show what is meant better than a serious example, where it would have been necessary

---

[1] This was the view of Tannery.
[2] The *metodo risolutivo* is just the ἀναλυτικὴ μέθοδος. Galileo was a convinced Platonist.

to justify each step elaborately. We shall return to this subject when we come to the *Philebus*.

§ 171. As to the plan of teaching and study adopted in the Academy we have, as is natural, but little direct evidence, but what we have is at once trustworthy and instructive. In the first place, there can be no doubt that Plato gave regular lectures (συνουσίαι, ἀκροάσεις), and that his hearers took notes. Aristoxenos said that Aristotle 'was always telling' how most of those who heard the lecture on the Good were affected. They came expecting to hear about some of the recognised good things, and when they heard of nothing but Arithmetic and Astronomy and the Limit and the One, they thought it all very strange. We know from Simplicius that Aristotle, Speusippos, and Xenokrates had all published their notes of this very discourse. We may infer that Plato did not write his lectures, and that is confirmed by Aristotle's reference to his 'unwritten dogmas' (ἄγραφα δόγματα). As we know, Plato did not believe in books for serious purposes. In the *Seventh Epistle* he complains that, even in his lifetime, some of his hearers had published accounts of his doctrine of the Good, which, however, he repudiates. The passage is worth quoting. He says:

> There is no writing of mine on this subject, nor ever shall be. It is not capable of expression like other branches of study; but, as the result of long intercourse and a common life spent upon the thing, a light is suddenly kindled as from a leaping spark, and when it has reached the soul, it thenceforward finds nutriment for itself. I know this, at any rate, that if these things were to be written down or stated at all, they would be better stated by myself than by others, and I know too that I should be the person to suffer most from their being badly set down in writing. If I thought they could be adequately written down and stated to the world, what finer occupation could I have had in life than to write what would be of great service to mankind, and to reveal Nature in the light of day to all men? But I do not even think the effort to attain this a good thing for men, except for the very few who can be enabled to discover these things themselves by means of a brief indication. The rest it would either fill with contempt in a manner by no means pleasing or with a lofty and vain presumption as though they had learnt something grand (341 c–e).

This is not mystery-mongering, as has been said; it is simply a statement of the true theory of all higher education. To be of any use, philosophy must be a man's very own; it ceases to be philosophy if it is merely an echo of another's thought. The passage is also a salutary warning to the interpreter of Plato. He may, in a measure, recover the dry bones of his deepest thought; the spirit of it is less easy to reproduce.

§ 172. We are to think, then, of Plato lecturing in the Academy without notes, and of his more attentive hearers taking down what they could. But the set discourse, though necessary, was by no means the most important part of the work. It was better than a book, no doubt, but it was only preparatory to the real thing. Its function is to rouse the soul, to turn it to the light, but the soul must see the light for itself. The Academy was no mere lecture-hall; it was an institute for scientific research. Simplicius, who had the library of the school at his disposal, tells us that Plato, who held that the movements of the heavenly bodies must be regular, 'propounded it as a problem' to the mathematicians of the Academy to find on what hypothesis (τίνων ὑποτεθέντων) their apparent irregularity could be explained so as to 'save the appearances'.[1] The word 'problem' calls for special attention in this connexion. Both it and 'protasis', the verb corresponding to which (προτείνειν) has been rendered 'propound' (proponere) in the passage just referred to, originate in the Greek custom of asking riddles at banquets, and the convivial associations of the words bear witness to the idea of scientific research as a common life (τὸ συζῆν). That accounts in turn for investigation taking the form of a quest for solutions (λύσεις) of certain problems (προβλήματα) or difficulties (ἀπορίαι). We have a collection of such in the Aristotelian corpus, which is obviously derived from the work of his school, and the passage of Simplicius just quoted shows that the method originated in the Academy. It is, of course, the beginning of the system of education through original research.

It is to be observed further that Plato by no means confined the researches of his students to subjects of special interest to himself, such as mathematics and astronomy. No doubt they had all to go through a preliminary course of mathematical training, but there is abundant evidence that biological studies were also pursued with enthusiasm. The satire of the comic poets was largely directed to this side of the Academy's activity. Epikrates (fr. 5) laughs at Plato, Speusippos and Menedemos for investigating by the method of division to what genus the pumpkin belongs. Speusippos, Plato's nephew and successor, wrote many books on the classification of animals and vegetables, and the few fragments that remain deal,

[1] Simpl. de Caelo, pp. 488. 21; 492. 31 (Heiberg).

for instance, with shell-fish and fungi. In the *Critias* (110 d *sqq.*) Plato himself surprises us by an account of the geological history of Attika and its economic consequences which is almost on a level with the most modern discussions of the kind. The biological work of Aristotle belongs to the early period of his life, and it is natural to bring that into connexion with these facts. It remains to be said that we must of course represent the Academy to ourselves as well provided with scientific apparatus and collections. Aristophanes takes it for granted in the *Clouds* that a scientific school would possess maps and astronomical models as a matter of course, and, if that was so in the fifth century, it may certainly be assumed in the fourth.

THE PROGRAMME OF STUDIES

§ 173. We may fairly take the higher education of the Guardians outlined in the *Republic* as a guide to the course of study followed in the Academy. We are expressly told that the mathematical part of the course is to occupy the ten years from twenty to thirty, and it has all the appearance of a regular programme. It would, however, be a mistake to suppose that what is said about the sciences in the *Republic* represents the mature thought of Plato on the subject. It was written either before the foundation of the Academy or very shortly after, and the theories most characteristic of Plato's teaching are not yet elaborated. He is quite conscious of that. What he proposed was a thorough criticism of the hypotheses of all the sciences, and that had not yet been carried out. That is what he means by the 'longer way', which has yet to be travelled (435 d, 504 b). We must be prepared to find, then, that in some important respects the philosophy of the exact sciences given in the *Republic* is completely transformed at a later date.

The programme is based on the principle that the function of education is the conversion (περιστροφή) of the soul from the contemplation of Becoming (γένεσις) to that of Being (οὐσία). As we have seen, that distinction is Pythagorean, and it is therefore natural that the course should consist of the four Pythagorean sciences which survived in the medieval *quadrivium*, though with this distinction, that plane and solid geometry are distinguished, so as to give five studies (μαθήματα) instead of four. If we take these in order, we shall see the point of view from which Plato started.

1. *Arithmetic*. At this stage, Arithmetic is to be studied, not for utilitarian or commercial purposes, but with a view to understanding the nature of numbers by thought alone. It arises from the ambiguity and relativity of sense perception. What appears one to the senses also appears as many from another point of view. Two appear as one and one as two, so it is the function of thought to distinguish and separate these from the confusion in which they are presented by sense. It is the business of Arithmetic to consider numbers by themselves, not visible or corporeal numbers. A visible or tangible unit admits of division, and so is many as well as one, but unity itself is indivisible. Visible and tangible units are not necessarily equal to one another, but the units of the arithmetician are all absolutely equal. Such units cannot be apprehended by sense, but only by thought, and that is what gives the study of arithmetic its educational value (524 b — 526 c).

2. *Plane Geometry*. Geometry too is to be studied for other than utilitarian ends, for which, indeed, a very slight knowledge of it is required. Though geometers talk of performing certain operations, such as 'squaring' and 'applying' and 'producing', that is only a manner of speaking, and Geometry too has to do with Being, not with Becoming. Its objects are certain spatial relations which simply *are*, whatever we may do, and do not come into being in virtue of our constructions. This study too, then, is of value as purifying an instrument of the soul (527 a–e).

3. *Solid Geometry*. Sokrates is about to pass from Geometry to Astronomy, but recollects himself and points out that there is a science intermediate between them, that which deals with the 'third increase' (τρίτη αὔξη), that is, with the cube, and generally what has three dimensions, depth as well as length and breadth. 'But', says Glaukon, 'that does not appear to have been invented yet.' Sokrates answers that this is because in the first place no state holds such studies in honour, and in the second, because a director (ἐπιστάτης) is required to guide them. If the state were to second the efforts of such a director, they would soon be perfected. Even as it is, their extreme elegance (χάρις, τὸ ἐπίχαρι) causes them to make some progress (528 d).

As has already been indicated, this remarkable passage appears to refer to the fact that, though the Pythagoreans had made a beginning, the theory of the five regular solids was completed for the first time by Theaitetos, while the problem of the duplication of the cube was not solved till a still later date. The term Stereo-metry is not used here; it appears for the first time in the Epinomis (990 d).

§ 174. The remaining studies deal with motion, and it is hinted that there may be more than the two mentioned.

4. *Astronomy*. Astronomy is not to be studied merely for its use in agriculture, navigation, or strategy, or even because it turns our eyes upwards to a higher world. The visible motions of the heavenly bodies with all their labyrinthine intricacy are related to true astronomy only as the diagrams analysed by the geometer are related to his science, that is to say, these apparent motions must be regarded merely as illustrations ($\pi\alpha\rho\alpha\delta\epsilon i\gamma\mu\alpha\tau\alpha$). We must treat them as 'problems' ($\pi\rho o\beta\lambda\eta\mu\alpha\sigma\iota\nu$ $\chi\rho\omega\mu\epsilon\nu o\iota$), not as solutions. What we have to study is 'the true motions with which the real velocity and the real slowness move in relation to one another, in the true numbers and the true forms, and carry their contents with them' (529 d).

This sentence is easily misunderstood and requires elucidation. In the first place, the visible motions of the heavenly bodies are what we call their apparent motions, which are of great complexity and at first sight seem quite irregular. The planets move at one time from east to west among the stars, at another from west to east, and sometimes they are stationary altogether. That is the 'problem' we have to solve. The 'real velocity' ($\tau\grave{o}$ $\grave{o}\nu$ $\tau\acute{a}\chi o\varsigma$) is spoken of simply as opposed to the apparent velocity. We should not think it necessary to add 'the real slowness', but that is only an instance of the Greek tendency to 'polar expression', and has no serious importance. We may speak of a lesser velocity as a 'slow-ness' if we please. Then this velocity is spoken of as carrying its 'contents' ($\tau\grave{a}$ $\acute{\epsilon}\nu\acute{o}\nu\tau\alpha$) with it. That is because the Greeks were in the habit of attributing the orbital revolution to the orbit itself, and not to the celestial body, which was regarded as occupying a fixed place in its orbit. That again is due to their regarding all orbital revolution as similar to that of the moon, the only case which can be adequately studied without a telescope. The moon always presents the same face to the earth (or nearly so), and, in the absence of any indication to the contrary, it was not unreasonable to suppose the other planets did the same. We say the rotation of the moon upon its axis takes the same time as its revolution round the earth; the Greeks expressed the same fact by saying the moon does not revolve at all relatively to its orbit. That is why Aristotle can urge the fact of the moon's always presenting the same face to us in support of the view that none of the heavenly bodies rotate. To us that is just what proves the moon does revolve on its axis, but Aristotle is thinking of the orbit (or rather, in his case, the sphere) to which the moon is attached. All this explains why it was natural to speak of the heavenly bodies as the things 'in the velocity' (ἐνόντα, sc. τῇ ταχύτητι).[1] The 'true numbers' are the number of days and years the revolutions take, and the 'true forms' are the circles, spirals, or whatever they may prove to be, which they trace. What is meant, then, is simply that we must have a science which will exhibit the true motions of the heavenly bodies and not the motions they appear to have. The apparent motions of the heavenly bodies no more express the laws of solid bodies in motion than the diagrams of the geometer embody the truths of geometry.

It is amusing to observe that such a utilitarian thing as 'Greenwich time' has to take account of this. Our watches are set, not by the visible sun, but by an 'intelligible' sun called the 'mean sun', which only coincides with the visible sun four times a year, and then only for an instant. That this illustration is not too far-fetched is shown by the fact that the apparent anomaly of the sun's annual course was just one of the problems we know to have been investigated in the Academy.[2] It may be added that this is fatal to the interpretation which makes Plato's astronomy refer to some imaginary 'ideal' heavens. If it had, why should he have troubled himself about the sun's anomaly? It would have been so easy to say that the intelligible sun had a uniform velocity, and to disregard the shortcomings of the visible sun.

5. *Harmonics.* The next study is Harmonics, which the Pythagoreans regard as the counterpart of Astronomy. As the one deals with motions apprehended by the eye, so does the other deal with motions apprehended by the ear. The same principles will apply here. Not to speak of those who attempt to determine the harmonic intervals by ear, even the Pythagoreans themselves, who express them by numerical ratios, do not sufficiently emancipate themselves from the sound as heard.[3] It is not enough to say that such

[1] Adam's interpretation of this passage is sufficiently refuted by the fantastic account he has to give of τὰ ἐνόντα.
[2] Simplicius *in Phys.* p. 292. 22 (Diels).
[3] Aristoxenos represents the first class for us and Archytas the second.

and such an interval is expressed by such and such a ratio; we ought to consider which numbers are consonant with one another and which are not, and to ask the reason of this in both cases. Here, as in the case of Astronomy, we have an anticipation of the science of a later age. The sounds we hear are produced by a succession of 'beats' (πληγαί) of the air (we should say, of waves), and the business of the musical theorist is to express the differences of the musical intervals in terms of these, and not merely in terms of the length of strings. So far as the Pythagorean system goes, it would seem that the consonances might be expressed by any other ratios just as well as those which have been experimentally discovered. In fact, the Pythagorean intervals are a problem and not a solution. The fact that some intervals are consonant, while others are not, must be due to something in the nature of number itself.

§ 175. All these studies, however, are but the prelude to the strain we have really to learn, and that is Dialectic. We know already what Dialectic means in the Sokratic sense. It is the art of question and answer, the art of giving a rational account of things and of receiving such an account from others (διδόναι καὶ δέχεσθαι λόγον). Even Xenophon knew that Sokrates made those who associated with him 'dialectical', though he attributes to him an erroneous etymology of the word.[1] But here something more is meant than the art of reasoning, or at any rate something more special. In the *Euthydemus* (290 c) we are told that arithmeticians, geometers, and astronomers must hand over their discoveries to the dialectician for examination. Here we learn (533 b) that the weakness of the method of hypothesis, as described for instance by Sokrates in the *Phaedo*, is just this, that the hypothesis itself is only established by the consistency of its consequences; it has not itself been examined in the light of any higher principle. We are told, accordingly, that, though geometers and the rest do in part attain reality, they only see it 'in a dream'. So long as they use hypotheses and refuse to let them be moved, because they can give no account of them, they cannot be said to behold true Being with a waking vision. If we take for our starting-point what we do not know, and our end and all the intermediate steps are only a con-

---

[1] *Mem.* iv. 5. 12. He makes him derive the verb διαλέγεσθαι from διαλέγειν κατὰ γένη τὰ πράγματα. That is just like the derivation of σοφιστής from ὁ τῶν σοφῶν ἴστης (= ἐπιστήμων) in *Prot.* 312 c or that of ὑπόθεσις from ὑποτίθημι, 'lay a foundation', implied in *Rep.* 511 b. The *Cratylus* is full of such things, so Sokrates may really have said it.

catenation (συμπλοκή) of what we do not know, that is a mere agreement (ὁμολογία) not to raise ultimate questions, and cannot become science in the true sense of the word.

The defect of the special sciences is, then, that they depend on hypotheses of which they can give no account, and are therefore obliged to use sensible diagrams. We are told quite distinctly that Dialectic proceeds by 'destroying the hypotheses' (ἀναιροῦσα τὰς ὑποθέσεις). This has given much trouble to some interpreters, who find it hard to believe that Plato desired, for instance, to 'destroy' the hypothesis of three kinds of angles, which he expressly mentions in this connexion (510 c) as fundamental in geometry. It is impossible, however, to take the word I have rendered 'destroy' (ἐναιρεῖν, tollere) otherwise; for we have seen (§ 125) that it is a technical term in this context. Further, the view of science taken in the *Republic* really does demand the destruction of the hypotheses of the special sciences. The hypothesis of three kinds of angles has a spatial character, and that is just why the geometer is forced to use sensible diagrams. The ideal is that Arithmetic, Geometry, and the rest should all be reduced to one science, and this cannot be done so long as their special hypotheses remain. It is only when these have been removed that we can ascend to a first principle which is no longer a postulate (to an ἀνυπόθετος ἀρχή), namely, the Form of the Good. Then, and not till then, can we descend once more without making use of sensible diagrams of any kind. The whole of science would thus be reduced to a sort of teleological algebra.

EUKLEIDES AND PLATO

§ 176. We shall understand this point of view better if we consider how natural it was that, when Plato set himself to draw up a scheme of scientific study for the Academy, he should be influenced by the teaching of Eukleides of Megara. He had taken refuge with him after the death of Sokrates, and the prominence given to Phaidon as the narrator of the last discussion of Sokrates on earth points in the same direction, for the school of Elis founded by him was closely related to that of Megara. Plato was also influenced, of course, by the Pythagorean associates of Sokrates, but it looks as if he did not become personally intimate with the leading Pythagoreans of his day till later. He would have little time for that during his first visit to Italy and Sicily. This makes it necessary for us to learn all we can about Eukleides. It is not much, unfortunately, but the few statements we have rest on the best authority, and are of fundamental importance.

In the first place, as we have seen already (§ 117), Eukleides was an Eleatic, and the doctrines of the Megaric school in a later generation, as we know them from Aristokles,[1] still bear traces of their Eleatic origin. Accordingly, though we are not entitled to ascribe all these doctrines to Eukleides himself without more ado, we cannot go far wrong in crediting him with those that are definitely Eleatic in character. To begin with, we are told that the Megarics considered it their business to 'throw' (καταβάλλειν)[2] sensations and appearances and to trust to reasoning alone. That goes without saying in an Eleatic. We are also told that they held that Being was one and the Other is not, and that there was no such thing as coming into being or ceasing to be or motion. That is also sound Eleatic doctrine, and may be confidently attributed to Eukleides. It is impossible, then, to suppose that he could have accepted, and still less that he could have originated, the doctrine Plato attributes to Sokrates in the *Phaedo*, for there we have a plurality of forms which enter into the world of becoming. Eukleides accordingly, though present, takes no part in the discussion. On the other hand, he appears to have been deeply interested in the teaching of Sokrates on the subject of the Good. We still have a curious document written in the Doric dialect, in which certain Sokratic doctrines about goodness are clearly referred to.[3] It is generally recognised that it belongs to the end of the fifth century, and its 'eristic' character, taken in conjunction with its Doric dialect, strongly suggest Megara as its place of origin. At any rate, we know that Eukleides identified the Good with the One, which is also called by other names, such as God or Wisdom. It is only possible to guess his exact meaning, but the fact of the identification is certain, and its connexion with the teaching of Sokrates seems plain. As there is nothing else than the One, he inferred that there is no such thing as evil. The method by which it is shown that the senses and the things that appear to them are unreal, is to show that there are 'two statements' (δισσοὶ λόγοι)

---

[1] Aristokles was the teacher of Alexander of Aphrodisias. The statements referred to are preserved in Euseb. *Pr. Ev.* xiv. 17.

[2] See p. 113, *n.* 2.

[3] The δισσοὶ λογοι (formerly known as *Dialexeis*). It is printed in Diels, *Vors.*[3] ii. pp. 334 *sqq.* See Taylor, *Varia Socratica*, i. pp. 91 *sqq.*

which may be made with equal truth and cogency about all of them. That is what the Megarics called Dialectic and their opponents called Eristic. If we may trust Aristotle's account of the matter, the method had degenerated by this time into a mere quibbling about words. It does not follow that it was anything but a serious doctrine in the hands of Eukleides; for Plato had not yet cleared up the meaning of 'is' and 'is not', and we shall see good grounds for believing it was just his interest in the teaching of Eukleides that led him to do so. It is highly probable, then, that the account of Dialectic in the *Republic* was written under this influence, and in that case we can most easily understand it as an effort to do justice to the position of Eukleides without following him in reducing all the forms to the intelligible One, which is also somehow the Good. I have said (§ 129) that I regard the doctrine of the Good as Sokratic, but there are some things said about it in the *Republic* which seem to be Plato's own, for they are directed against the identification of the form of Good with Being on the one hand and Wisdom on the other, and these are the doctrines of Eukleides. According to the *Republic*, the Good is neither Being nor Knowledge, but the cause of both. It altogether transcends and is 'on the other side' of Being (ἐπέκεινα τῆς οὐσίας), as it transcends Knowledge. In some such way as this, it may have seemed to Plato at the time, the monism of Eukleides might be avoided, while all that was valuable in his system might be preserved.

The theory which would naturally follow from this way of regarding the Good would be one of 'emanation', and that is in fact the view which was associated with it when the doctrine was revived in later days. To a considerable extent Neoplatonism may be fairly described as a development of the thought that was in Plato's mind when he wrote this part of the *Republic*. We have no means of knowing how far Plato himself had gone in this direction. He could not in any case have made Sokrates the mouthpiece of such a theory; and, as has been indicated, he has probably strained historical verisimilitude to some extent in saying as much as he does. We shall never know more on the subject, for he never speaks in this way of the form of Good again, and Aristotle never even alludes to this passage. As we shall see, the solution that finally commended itself to Plato was reached on other lines, and we have now to consider the steps by which he finally emancipated himself from the Megaric doctrine.

XIII

Criticism

§ 177. Plato's emancipation from the influence of Eukleides seems to have been gradual. For about twenty years he carried on his work in the Academy without interruption, and it does not appear that he published any more dialogues till towards the end of that period. His hands were probably too full. A time came, however, when he felt it necessary to define his attitude to other philosophers, and that could only be done by writings addressed to a wider circle than the school. We cannot estimate the interval of time which separates the *Theaetetus* from the *Republic* and the *Phaedrus*, but it was probably one of a good many years. When Plato began to write dialogues again they had a different character from those of his early life. This is marked first of all by a significant change in form. Some of the very earliest dialogues had been simple dramatic sketches in direct speech, but this form soon proved inadequate for Plato's purpose, so long as that was mainly to give a picture of Sokrates as he lived and moved. Unless interpreted by action it makes too great a demand on the reader, who has to supply the *mise en scène* and the stage directions himself. Narrated dialogue, on the other hand, allows of descriptions and comments which make the picture live, and all the most artistic of Plato's dialogues are therefore narrated. When, however, the scientific interest begins to prevail over the artistic, this form becomes very cumbrous. We see it at its worst in the *Parmenides*, the formula of which is 'Antiphon said that Pythodoros said that Parmenides said'. In the *Theaetetus* there is an express reference to this question of form. Like the *Phaedo* and the *Parmenides*, that dialogue opens with a short dramatic introduction; but this leads up, not to a narrated dialogue as in their case, but to one which is also dramatic in form. That, we are told (143 c), is to avoid the troublesome repetition of such phrases as 'And I said', 'He assented', 'He agreed'. It is true that the *Parmenides* is probably a little later than the *Theaetetus*, but they both belong to the same period, and Plato may well have been engaged on the one when he produced the other. If so, we can easily understand his conceiving a distaste for the narrative form. At any rate, he never made use of it again, and his latest dialogues are simply dramatic, just as his earliest had been.

§ 178. Philosophically, the distinguishing feature of these dialogues is Plato's preoccupation with the Megarics. The *Theaetetus* is dedicated to Eukleides, or rather to his memory; for it is not likely that he was still living. Plato does not introduce living characters if he can help it. He was about to criticise the doctrine of Eukleides, and the *Theaetetus* is meant to lead up to that criticism, but he still cherished, we may suppose, a feeling of regard for the man. Nor is there anything in the dialogue that directly impugns his doctrine. It does not, we shall see, go far beyond the possibilities of discussion within the Sokratic society itself. The rift, as has been pointed out (§ 129), was probably in existence before the death of Sokrates, but was regarded as a difference within the school. For the same reason, there is no difficulty in making Sokrates the chief speaker. And yet the point of view is no longer strictly Sokratic. Plato is now as much impressed by the dangers of a one-sided intellectualism as by those of a one-sided sensationalism. He avoids the doctrine of forms altogether in this dialogue, though there are points in the argument where we should expect it to be discussed. It was taking another shape in his mind by this time, and he could not make Sokrates the mouthpiece of that.

§ 179. This brings us face to face with the very important question of the place assigned to Sokrates in the dialogues of Plato's maturity. The discussion narrated in the *Theaetetus* is supposed to have been taken down by Eukleides and revised and corrected by Sokrates himself (143 a). Further, it is supposed to be read aloud at Megara years after the death of Sokrates. The informal discussion of the earlier dialogues has become a deliberate statement of doctrine intended to be read and criticised. As, however, it only states a problem which had really been raised by Sokrates, and does not give the solution, there is no difficulty in his being the chief speaker, though by a curious device, certain doctrines are said to have been known to him only 'in a dream'. The *Parmenides* is also represented as a deliberate statement; for it

is supposed to have been learnt by heart and repeated long afterwards, a fiction which would seem more credible then than in this
age of books. This dialogue contains a direct criticism of the
doctrine of forms as that is stated in the *Phaedo* and the *Republic*,
and the introduction of Parmenides as the chief speaker suggests
that it was the Eleatic criticism that in fact forced Plato to seek for
a more satisfactory formulation of it. He was bound to make his
position clear; for, whether he himself had ever held the doctrine
criticised or not, he had certainly done a great deal to propagate it
by his Sokratic writings. Clearly Sokrates cannot be the chief
speaker here, but it would have been unseemly to introduce
Eukleides, for instance, as criticising him. So Plato takes advantage
of the visit of Parmenides and Zeno to Athens almost a century
before to put the criticism into the mouth of the founder of the
school to which Eukleides belonged. It would have been too much,
however, to represent Parmenides as asserting the reality of 'not
being', which is the theme of the *Sophist*, so the leading part in that
dialogue and its sequel, the *Statesman*, is taken by an Eleatic
stranger, who is a very unorthodox disciple of the great Parmenides.
Plato seems to mean by introducing this enigmatic figure, who
certainly expresses his own views, that he himself, rather than the
disciples of Eukleides, was the true successor of Parmenides. In
the *Philebus* we seem to come nearer Plato's own philosophy than
we do anywhere else, and yet Sokrates is once more the chief
speaker. That is a problem we shall have to face later. In the
Timaeus and *Critias* Sokrates is only a listener, and in the *Laws* he
does not appear at all. We are told in the *Phaedo* that Sokrates had
rejected all attempts at a mechanical explanation of the world, and
the *Timaeus* contains such an attempt. As to the works which deal
with human history and institutions, like the *Critias* and the *Laws*,
we learn from the *Timaeus* (19 a–d) why Sokrates can take no part.
He could paint the picture of an ideal state, but he could not make
the figures move. He is made to confess that he could not, for
instance, represent his state as engaged in the struggle for existence
with other states; to do that men are required who by nature and
training have a gift for practical politics as well as for philosophy.
This is a very valuable passage as evidence that Plato was conscious
that some themes were appropriate for Sokrates and others were
not. The implied criticism of his master's political teaching should
also be noted. Plato knew very well that, on its constructive side,

it was too uncompromising and on its critical side too negative. That is partly why so many followers of Sokrates turned out reactionaries rather than statesmen.

THE THEAETETUS

§ 180. The purpose of the *Theaetetus* is to clear the ground by showing that knowledge cannot be identified either with sensation or with thought. Theaitetos, after whom the dialogue is named, was one of the original members of the Academy and one of the most distinguished, and we gather that he died of wounds and dysentery after a battle at Corinth, which was probably that of 369 B.C. It was certainly before this dialogue was written; for the beautiful description of his character in the introduction can only be read as a tribute to a gifted disciple too soon lost. His eminence as a mathematician is skilfully suggested by the story of how, when a mere lad, he discovered a general formula for numbers of which the square root is irrational. It seems probable that his death was still recent when the dialogue was composed, and for that and other reasons it is most probably dated in 368 B.C. or a little later, when Plato was about sixty years old. The other speakers are the 'younger Sokrates', the friend of Theaitetos, and like him an original member of the Academy, and the mathematician Theodoros of Kyrene. He had been a follower of Protagoras and a friend of Sokrates. He therefore belongs to an earlier generation than the two lads whose teacher he is, and had certainly passed away long before this dialogue was written. The dialogue is supposed to take place just before the trial of Sokrates (210 d), that is to say, more than thirty years before it was composed.

§ 181. The first serious answer given by Theaitetos to the question, 'What is knowledge?' is that it is sensation ($a\emph{\"\i}\sigma\theta\eta\sigma\iota\varsigma$). That definition agrees with what Protagoras said in another form about knowledge, namely, that man is the measure of all things, of what is that it is, and of what is not that it is not. This means that as a thing appears to me, so it is to me, and as it appears to you, so it is to you. Instead of saying 'as a thing appears to me', we may equally well say 'as I am sensible of it', for instance, 'A wind appears to me cold' is the same thing as 'I am sensible that a wind is cold'. In a word, appearance ($\phi a\nu\tau a\sigma\iota a$) and sense ($a\emph{\"\i}\sigma\theta\eta\sigma\iota\varsigma$) are the same thing in the case of hot and cold and the like. Sensation, then, is always sensation of what is, and cannot err; for what *is* is that of which I am sensible (152 a–c).

That, however, was only a dark saying of Protagoras addressed to the vulgar crowd; to the initiated he told the truth, and the truth is this. It is not true to say that what appears *is*. In reality nothing *is*, everything is becoming, as Herakleitos and others have taught. Motion is the cause of growth, while rest is the cause of decay and ceasing to be. Motion is good, and rest is evil. You cannot rightly use the terms 'something', 'such a thing', 'one', 'is'; for, if you say 'Something is great', it will appear small from another point of view, and so with the rest (152 d).

In the light of this principle let us consider the case of sight. When we use the words 'white colour', we must not suppose that what we mean by these words is either something outside the eyes or something in the eyes. We must not suppose it to be in any place at all. We must say rather that it results from the impact (προσβολή) of the eye on the appropriate movement (πρὸς τὴν προσήκουσαν φοράν) outside it, being neither what impinges nor what is impinged upon, but a something between the two having a proper character of its own for each individual (154 a). Thus no one knows whether what appears to him is the same as what appears to another, and everyone knows that what appears to himself in one way at one time appears to him differently at another. And so with other objects; for instance that which after measurement and comparison we call great, that which after touching we call hot, become respectively small and cold by the presence of greater or hotter objects. Six dice compared with four are 'more' and 'half as many again'; compared with twelve, they are 'less' and 'half', yet they are not changed in themselves. They become more and less, and yet nothing has been added to them or subtracted from them (153 d — 154 d).

On the other hand, if we look into our own thought, we shall agree in the three following propositions: (1) Nothing can become greater or less either in size or number so long as it is equal to itself; (2) Nothing can increase or decrease to which nothing is added or from which nothing is taken away; (3) Nothing can be what it was not before without becoming and having become. But all these propositions are in direct contradiction to the instance of the dice which we considered above, or again to such a case as this — 'I, Sokrates, am now taller than you, Theaitetos; in a year, I shall be smaller (for Theaitetos is still a growing lad), though nothing will have been taken from me, nor shall I have become, though I shall be, what I was not before' (154 d — 155 c).

Let us go deeper into the mysteries of those wise men of whom we spoke, taking care that none of the uninitiated hear us, the 'hammer-

and-tongs persons' (ἀντίτυποι ἄνθρωποι), who think that nothing is but what they can clutch in their hands, and refuse the right of being to actions and processes and everything invisible. The hidden truth is this. Nothing is but motion, but there are two forms (εἴδη) of motion, either of infinite extent, the one having the power of acting, the other of being acted upon. The mutual intercourse of these motions begets an infinity of offspring (ἔκγονα), each of which is a twin, being partly sensation and partly the sensible, the one always simultaneously accompanying the other. Of the infinity of sensations many have received names, warming and cooling, sight, hearing and smell, pleasure and pain, desire and fear, and so forth. The corresponding sensible things are colours, sounds, and so forth. These motions are quick and slow; those that are slow take place in one spot and in relation to what is in contact with them, and are thus the producers; those that are produced are swifter, for their motion is from place to place (155 d — 156 d).

Thus what we call seeing may be analysed as follows. On the one side there must be the eye, on the other something commensurable (σύμμετρον) with the eye. These are the 'slower motions' which take place in one spot. If they come into one another's presence, from the former to the latter there is a motion, sight; from the latter to the former there is a motion, whiteness. These are the 'swifter motions' which pass from place to place. This whiteness cannot be said to *be anything*; it is continually *becoming* as a result of motion. Nor can we even say that what acts or what is acted upon *is anything* that can be fixed and individualised in thought; for the one is not until it meets the other, and the one in one combination appears as the other in another combination (156 d — 157 a).

Strictly speaking, then, we must not admit any terms such as 'this', 'that', 'something', but must think of everything as a process of becoming, being destroyed, being changed, and this both in the case of particular sensible qualities and of aggregates (ἀθροίσματα) of particular sensible qualitities, such as what we call 'man', 'stone', and every individual object (157 c).

It only remains to consider the question of the sensations of dreaming, insane and diseased persons. We cannot prove that what we call dreaming is not waking, and *vice versa*; for in both states the soul upholds the truth of what appears to it at the moment, and so in the case of insanity and disease, except that these states last longer than sleep. The answer is simple. Sokrates awake or in health is, taken as a whole, other than Sokrates in sickness or asleep. Accordingly, any natural agent will act upon him otherwise in these different states, and the resultant of the agent and what it acts on will be different. Now the resultant is what it is, not in itself, nor relatively to the agent only, nor relatively to Sokrates only, but relatively to both. When someone becomes sensible, he becomes sensible *of something*, and, when something becomes sensible, it becomes sensible *to someone*, and what the person is or becomes, he is or becomes relatively to that thing, and so with the thing. The being or reality (οὐσία), then, of the moment (*i.e.* the coexistent, correlative sensation and sensible) is bound to both the agents of which it is the resultant; and, from the side of the person, sensation, the momentary state, is true; for it is a sensation of what the person at the moment *is* (157 e — 160 d).

§ 182. This is obviously a well-thought-out and coherent theory of sensation. We are not told whose it was, though it is made quite plain that it was not to be found in the book of Protagoras (§ 92). There are certain points in it which remind us of what we are told about the Herakleitean Kratylos, who criticised his master for saying that we cannot step twice into the same river. We cannot do so even once. And yet, if the theory just expounded were his, we should surely hear a great deal more about him than we do. On the other hand, it can hardly be an improvised fiction; it is too strongly characterised and too personal for that. It is, of course, quite on the lines of the view of sensation everywhere attributed to Sokrates, so there is no difficulty in putting it into his mouth; but it must clearly have been worked out by someone who believed in it as an adequate account of knowledge. On the whole, it seems best to regard it as in this form Plato's own. Aristotle tells us that in his youth Plato had been familiar with the doctrine of Kratylos, and had adopted it,[1] and there is an earlier dialogue called by the name of that thinker, in which Herakleitean doctrine is discussed. Aristotle further tells us that Plato continued to hold this doctrine to the end, and there is certainly nothing in it, as an account of sensation, that he need ever have wished to retract. In fact, a thorough-going sensationalism is the necessary foundation of Platonism. I assume, then, that the doctrine is that of Kratylos, while the elaboration of it is Plato's. That will account for the obvious zest with which he expounds it, and his equally obvious

[1] It is probable, indeed, that this is only Aristotle's inference from the *Cratylus* and the *Theaetetus*, but it is a fair inference.

annoyance at the cheap objections which may so easily be made to
it.

These objections are certainly captious enough, and Sokrates
himself protests that it is treating Protagoras unfairly to urge them.
He even undertakes to reply to them in the name of Protagoras,
since he himself is dead. They have a certain historical interest;
for some of them reappear in the eristic of the later Megaric
school, and that of itself suggests they may have originated in the
circle of Eukleides. To discuss them here would merely divert the
reader's attention from the main argument. As Sokrates says
(165 d), there is no end to the attacks which might be made on the
senses by one of these 'mercenary sharpshooters', who take you
captive by the spell of their wisdom, and will not let you go again
without a ransom.[1] He proceeds, accordingly, to restate the theory
of Protagoras in a form which secures it against cheap criticism of
this kind.

§ 183. As restated by Sokrates, the doctrine of Protagoras is as
follows. However true it may be that the sensations of each individual are his and his only (ἴδιαι ἑκάστῳ), and that what *is* (if the word
is to be used at all) is what appears to the individual and to him
alone, Protagoras never intended to deny the distinction between
wise and unwise. He would say that the wise man is one who is
able to change bad beliefs to good. Belief, or what appears to one
man, differs from belief, or what appears to another, not as true
from false (for what appears to the individual *is*, and is therefore
true and the only truth), but as good from bad, healthy from
diseased, and the wise man is he who by his words can make what
is good appear, and therefore *be*, good for the state and the individual alike.

Let us examine this. We shall see the bearing of it best if we
consider questions of expediency or the advantageous (τὸ ὠφέλιμον).
In such questions it will be admitted that one man is a better
adviser than another, even by those who maintain that such
distinctions as right and wrong are only conventional, that is, that
they have no independent reality by nature, but depend for their
existence and duration on the opinion of the community. No one,
in fact, would maintain, except as a mere form of words, that what
a state thinks advantageous for it *is* therefore advantageous for it.

---

[1] The reference to the Megarics is unmistakable here. The rift within the
Sokratic school is evidently widening.

This will be still more obvious if we consider the whole 'form' ($\epsilon\hat{\iota}\delta os$) to which the advantageous must be referred. The general characteristic of it is that it has to do with the future. Now we may say that the present sensation of the individual is the only test ($\kappa\rho\iota\tau\acute{\eta}\rho\iota o\nu$) by which we can judge what *is*, but it will not be maintained that it is also the test of what *is to be*. With regard to that, the belief of the professional or the specialist always carries more weight than that of the layman. Where the future is concerned, it is not everyone, but the man who is wiser than others, who will be the 'measure', and Protagoras himself admits this; for he holds the wise man to be the man who can replace worse by better beliefs with regard to these very things. We see, then, that when we state the doctrine of Protagoras sympathetically, it at once takes us beyond sensationalism. It is no longer true, even according to him, that what appears to me *is* to me, and what appears to you *is* to you. This is specially noted (179 b) as the argument which is most fatal to the doctrine of Protagoras, though there is another which also disproves it. Protagoras must admit that the beliefs of other people are valid for them, and most other people do not believe the theory of Protagoras to be true. Therefore it is not true for them.[1]

§ 184. This piece of reasoning is interrupted by a magnificent digression on the philosophic life, conceived as it was in the *Gorgias* and the *Phaedo*. It is impossible to summarise a passage like this; it must be read as it stands. Still, we are bound to ask ourselves why it is inserted here. It comes in the middle of a discussion intended to show that the wise man is the best judge of what is advantageous for the community, and yet it describes in glowing colours the aloofness of the philosopher from practical concerns of every kind. The world is of necessity evil, and the philosopher will strive to escape with all speed from it to a better. The only way to do this is to become likened unto God, so far as that may be, and this likeness is to be attained by the cultivation of holiness and wisdom, and especially of geometry and astronomy. That is just the doctrine Plato consistently attributes to Sokrates, but it can hardly be an adequate representation of his own attitude to life at the time he wrote the *Theaetetus*. He was shortly to become involved in politics of a decidedly practical nature, as we shall see, and the Academy was as much a school for statesmen and legis-

[1] This is the argument which came to be known as the $\pi\epsilon\rho\iota\tau\rho\sigma\pi\acute{\eta}$ or 'turning the tables'. It was also used against Protagoras by Demokritos (Sext. Emp. vii 389).

lators as anything else. In the *Timaeus* Sokrates admits, as we have
seen, that practical politics is something foreign to his interests,
and we might therefore say that the present passage is inserted to
keep the picture of him true to life, at a time when Plato was
entering on a course his master would have shrunk from instinctively. I believe that to be true, but it is not the whole truth.
I believe that Plato, though he had learnt the duty of philosophers
to descend in turn into the Cave,[1] still felt that the life here
described was in truth the highest. It is not uncommon for a man
of action to feel intensely the superiority of the contemplative life;
and it is not unnatural for such a man, if he is also a great artist, to
sing the praises of what has become for him an impossible ideal,
though he may recognise it in his inmost heart as saving truth. In
the 'digression' of the *Theaetetus* I think we may see Plato's
reluctant farewell to the theoretic life. At any rate, he tells us
himself that it is a digression unconnected with the main theme of
the dialogue, and he must have had some motive for inserting it.

§ 185. We must now examine the claims of the theory of universal motion to give an account of knowledge. We must not
forget that Melissos and Parmenides have asserted an exactly
opposite theory, namely, that all is one and at rest in itself, having
no space to move in. We stand, then, in a cross-fire between two
hostile camps. Let us attack 'the streamers' (οἱ ῥέοντες) first. We
shall see that, on their theory, knowledge is impossible (179 d —
181 b).

When we say 'everything moves', what do we mean by 'moves'?
There are two forms (εἴδη) of motion: (1) motion from place to place
(φορά); (2) motion from state to state (ἀλλοίωσις). In other words,
motion is either locomotion or alteration; and, if motion is universal,
it must include both. Since, then, everything not only moves its place,
but also alters its state, we cannot ascribe any quality to what moves;
for what we call qualities (ποιότητες) are nothing but perpetual processes going on between what acts and what is acted upon, and
accordingly, in the very moment of being named, the quality is gone.
Similarly, as we may not speak of sensible qualities, so we may not
speak of sensations; for each sensation is in process, and cannot be
called sight, hearing, or the like, any more than not-sight, not-hearing,
and the like. And, if we cannot speak of sensation, we cannot speak of
knowledge, which we identified with sensation, and the answer of
Theaitetos was no answer, and the attempt to prove it by the theory
of universal motion has only resulted in proving that all answers are

---

[1] *Rep.* 520 c: καταβατέον ἐν μέρει.

equally right. In fact, we are not entitled to distinguish one answer from another; for such words as 'thus' and 'not thus' imply fixity, not motion (181 b — 183 b).

Sokrates declines to examine the 'partisans of the Whole' (οἱ τοῦ ὅλου στασιῶται),[1] Melissos and Parmenides, for the present; we must come back to the original answer of Theaitetos.

§ 186. In ordinary language we speak of 'seeing with the eyes', 'hearing with the ears', and so on, but strictly we ought to say, not that the eyes are that *with which* we see (ᾧ ὁρῶμεν), but that they are the instruments (ὄργανα) through which (δι᾽ ὧν), or by means of which, we see. For we cannot suppose ourselves to be like so many Wooden Horses, each with a number of sensations sitting inside; we must suppose that there is some one constituent element (εἶδος) in us — call it soul or what not — in which all these sensations converge, and to which they serve as instruments when we are sensible of objects. This distinction between the one identical element and the instruments employed by it may be made clear as follows. The instruments through which we are sensible of hot, hard, light, sweet things are various parts of the body. Each of these instruments has a specific power (δύναμις), and that which one can do another cannot; we cannot be sensible of sound by means of sight, nor of colour by means of hearing. If, then, we have a thought of anything which is common both to sound and colour, this must be due to some other instrument than seeing or hearing, and it is certain that we do have thoughts of things which are common to the objects of different senses. Let us see what these are (184 b — 185 a).

To begin with, we have such thoughts as 'colour and sound are', 'each is other than the other and the same as itself', 'both are two', 'each is one', 'they are like or unlike one another', and so on. What, then, is the power and what is the instrument through which it acts, by which we are enabled to find this common element to which we give such names as being and not-being (οὐσία καὶ τὸ μὴ εἶναι), likeness and unlikeness (ὁμοιότης καὶ ἀνομοιότης), sameness and otherness (τὸ ταὐτόν τε καὶ τὸ θάτερον), unity and number (τὸ ἓν καὶ τὸν ἄλλον ἀριθμόν), odd and even (περιττὸν καὶ ἄρτιον), fair and foul (καλὸν καὶ αἰσχρόν), good and bad (ἀγαθὸν καὶ κακόν)? Not one of these common properties (κοινά) has any specific instrument by which it is apprehended, as was the case with such

---

[1] Cf. *E. Gr. Ph.*[2] p. 140, n. 1.

properties as sweetness, hardness, and so forth; it seems rather that in those cases the soul is its own instrument (αὐτὴ δι αὐτῆς ἐπισκοπεῖ), and acts by itself (καθ' αὐτήν).

The simple sensation, then, of the sensible qualities of things takes place through the affections of the body (τὰ τοῦ σώματος παθήματα); such sensation begins with birth and is common to man and beasts. On the other hand, the apprehension of the common qualities of things implies comparison and reflexion (τὸ ἀναλογίζεσθαι, συλλογισμός, συμβάλλειν), whether of the most common property, that of being, or of those of sameness and difference and the rest, or of those of fair and foul, good and bad, the investigation of which last implies comparison in a pre-eminent degree in the bringing of past and present into relation with future, which requires time and effort and education (185 a — 186 c).

It is at this point that we should expect Sokrates — the Sokrates we have learnt to know from the *Phaedo* and the *Republic* — to introduce the doctrine of incorporeal and intelligible forms; but nothing whatever is said about them either here or in any other part of the dialogue. Instead, we have the beginnings of a theory of what were afterwards called Categories, and these are regarded as certain common predicates which the soul apprehends without the instrumentality of sense, and by means of which it organises the manifold of sense. It is also to be observed that these common predicates apprehended by the soul alone include not only categories of reality (οὐσία), but categories of value (ὠφελία). The practical is becoming more promiment than it was in the earlier dialogues.

§ 187. Now, if there are predicates of this kind which are common to the sensations of all the organs of sense, and are apprehended by a purely mental activity, it follows that we cannot identify knowledge with sensation. The apprehension of being is essential to knowledge. Being and truth cannot be apprehended in the affections of the body, but only in the soul's reflexion about them. We must, therefore, look for knowledge under the name which describes the proper activity of the soul when it is concerned with what is. That name is *judgement* (τὸ δοξάζειν). Is that to be identified with knowledge? (186 c — 187 a).

The definition of judgement is not given till later, but it will be convenient to state it here. Thought (τὸ διανοεῖσθαι) is the dis-

course (διάλογος) that the soul holds alone with itself. When it
has come to a determination, whether slowly or by a swift dart at a
conclusion, and is at last at one and no longer at variance with
itself, we call this its *judgement* (δόξα). Here we have a very remarkable change in terminology. In the *Republic* the word (δόξα), which
is now used to signify the completed result of thought (διάνοια),
means something lower than thought, and covers 'imagination'
(εἰκασία) and belief (πίστις). Plato is preparing to attack the problem
of predication in his own way, and he wants a word for 'judgement',
and this seems the most natural to take. We must understand the
term here in the sense in which it is defined, and not in that which
it bears in earlier dialogues. It is the characteristically Platonic as
distinct from the Sokratic use of the word. It recurs in the later
dialogues, and in certain Academic passages of Aristotle. We have
to ask, then, whether knowledge is to be found within this activity
of the soul. Does simple judgement contain in itself the guarantee
of truth?

§ 188. The second section of the *Theaetetus* is accordingly
devoted to showing that no representation of the independent
(αὐτὴ καθ' αὐτήν) action of the soul can be made to explain the
undoubted fact of the distinction between true and false judgement.
It is shown that thought alone is as incapable of yielding knowledge as sensation alone, nor is it clear how any combination of
sensation and thought can yield knowledge.

In the first place, we can only say that *true* judgement (ἀληθὴς
δόξα) is knowledge. True judgement or thought is to judge something
to be what it is; false judgement or thought is to judge something to
be other than it is. But this at once raises a difficulty. How can
thought as such be other than true? How can there be a false
judgement at all? So long as we confine ourselves to the independent activity of soul, it would seem that false judgement is as
impossible as we have seen false sensation to be. Three possible
accounts of it are examined, and are all found to be equally unsatisfactory. They either imply that it is possible to know and not
to know the same thing at the same time, or that we can judge
without judging anything, or that it is possible to judge one thought
to be another. To identify knowledge with the work of the mind is,
therefore, open to the same objections as its identification with
sensation. All judgements will be equally true, and the distinction
between knowledge and ignorance, wisdom and unwisdom, will

disappear. Thought, in fact, can be attacked with precisely the same weapons as sensation (187 b — 190 e).

§ 189. It might seem more hopeful to regard true judgement as the reference of an impression of sense to the right or corresponding mental counterpart. We might suppose that memory is like a waxen tablet in the soul on which images are impressed. It is impossible that two impressions on this tablet should be confused, or that a sensation which makes an impression on it should be confused with another simultaneous sensation. It is, however, possible that there should be error in the reference of a sensation to the memory-image left by a former sensation, if that image was not sharply impressed or if it has been worn out. That would be false judgement. This, however, is still unsatisfactory; for it would restrict true judgement, and therefore knowledge, to judgements about actually present sensations. It would not explain, for instance, how some people can judge that $5+7=12$, and others that $5+7=11$, where there is no present sensation of such a number of objects. To explain this, we should have to make a distinction between having and possessing knowledge (ἕξις ἐπιστήμης and κτῆσις ἐπιστήμης), of which the latter may exist without the former, just as we may possess a coat without actually having it on. Let us compare the mind to a dovecot in which we have shut up a number of birds that we have caught. We *possess* these birds, indeed, but we cannot be said to *have* them till we have caught them again. Now we may catch the wrong bird, and in the same way we may catch the wrong piece of knowledge, and that will be false judgement.

Even that, however, is unsatisfactory, unless we suppose there are ignorances flying about in our mental dovecot also. But that will not do either; for, when we have caught our bird, it is a bird in the hand and we know what it is. We are not any nearer an explanation of false judgement than we were before (191 b — 200 d).

Finally, it is certain that there may be true judgement without knowledge. The pleaders in the law courts operate by means of persuasion and not by means of instruction, and yet the jury may be led by them to form a true judgement. This suggests to Theaitetos a definition which he has heard of knowledge, namely, that it is true judgement accompanied by a rational account of itself (ἀληθὴς δόξα μετὰ λόγου). Sokrates identifies this definition of knowledge with an elaborate theory he has heard 'in a dream'. There are some persons who maintain that the real is unknowable. Our sensations are produced by simple elements ($\sigma\tau o\iota\chi\epsilon\hat{\iota}a$) which are unknowable just because they are simple. They can only be named and cannot be defined, nor can we predicate anything of them, not even 'being' or 'this'. Such properties as these are common to all sorts of things and cannot be regarded as properties of the simple reals. These can, however, be apprehended by sense, and we can give them names ($\dot{o}v\dot{o}\mu a\tau a$). They can also combine with one another just as letters ($\sigma\tau o\iota\chi\epsilon\hat{\iota}a$) can form a syllable ($\sigma\upsilon\lambda\lambda a\beta\dot{\eta}$). If we combine their names, we get a statement or proposition ($\lambda\dot{o}\gamma os$), and that makes their combinations knowable (201 a — 203 b).

§ 190. The 'dream' of Socrates reminds us of the 'mystery' of Protagoras, and we feel that they are both devices for going beyond historical verisimilitude. There is also the same difficulty about the authorship of this theory, as there is about that of the sensationalist theory described in the early part of the dialogue. In the first place, it must be observed that it is a thoroughly idealist theory in the modern sense of that word. The simple reals are themselves unknowable, and all our knowledge is the work of the mind. In this respect it is the exact counterpart of the earlier sensationalist theory. Thought is everything here as sensation was everything there. Now there can be no doubt that the definition of knowledge as true judgement accompanied by a rational account of itself or ground ($\mu\epsilon\tau\dot{a}$ $\lambda\dot{o}\gamma o\upsilon$) belongs to the Sokratic school. It is the definition adopted by Diotima in the *Symposium* (202 a), and it is also taught in the *Meno* (97 e *sq.*). It is more difficult to say where the elaboration of it we find here comes from. Aristotle appears to allude to it in a passage of the *Metaphysics*, in the course of which he makes a remark about the view of Antisthenes 'and such uncultivated people' that it is impossible to define the 'What is it?', because a definition would be a 'long enumeration' ($\mu a\kappa\rho\dot{o}s$ $\lambda\dot{o}\gamma os$), and on the strength of this the whole theory has been attributed to Antisthenes. But all Aristotle says is that the theory in question appears to give plausibility to the view of Antisthenes, and, whatever we may think of it, it is not a theory likely to have been set up by 'uncultivated persons'.[1] Antisthenes denied the

---

[1] *Met.* B, 3. 1043 b, 5 *sqq.* Antisthenes is not mentioned till b, 24, and the passing manner in which he is alluded to seems to me to exclude the idea that Aristotle was thinking of him at all when he began the chapter.

possibility of predication, whereas, according to this theory, knowledge consists of nothing else. Nor is there any reason why Sokrates should 'dream' of Antisthenes. The suggestion made long ago by Lewis Campbell that the theory is that of 'some Pythagorean' is much more plausible.[1] The terminology of letters (στοιχεῖα) and syllables (συλλαβαί) is characteristic of the Pythagoreans, and we can see quite well how these Pythagoreans who refused to adopt the Sokratic doctrine of the participation of sensible things in the forms might find themselves driven to some such theory as this. In any case, the importance of the discussion is missed altogether if it is not clearly understood that the doctrine discussed is the exact opposite of the sensationalism Protagoras is said to have revealed 'in a mystery', and that it is rejected as equally unsatisfactory.

§ 191. For, when we come to examine it, we find that this theory leads to very great difficulties. How are we to conceive the relation between the prime elements and the complexes which are the objects of knowledge? Either the syllable is only the sum of the letters, in which case it is impossible to see how it should be more knowable than they are, or it is an indivisible unity, in which case it cannot be known either, since that would imply the separate apprehension of its parts.

Further, we must ask precisely what we mean by an 'account' (λόγος) in this connexion. Obviously we do not mean merely the expression of a judgement in articulate language. Nor can we mean a simple enumeration of the elements which make up a thing. Rather, we must mean a statement of the thing's *differentia* (διαφορότης), that which marks it off from all other things. If, however, we mean by this that we have merely a judgement (δόξα) as to the *differentia*, that brings us no further forward; while, if we mean that we have knowledge of the *differentia*, our definition will be circular. 'True judgement with a knowledge of the *differentia*' is not a definition of knowledge.

The conclusion of the *Theaetetus*, then, is that knowledge can neither be sensation nor the work of the mind. Sensation is merely a resultant of motion, and gives us no reality outside itself. Thought alone merely yields combinations of names. Nor have we been able to show, except by clumsy images, how knowledge

---

[1] Introduction to the *Theaetetus*, p. xxxix. The theory would harmonise well enough with what we are told of the doctrine of Ekphantos of Syracuse.

can be due to any combination of sensation and thought. On the other hand, we have incidentally made several discoveries as to the nature of knowledge. We have found, in the first place, that it implies certain 'common' or generic predicates, and, secondly, that to know a thing we must know its *differentia*. A mere apprehension of its common properties would not be an apprehension of *it* at all. The next dialogue we have to consider really deals with the same difficulties, though from another point of view.

THE PARMENIDES

§ 192. The *Parmenides* is a criticism of the doctrine of forms as stated in the *Phaedo* and *Republic*, and the selection of Parmenides as the chief speaker points to the conclusion that the objections to the theory of participation contained in the first part of the dialogue are of Eleatic origin. We know from the *Theaetetus* that Plato was busy with Eukleides about this time. Besides that, we have a remarkable piece of external evidence to the same effect. The most telling argument against participation is that known as 'the third man', which we shall come to presently. We have unimpeachable evidence that this argument was introduced in some work or other by the 'Sophist', Polyxenos.[1] He had been a pupil of the 'Sophist' Bryson, who had been an associate of Sokrates along with Eukleides, and with him had founded the 'Eristic' of Megara. He also stood in close relations of some kind with the Academy.[2] Now the detractors of Plato asserted that he plagiarised the lectures (διατριβαί)[3] of Bryson, and that is most easily explained if we assume that Bryson was the original author of this argument.

But, if these arguments are Eleatic in origin, it follows that they are not directed against the reality of the intelligible, but against that of the sensible. It would have been absurd to make Parmenides the mouthpiece of an attack upon the One, and all we know of the Megaric doctrine goes to show that it denied all reality to the world of sense. The arguments of the *Parmenides* are not directed,

---

[1] Alexander on Ar. *Met.* 990 b, 17. He quotes Polyxenos from Phanias of Eresos, a disciple of Aristotle and friend of Theophrastos. See Baümker in *Rhein. Mus.* xxxiv. pp. 64 *sqq.* The word εἰσάγειν used by Phanias does not necessarily imply that Polyxenos invented the argument. Cp. εἰσάγειν, 'to bring on the stage'.

[2] This appears from the comic poet Ephippos, fr. 14 Kock. It is not clear whether Bryson was a member of the Academy, but he may have been. It makes no difference. What is important is that he was an associate of Sokrates.

[3] Theopompos, *ap.* Athen. 509 c.

then, against the doctrine of forms as such, but against the Sokratic theory that sensible things come into being and cease to be by partaking or ceasing to partake in the forms. An argument like the 'third man' is clearly double-edged. It may be used to show the impossibility of an αὐτοάνθρωπος, but it will serve equally to demonstrate the unreality of particular men. Plato was, of course, far too interested in the world of experience to accept the acosmism of Eukleides, but he was clearly impressed by the force of the arguments against 'participation' as an account of the relation between the sensible and the intelligible. His own account of that is not, however, given in the *Parmenides*.

§ 193. The subject of the dialogue is introduced as follows. One of Zeno's arguments against the opponents of Eleaticism was that 'if things are a many, they must be both like and unlike'. The precise meaning of this does not concern us here; what we have to deal with is the solution of the difficulty proposed by Sokrates, who is not an old man, as in the *Theaetetus*, but 'extremely young' (127 c). He asks Zeno whether he does not believe in 'forms' which are 'apart from' the things of sense, but in which these things 'participate'. If that is the truth, there is no reason why sensible things should not participate at once in the form of likeness and in the form of unlikeness. A man, for instance, is both many and one; he has many parts, but he is one man among others. Why should not a sensible thing be at once like one thing and unlike another, thus partaking in both forms? To show that stones, sticks, and the like are both many and one is not to show that One is many or Many is one. What would be surprising would be if a man should set up separate forms such as Likeness and Unlikeness, One and Many, Motion and Rest (*i.e.* the common predicates (κοινά) of the *Theaetetus*), and should then show that these can mingle with and be separated again from each other. It would be still more surprising if he could show that the same contradictions which have been shown to exist in the things of sense were also to be found in forms apprehended by thought (129 a — 130 a).

The theory here stated by Sokrates is precisely that of the *Phaedo*, where we are told that Simmias may be greater than Sokrates and smaller than Phaidon, though Greatness and Smallness exclude one another (102 b). It is to be noted, however, that, even in the *Phaedo*, a doubt is expressed as to the adequacy of the term 'participation', for the relation between a subject and its predicates (100 d). If the *Phaedo* is in the substance historical, it will follow that the Sokrates of the *Parmenides* is just Sokrates himself before he had begun to feel these doubts. That Plato should have meant his own earlier self will only be credible to those who can believe that in the *Phaedo* he made use of Sokrates as a mask for his own personality, while the view that by Sokrates here he meant some callow Academic who held his own theory in a crude form should be credible to no one. We might be reluctantly convinced that Plato used Sokrates as a disguise for himself; but it would surely have been impious to represent his own immature disciples under the revered name of his master. The fact that it has to make assumptions of that kind ought to be fatal to this line of interpretation.

§ 194. Parmenides, who has evidently heard of 'forms' before (130 a), and who is delighted by the philosophic aptitude of Sokrates, as shown by his theory of 'participation', begins by asking him whether, in addition to the mathematical forms, which have been mentioned so far, he also believes in forms of the Just, the Beautiful and the Good, and, as might have been expected from the *Phaedo*, Sokrates at once assents. The next question is whether he believes in forms of Man, Fire, and Water. Sokrates confesses that he is in a difficulty about these. We have seen what this means (§ 73). As to things like mud, hair, and dirt, though he has sometimes been troubled by the thought that they must have forms too, he had finally renounced the idea. That, says Parmenides, is because Sokrates is still young, and philosophy has not yet laid hold of him completely as it will do some day. Then he will despise none of these things; at present he is too much influenced by popular opinion (130 e).

In the mouth of Parmenides this remark must be ironical. He must mean that, if such things as hair, mud, and dirt, are in any sense real, they are quite as much entitled to have 'forms' as the objects of mathematics. From Plato's point of view, on the other hand, the passage has probably another bearing. The doctrine of forms, as hitherto stated is only plausible because it is confined within certain limits. It is adequate in mathematics, where it originated, because in that region even the particulars are objects of thought and not of sense. In morals and aesthetics it is almost as satisfactory; for actions in their moral aspect are not really objects of sense, and beauty is a direct revelation of the form. On the other hand, it is a serious weakness in the doctrine that it can only be applied with difficulty in physics and biology, and that it breaks down altogether when we come to things common and unclean. If, now, we remember the way in which Plato insists in the *Theaetetus* on the distinction between the 'common' predicates (κοινά) which the soul apprehends by itself, and the objects of the several senses, we shall be inclined to think that he is preparing the way for a restriction of the doctrine to the former, while suggesting at the same time that this very restriction may so modify the doctrine that it will enable us to understand the whole world of experience, even in its humblest manifestations. There is no inconsistency in the restriction of the doctrine to purely intellectual categories, and the extension of the operation of these categories to the whole of the sensible world. Nor is any weight to be attached to the fact that in the *Timaeus* we have forms of Fire and the other elements; for there the speaker is a Pythagorean, and we have seen reason to believe that it was just in the construction of the elements that the later Pythagoreans made most use of the forms.

§ 195. Leaving this question for the present, Parmenides goes on to discuss the difficulties involved in the specially Sokratic conception that the many sensibles 'partake in' the one form, or that the one form is 'present to' or 'in' the many sensibles.

In the first place, these sensibles must either all contain the whole of the form or each of them only a part of it. In the first case, the whole form will be present in each particular thing, which means that it will be in more places than one, and so will be separate from itself and divided. Sokrates suggests that it may be like the day, which is present in many places and yet one, but Parmenides will not accept this comparison. If a number of people are covered by the same sailcloth, each one of them is covered only by a part of it. We come, then, to the other alternative, that the forms are divisible, and that what partakes in a form contains only a part of it; or, in other words, that only a part of the form is present in each of the many sensibles. In that case, however, the forms will not serve to explain anything. A part of the form of magnitude, if there could be such a thing, would be less than the whole, and a thing could not become great by participating in it, and many other absurd consequences would follow.[1]

[1] For the details of these I must refer to Professor Taylor's article in *Mind* (N.S.), vol. xii. No. 45.

Further, the very grounds on which Sokrates bases the doctrine of the one form in which innumerable sensible things partake would really compel him to assume also the existence of equally innumerable forms. If we require a form to explain the participation of particular things in a common predicate, we also require a form to explain the participation of the form itself and the particular things in a common predicate, and so on *ad infinitum* (132 a).

Sokrates hereupon suggests that perhaps the forms are really thoughts (νοήματα), and that they may only exist in souls, to which Parmenides replies that a thought must be a thought of something real, and further that, if the forms are thoughts, the things that partake in them must be thoughts too. It would also follow either that all things think or that there are unthought thoughts.[1]

The next suggestion made by Sokrates is that the forms may be 'patterns' (παραδείγματα), and that the true account of the participation of sensible things in them may be that they are 'likenesses' (ὁμοιώματα) of them.[2] But, says Parmenides, if the things are like the forms, the forms will be like the things, and we shall require another pattern which both resemble to explain their likeness. We are confronted once more by an infinite regress.

But there are far more serious difficulties than these. It would be very hard to refute anyone who said that these forms, if they are such as we describe them, are unknowable. We have said that they are 'alone by themselves' and not in our world (ἐν ἡμῖν), and therefore, as they are relative by nature, they can only be relative to one another. On the other hand, their 'likenesses' in our world can only be relative to one another and not to the forms. A man is not the master or slave of 'mastership itself' or of 'slavery itself', but of another man; while, on the other hand, 'mastership itself' is relative to 'slavery itself', and not to a particular slave. In the same way 'knowledge itself' is relative to 'truth itself', but our knowledge is relative to the truth in our world. But, if that is so, the forms must be entirely unknown. If we try to avoid this by saying that God has 'knowledge itself', and therefore knows the forms, the result is still worse. It will follow that God cannot know us or

[1] The last point is somewhat obscure, but it does not affect the main argument. Observe how clearly Conceptualism is formulated, and how deliberately it is rejected.

[2] According to Aristotle this was the Pythagorean view (*Met.* A. 6). We can, therefore, draw no inference from its prominence in the *Timaeus*, where the speaker is a Pythagorean, least of all the inference that Plato himself adopted this view in later life.

anything that we know; for the knowledge he has is not relative to the truth of our world. Nor can he be our Master; for 'mastership itself' is not relative to us (134 d–e).

§ 196. This section is based on the argument of the 'third man', which has already (§ 195) been used to throw doubt upon the theory of participation. It will be well to give it here in the form in which Phanias of Eresos quoted it from Polyxenos.[1] 'If a man is a man in virtue of participation or partaking in[2] the form or the αὐτοάνθρωπος, there must be a man who will have his being relatively to the form. Now this is not the αὐτοάνθρωπος, who *is* the form, nor the particular man who is so in virtue of participation in the form. It remains, then, that there must be a third man as well who has his being relative to the form.'[3] I understand this to mean that, as it is impossible for the particular sensible man to stand in any relation to the form, and, as the form cannot be related simply to itself, the theory of participation explains nothing. The only 'man' who could participate in the form of Man would be a third man in the intelligible and not in the sensible world, and it is quite superfluous to assume anything of the sort. It will be observed that, as has been suggested above, this argument is directed against the reality of the sensible and not of the intelligible. It is first and foremost an argument against the theory of participation, and it is only an argument against the doctrine of forms in so far as that implies many particular forms of man, etc., instead of a single absolute One. That explains further how it is that, while Aristotle uses the argument against the doctrine of forms, he also thinks it necessary to refute it.[4] It was intended to support a position with which he had still less sympathy.

§ 197. It almost seems as if we should be driven to the conclusion that the forms are unknowable, and that would be the end of all philosophic discussion. It would destroy dialectic (τὴν τοῦ διαλέγεσθαι δύναμιν). It is hinted, indeed, that a solution may be found (135 a), but this is not followed up for the present. Instead of that, Parmenides, who could hardly be expected to undertake the task of justifying the world of experience, proposes to dismiss

---

[1] See above, p. 254, *n.* 1.
[2] It is important to notice that Polyxenos uses for 'participation' two terms (μετοχή, μετουσία), which are never used by Plato. That goes to show that the argument was not specially directed against Plato's statement of the theory.
[3] I have adopted the transposition of Baümker (*Rhein. Mus.* xxxiv. p. 75).
[4] *Soph. El.* 178 b, 36 *sqq.*

that from consideration altogether, and to consider the difficulties that arise in the world of forms itself. The argument is still on Megaric ground; for we know that Eukleides rejected the multitude of forms and reduced them all to the One.

At the beginning of the dialogue (129 e *sq.*) Sokrates had declared himself unable to understand how the forms themselves could enter into combinations with one another, and still more how a form can be both one and many, like and unlike, at rest and in motion. It is easy enough, he repeats here (135 e), to see how sensible things can have different predicates; the real difficulty arises when we apply this to the forms. The way to deal with a problem of this kind, says Parmenides, is the method of hypothesis, and that both in its positive and negative application. We must trace out all the consequences (συμβαίνοντα) of the hypothesis that *it is* and also of the hypothesis that *it is not*. For instance, if we take the hypothesis Zeno examined, '*If things are a many* . . .', we should go on next to the consequences of the hypothesis '*If things are not a many* . . .', and in both cases we should ask what are the consequences, not only to the subject of the hypothesis itself, but also to the rest, and in each case we should consider the consequences to the subject of the hypothesis and to the rest both in themselves and in relation to one another. The same method must be followed in the case of all the forms, such as likeness and unlikeness, rest and motion, coming into being and ceasing to be, being and not being, and so forth (or, in other words, the 'common' predicates of the *Theaetetus*).

§ 198. Parmenides naturally takes his own doctrine of the One as the hypothesis to be examined. Plato has his own reasons for this, as we shall see, but there is no ground for thinking that either Parmenides or Sokrates is supposed to be conscious of them. Parmenides is not represented as accepting the consequences of his argument — he could not do that without destroying his own system — and he expressly declares that the result of his examination of the first hypothesis is impossible (142 a). Sokrates is reduced to silence, but we cannot suppose him to be convinced. The whole thing is treated as a mental gymnastic (γυμνασία), a 'laborious game', valuable chiefly for the training it gives in method. Plato means more than that, however, and he gives us the hint in the dialogue itself. We must remember that the discussion is about forms alone, and we are expressly warned against the idea that 'the rest' of which he speaks are the things of sense (135 e). They are just the other forms. Now Sokrates had said (129 d *sqq.*) that he would be very much astonished if anyone could show that the forms were capable of combination with one another. That form of separation (χωρισμός) had been clearly taught in the *Phaedo*, for instance. Sensible things could participate in the forms, but the forms excluded one another. He would be still more astonished, he adds, if anyone could show that there was the same sort of confusion and uncertainty in the forms as there is in the sensible things which participate in them, and that is exactly what Parmenides does show. If you take such forms as One and Being abstractly (χωρίς), they at once partake of and begin to pass into one another and all the other forms, including even their opposites. They are just as bad as water, which is cold to one hand and hot to the other, or any other of the sensible things which we have seen to be in continual flux. In fact, Parmenides proves that, if we take the intelligible world by itself, it is quite as unsatisfactory as the sensible, and by taking the One as his example, he really refutes the Megaric doctrine, and that with the weapon of the Megarics themselves. It adds to the humour of the situation that this refutation is ruthlessly carried out by the revered Parmenides, and it is even possible that we are to regard the description of his own work given by Zeno in the introduction as a hint of the light in which Plato wishes us to look at the second part of our dialogue. Zeno says:

> My work makes no sort of pretence to have been written with the object you mention (*i.e.* to prove the doctrine of Parmenides in another way). . . . It argues against those who maintain a multitude, and gives them back as good or better than they gave, by trying to show that their hypothesis will have even more absurd consequences than his, if it is thoroughly discussed (128 c–d).

Just so we may say that Plato has no idea of proving the hypothesis of his master, Sokrates, but he does propose to show that the hypothesis of the Megarics has even more absurd consequences than his if it is adequately followed out.

§ 199. It is from this point of view we must judge what strikes a modern reader as the arid and repellent form of the discussion with its occasional suggestion of sophistry. It is a display of the dialectical method introduced by Zeno and assiduously cultivated by his successors at Megara. Now Plato's dramatic power is by no means extinguished yet, and whatever impression it makes upon us, we may be sure that his contemporaries would keenly appreciate the virtuosity with which he plays on this alien instrument. It should be added that, so far as the arguments are sophistical — and one or two of them must certainly have been known by Plato to be so — that is probably quite deliberate. We shall see that he was coming to regard the disciples of Eukleides more and more as 'eristics', just because, as we saw in the *Theaetetus*, arguments confined to the objects of thought alone consist of judgements which are only combinations of names. There is, in fact, no dialogue where it is more important to remember the dramatic character of Plato's writing than this, and where it is more important to realise the contemporary situation. It seems to me quite possible that to Plato's circle the second part of the *Parmenides* seemed highly entertaining. Men who had laughed at the *Euthydemus* would find a subtler enjoyment here. I suspect, however, that Bryson and his friends were not pleased. In introducing Helikon some years later to Dionysios II. as a disciple of Eudoxos, Isokrates, and Bryson, he says,[1] 'And what is rare on the top of all this, he is not unpleasant to deal with, and he does not strike me as malicious, but rather as easy-going and simple. I say this with fear and trembling, seeing that I am expressing a judgement about a man, and man is not a bad animal, indeed, but a changeable one.' We shall have occasion to note other traces of the growing estrangement of Plato from the Megarics. Let us now consider the hypotheses.[2]

§ 200. There are properly speaking eight hypotheses to be examined, but there is a sort of corollary to the first and second, so that there appear to be nine.

Hypothesis I. — If it is One, what will be the consequences for itself? (137 c).

If it is One, it cannot be Many, and therefore it cannot have parts, and cannot be a whole (for that implies parts). Not having parts, it cannot have beginning, middle or end; it has therefore no limits and is infinite. Further, it will have no figure; for figure implies parts. Further, it will be nowhere; for what is anywhere must either be contained in something else or in itself. It cannot be contained in

[1] *Ep.* xiii. 360 c.
[2] I have thought it right to analyse these somewhat fully as a guide to students of the *Parmenides*. From what has been said, it will be clear that the reader may omit them if he likes.

anything else; for it would then be in contact at different points with what contained it, and that implies parts. Nor can it be contained in itself; for then it would be both container and contained, and so two, not one.

It cannot be in Motion or at Rest. If it suffered alteration (ἀλλοίωσις), which is one form of motion, it would no longer be one. It cannot have spatial motion (φορά), which is the other form of motion, either motion of rotation (περιφορά), for that implies a centre or axis of rotation, and so figure and parts, or motion of translation, since it has no place. Further, it would have to be at once in the same place and not in the same place, which implies parts. Nor can it be at rest, since it is nowhere in space, neither in itself nor in anything else, and cannot therefore be where it is (ἐν ταὐτῷ).

Nor can it be the Same as or Other than itself or anything else. It cannot be other than itself, for then it would not be one; it cannot be the same as anything else, for then it would be the same as what is other than one; it cannot be other than anything else, for it is only the other that can be other; it cannot be the same as itself, for if same were one, how could anything be the same as many?

It cannot be Like or Unlike itself or anything else, for the like is what has an identical property, and the only property of what is one is to be one.

Nor can it be Equal or Unequal to itself or anything else. If it were equal, it would have the same measures, but it does not participate in the same. If it were unequal (greater or less), it would have as many parts as measures, and so would not be one.

It cannot be older or younger than itself or anything else, or the same age, since all these imply inequality or equality. It cannot, therefore, be in time at all; for what is in time is always becoming older than it is at a given moment, and therefore at the same time younger than it is, and also, since this becoming lasts no longer or shorter time than what becomes, it is always the same age as itself.

Further, since it does not participate in time, it does not participate in Being; for it has not become and has not been, it will not become and will not be, it is not becoming and it is not.

And, if it cannot *be*, it cannot be *one*, and cannot be named, spoken of, judged of, known, or perceived by the senses.

As this result seems impossible, let us put the hypothesis in another form. Let us consider One, not merely as one (τὸ ἓν ἕν), but as being (τὸ ὂν ἕν).

Hypothesis II. — If One is, what are the consequences for itself? (142 b, 1 — 155 e, 3).

If One *is*, it partakes in Being (for *is* and *one* do not signify the same). Therefore One as being (ἓν ὄν) must be a whole of which one and being are parts. But, since each of these parts partakes in turn both of one and being, each can be further subdivided into two parts, and what always becomes two is not one but an infinite multitude.

Again, if we take One by itself, it is other than being. But One is not Other, and Being is not Other, therefore Other is other than either. Any pair of these three must be called two or both, and each of two is necessarily one. If we add One to any of these pairs, we get three, and three is odd while two is even; and two gives twice and three gives thrice, so that we have twice two and thrice three and twice three and thrice two. And so we may get any combination of odd and even numbers, and thus an infinite multitude, every part of which partakes in Being, so that Being is infinitely divided into parts. But each of these parts is one, so One is divided into as many parts as Being, and therefore not only One as being but One as one is an infinite multitude.

One as being is a whole, and parts are only parts as parts of a whole, and the parts are contained in the whole. Now that which contains is a limit. But, if it is limited, it will have extremes, and, if it is a whole, it will have beginning, middle and end. But, as the middle is equally distant from the extremes, it will have figure, either rectilinear, or circular or mixed, and will be finite.

Further, since all the parts which make up the whole are contained in the whole, it must be in itself; and, since the whole is not contained in the parts, it must, regarded as a whole, be in something else. Therefore it will be both at Rest and in Motion.

Further, it will be the Same as itself and everything else, and Other than itself and everything else. It is other than itself because it is both in itself and in something else, and other than everything else, since these are not one. But it is also the same; for otherness cannot be a property of anything. Therefore One and what is other than One, cannot be other because of otherness, nor can they be so in themselves. Nor can they stand in the relation of whole and parts; for what is not One does not partake in number. Therefore they are the same.

Consequently, it must be Like and Unlike itself and everything else, for One is other than everything else in the same way as everything else than One, and therefore they are alike in so far as they are other. On the other hand, they must be unlike in so far as they are the same; for opposite antecedents must have opposite consequences.

Further, it will be in contact with itself and with what is other than itself, since it is contained in something other. But, as contact always implies at least two, since the number of points of contact is always one less than that of the things in contact, it cannot be in contact either with itself or anything else.

Further, it will be Equal and Unequal to itself and everything else. If it were smaller, Small would be in it, either as a whole or in a part of it. If it were in it as a whole, it would either pervade it completely, in which case it would be equal to it, or exceed it, in which case it would be greater. And the same contradiction arises if it is in a part of it. The same applies *mutatis mutandis* to the Great. Besides, Great and Small are relative to one another and not to One. Therefore One is equal to itself and to what is other than itself. But One is in itself, and therefore contains and is contained by itself, and is therefore greater and smaller than itself. And, since there is nothing besides One and what is other than One, and, since everything that is is in a place, what is other than One is in One, and One is therefore greater than what is other than One. But, for the same reason, One is in what is other than One, and therefore smaller than it. The same reasoning will apply to the parts as to the whole.

Further, it will participate in time; for it *is*, and to be is just participation in being along with present time. But as time (of which the present is a part) is always advancing, One, as sharing in this advance, is always becoming older, and therefore at the same time younger, than itself. But it cannot advance from past to future without passing through the present; and so, when it comes to the present, advance is arrested, so that the growing older and younger are already complete in the present. But the present lasts for the One as long as it is; for it is always now whenever it is. Therefore the present lasts as long as time for the One, and its being older and younger coincides with its becoming older and younger. Further, since it is not and does not become for a longer time than it is and becomes, it is always the same age as itself.

In the same way it is older than what is other than itself. What is other than One must be more than One, and being a multitude must partake in number, and One comes into existence before all other numbers. But it is also younger than what is other than One; for it has beginning, middle, and end, and the beginning comes first into existence and the end last, and One only is when the end has come into existence. Therefore One only comes into existence after its parts. On the other hand, each part is itself one, and so One came into being simultaneously with the beginning and with every subsequent part, and must therefore be the same age as what is other than One.

So much for its *having become* and *being* older and younger than what is other than One; we have still to consider its *becoming* older and younger. On the one hand, it does not become either older or younger than what is other than One; for, if the difference of two ages is given, the addition of equal to unequal times does not alter the (arithmetical) ratio between them. On the other hand, it does become older and younger; for, if the difference of two ages is given, the addition of equal to unequal times does alter the (geometrical) ratio between them.

Therefore One partakes of past, present, and future; it was, it is, it will be; it has become, is becoming, and will become. It can be the object of knowledge, judgement, and sensation; it can be named and spoken of.

COROLLARY

We have seen that One is (1) one and many and neither one or many, and (2) that it partakes in time. We must now consider how the second conclusion affects the first (155 e, 4 *sqq.*).

If One is both one and many, and also partakes in time, it follows that it partakes in being at one time, viz. when it is one, and that it does not partake in being at another time, viz. when it is not one. To begin to partake in being is to come into being, to cease to partake in it is to perish; therefore One must come into being and cease to be (γένεσις καὶ φθορά). Therefore it must be compounded and decomposed again; it must be assimilated and dissimilated again; it must increase and decrease again and be equalised.

Further, it must pass from motion to rest, and again from rest to motion. But how is that possible? How can it stop when it is moving, or start moving when it is at rest? The transition from rest to motion or from motion to rest cannot be either rest or motion, and there is no time at which a thing is neither at rest nor in motion. Therefore the transition must be out of time altogether; it must be in that strange thing (τὸ ἄτοπον τοῦτο), the instantaneous (τὸ ἐξαίφνης), which has position but not duration in time. It is the instantaneous which makes all changes from one opposite to another possible, and it is in the instant of change that what changes has neither the one nor the other of its opposite qualities (155 e — 157 b).

Hypothesis III. — If One is, what are the consequences for the others? (157 b, 6 — 159 b, 1).

The others are other than the One, but they will partake in it both as a whole and as parts. For, since they are others, they are a multitude, and this multitude must have parts or it would be one. Again, it must be a whole and a whole must be one. For, if a whole were not one but many, each part would be part of a many of which it itself was one. Then each would be a part of itself and of each of the others, which is absurd. Therefore they are a whole, that is a complete one made up of them all. Further, each part is also one since it is distinct from the others. Therefore both as a whole and as parts the others partake in One.

Therefore they will be both finite and infinite. For, since they are more than one, they must be an infinite number; for, if we cut off in thought the smallest imaginable portion of what is distinct from One, it will be more than One, and therefore an infinite multitude. On the other hand, at the moment when any part partakes in One, it has a limit both with the other parts and with the whole, and the whole has in the same way a limit with the parts. Therefore it is finite.

So too they will be both like and unlike each other and themselves. As being all finite and all infinite they are like; while, as being both at once, they are unlike. And in the same way it would be easy to show that they are the same and other, at rest and in motion, etc., etc.

Hypothesis IV. — If it is One, what are the consequences for the others? (159 b, 2 — 160 b, 4).

The others will participate in the One neither as a whole nor as parts. For, since there is nothing which is at once other than one and other than others (for One and the others are everything), One and the others cannot be contained in the same thing. Therefore they are quite apart. Further, since One as such has no parts, no part of it can be in the others.

Further, since the others do not participate in One either as a whole or as parts, they are not a whole. Nor can they have multitude or number; for number consists of ones. Therefore they cannot have two properties, such as likeness and unlikeness, to One, nor even one property in themselves, such as Same, Other, Rest, Motion, etc.; for that would imply participation in One.

§ 201. The result of our positive hypotheses, then, is this, One is everything and nothing both in itself and in relation to the others, and the same is true of the others. We now turn to the negative hypotheses.

Hypothesis V. — If One is not, what are the consequences for itself? (160 b, 5 — 163 b, 6).

If we can say that One is not, One must have a meaning, and therefore it must be knowable and there must be knowledge of it. And, as it is other than everything else, it must have altereity (ἑτεροιότης). And it must partake in 'this', 'that', 'anything', etc.; for otherwise it could not be spoken of, nor could what is other than One be spoken of. There is nothing to hinder it partaking in many things, even if it is not. On the contrary, it must do so, if it is *that* One and can be named at all.

Further, in so far as it is other, it must be unlike the others and like itself.

Further, it must be unequal to the others; for, if it were equal, it would be, and would be in so far like them.

On the other hand, since Great and Small belong to the Unequal, and what possesses inequality must possess them; and further, since the possession of Great and Small implies that of Equal as a necessary intermediate, it will possess all three.

Further, it will participate in Being. For, if it is true that the One is not, then the One *is* a not-being. The very bond of its not being is that not-being is, just as the bond of what is is the not being of not-being.

But, if it has both being and not-being, there must be a transition, that is, a movement from the one to the other, and this movement must imply alteration (ἀλλοίωσις).

On the other hand, One, so far as it is not, and therefore is in no place, cannot move from place to place, nor move in the same place round a centre. Nor can it alter without ceasing to be the One which is distinct from the others. Therefore it is immovable and unalterable.

Further, it follows that, in so far as it is moved and altered, it comes into being and ceases to be; in so far as it is unmoved and unaltered, that it neither comes into being nor ceases to be.

Hypothesis VI. — *If there is no One, what are the consequences for itself?* (163 b, 7 — 164 b, 4).

If there is complete absence of being from One, it can neither partake nor cease to partake in Being. Therefore it can neither come into being nor cease to be; it can neither be in motion nor at rest; it cannot stand in any relation to what is, for that would be to partake in Being. Therefore it has neither greatness or smallness or likeness or unlikeness to itself or anything else. Neither is it in a place or in a time. Neither can there be knowledge, judgement or sensation of it; it cannot be spoken of or named.

Hypothesis VII. — *If One is not, what are the consequences for the others?* (164 b, 5 — 165 e, 1).

Since they are others, they must have something that they are other than. They cannot be other than One; for One is not. Therefore they must be other than themselves.

Further, they must be so, not as ones, but as multitudes or masses, of which each can be broken into an innumerable number of similar parts, so that we can never reach a smallest and least part, and that what seemed small appears great compared with each one of the multitude of which it is the sum.

Further, we never come to a beginning, middle, or end, but always to something before the beginning or after the end or in the middle of the middle.

The conclusion is that, if One is not, other things will appear both finite and infinite, one and many.

Hypothesis VIII. — *If there is no One, what will be the consequences for the others?* (165 e, 2 — 166 c, 1).

They will be neither one nor many; for many implies ones. Nor have they even an appearance of one or many; for they can have no communion with what is not, nor can anything which is not be present to anything else; for what is not has no parts.

Therefore we must deny of them not only the reality, but even the appearances of all the predicates which were formerly applied to them really or apparently, likeness and unlikeness, sameness and otherness, contact and separation, etc.

The conclusion of the whole matter is, then, that, whether we assume that One is or that One is not, it itself and what is other than it, regarded both in themselves and in relation to one another, all are and are not, all appear and do not appear.

§ 202. And so it ends. No one has a word to say about this portentous result. If, however, we attend to the hints given in the course of the dialogue itself, we shall hardly be far wrong in drawing the following conclusions from it. In the first place, the Megaric doctrine is refuted. If we postulate a One which is only one (as the Megarics did), we can say nothing whatever about it. Or if (as the Megarics also did) we identify One with Being, we shall have to predicate of it all sorts of incompatible predicates. 'Two statements' (δισσοὶ λόγοι) can be made about the One as well as everything else.

On the other hand, the Sokratic theory has also been refuted in the early part of the dialogue, and that by arguments taken from the Megarics. It was based on the view that, though sensible things may partake in opposite forms, these forms themselves exclude one another. As that is untenable, we must try to find some other way in which things participate (ἄλλο δεῖ ζητεῖν ᾧ μεταλαμβάνει).

The second part of the dialogue has shown once for all the impossibility of maintaining the isolation of the forms from one another. 'The others' are just as hard to grasp as 'the One'. If we regard them abstractly, we can say nothing whatever about them; while, if we regard them as being, we are compelled to ascribe contradictory predicates to them. In fact, the intelligible and incorporeal forms vanish under our hands just as the things of sense had done. It is clearly shown that we must now endeavour to understand in what sense the forms can participate in one another; for all the difficulties of the *Parmenides* arise from the assumption that they cannot.

XIV

Logic

THE SOPHIST

§ 203. The *Sophist* is linked externally to the *Theaetetus*, which is all the more remarkable that the evidence of style shows there was a distinct interval of time between the *Sophist* on the one hand and the *Theaetetus* and *Parmenides* on the other. The influence of Isokrates is strongly marked for the first time, especially in the avoidance of hiatus. In view of this interval of time, we shall be justified in looking for some real connexion between the dialogue and that of which it professes to be the sequel.

Sokrates, Theodoros, and Theaitetos, with the younger Sokrates, his friend and later a member of the Academy, are supposed to meet again on the following day to continue the discussion reported in the *Theaetetus*, but the fiction of the dialogue being read aloud at Megara is quietly dropped. The very title of the work is evidence of the growing coolness between Plato and the Megarics. Isokrates had already given the title of 'Sophists' to the Sokratics generally, but more particularly to the 'eristics', by whom he means mainly the Megarics. Plato adopts this way of speaking from Isokrates, and he also draws a hard-and-fast line between the Philosopher and the Sophist. That is made clear at the outset. A stranger from Elea is introduced, who is represented as a personal disciple of Parmenides and Zeno, and Sokrates at once professes alarm that he may prove to have a superhuman gift for cross-examination. Theodoros reassures him, and says he is far too good a man for an eristic; he is, indeed, a philosopher. Sokrates answers that it is hard to tell Philosophers from Sophists and Statesmen, and asks whether the Eleatics distinguished them. The Stranger replies that they did.

Now Plato seems to speak to us more directly than ever before by the mouth of this Stranger, who, for that very reason, is anonymous; and it seems, too, as if we were meant to understand once more that he claims to be the true successor of Parmenides, even though he is obliged to dissent from his central doctrine that 'not being is not'. What is this 'not-being' which nevertheless is? We shall find that it is identified with 'the Other', and one of the few facts we know about the Megarics is that they said 'What is is One and the Other *is not*.'[1] The name of Sophist is thus by implication applied to the Megarics, and it stuck to them. In fact, it more often means Megaric than not in the fourth century. We have heard of the 'Sophist' Bryson and the 'Sophist' Polyxenos already (§ 192). In Aristotle it is just the arguments of the Megarics that are technically called 'sophisms', and it is with these he mainly deals in his course on fallacies.[2] If this is correct, I do not think it fanciful to suggest further that the reluctance of the Stranger to differ from his master Parmenides with regard to his central doctrine (241 d) is a hint of Plato's own attitude towards Sokrates at this time.

Like several other dialogues, the *Sophist* appears to be made up of two wholly disparate sections bound together in an accidental way. It consists, as has been said, of a kernel and a shell. The shell is the attempt to find a definition of the Sophist by the method of division; the kernel is a criticism of categories, especially that of 'not being' (τὸ μὴ ὄν). The ostensible link between the two discussions is that the definition of the Sophist is found to imply the existence of 'not being', but that is by no means all. We find also that the reason why those who insist on the mere abstract unity of 'what is' (τὸ ὄν) cannot advance beyond contradictory argument (ἀντιλογία) like that of the *Parmenides*, is just that by so doing they have put it out of their power to divide any subject under discussion 'according to its forms' or 'kinds' (κατὰ γένη, 253 c–d). That is what the method of division aims at doing; but it requires to be justified against those who deny that forms are a many, and that defence can only take the shape of a proof that 'not being' (τὸ μὴ ὄν) *is*. Here, as in other cases, the real unity of the dialogue is left for us to discover if we can.

§ 204. It would be tedious to examine in detail the divisions by which the successive definitions of the Sophist are reached. They are not, of course, to be taken too seriously; but neither, on the other hand, are they wholly without purpose. They are marked, in

---

[1] Aristokles (*ap*. Eus. *P.E.* xiv. 17, 1; *R.P.* § 289).
[2] The Περὶ σοφιστικῶν ἐλέγχων.

fact, by a certain not ill-humoured satire, the objects of which it
will not be hard to guess after what has just been said. The Angler
is first selected for definition, merely as an illustration of the method
to be followed. That seems innocent enough; but it soon appears
that the Sophist too is a fisher, a fisher of men, and this leads up to
the definition of him as 'a paid huntsman of rich and distinguished
youths'. That suggests another definition from the point of view of
the art of exchange. He now appears as 'a wholesale exporter of
spiritual goods manufactured by others', though it is slyly added
that he does sometimes dispose of his goods in the home market,
and occasionally even manufactures them himself. Again, he may
be looked on as a fighting man, whose weapons are short questions
and answers; or, again, he may fall under the art of sifting and
purging. He purges the soul from beliefs that are a hindrance to
knowledge, and especially from the ignorance which consists in
thinking one knows what one does not know. Perhaps, however,
we are doing the Sophist too high an honour here, and this is a
higher art than his. We may have been deceived by a resemblance.

Obviously these last definitions do not apply to the great
Sophists of the fifth century. Protagoras and Gorgias are always
represented as averse to discussion by short questions and answers,
and it is Sokrates who forces this method upon them. Again, the
purging of the ignorance that consists in thinking one knows what
one does not know is in the highest degree Sokratic. We are forced,
then, to conclude that the persons aimed at are Sokratics, and the
doubt expressed at the end of the discussion is an insinuation that
they practised an imitation of the Sokratic method, though not
always in the true Sokratic spirit. Once more it can hardly be
doubtful who these are.

§ 205. The next section brings us to the real problem of the
dialogue. We shall find that the Sophist's art is one that produces
deceptive images and so gives rise to false judgements. On the
other hand, the distinction of an image from the object imitated,
and also the opposition of false judgement to true, imply that 'what
is not' in some sense is, and this Parmenides forbade us to assume.
The argument proceeds as follows:

> We have given several accounts of the Sophist, but that shows there
> is something wrong with our method. His art is called by a single
> name, and there must, therefore, be some element which all these
> accounts of it have in common, and to which they all lead up. Now

the account which seemed to point most clearly to this is the description of it as the art of Contradiction (ἀντιλογική). The Sophist professes to dispute on all things visible and invisible, in heaven and on earth, but it is impossible for one man really to understand all these things. Therefore the Sophist is a master of the Art of Appearance. He is like the painter who produces the appearance of solidity by lines and colours on a flat surface, and we may therefore call his art the Art of Imagery (εἰδωλοποιική). That art may be divided into two, that which produces an exact counterpart (εἰκαστική) and that which produces an apparent likeness by deliberately altering the real proportions (φανταστική). The Stranger is about to assign the Sophist's art to the latter when a pressing question of great difficulty emerges (232 a — 236 d).

How, indeed, can there be a deceptive image at all? And further, how is it possible to say or think what is false, without which there can be no deceit? In both cases we are forced to postulate that 'what is not' is (ὑποθέσθαι τὸ μὴ ὂν εἶναι), and that is just what Parmenides would not allow. If we say 'is not', we must apply (προσφέρειν) the words as a predicate to something. We cannot apply them to what is, and, if not, we cannot apply them to anything. But, if we are not speaking of anything, we are speaking of nothing, and are not in fact speaking at all. Nor can anything be applied (προσγίγνεσθαι) as a predicate to 'what is not'. We cannot even say that it is one or many; for number is, and we cannot predicate what is of what is not. But if 'is not' can neither be subject or predicate, it is unutterable and unthinkable. Nay, we have no right to say that it is unutterable or unthinkable or even to call it 'it' (239 a).

Applying this to the Sophist, we find (1) that we cannot without contradiction speak of him as producing an image; for, though an image is really an image, to be really an image is to be really unreal or really what is not (ὄντως οὐκ ὄν). Nor (2) can we speak of his producing an unreal appearance (φάντασμα) without contradiction; for that implies a judgement either that 'what is' is not or that 'what is not' is, and we have seen that such judgements are impossible. There is nothing for it, then, but to consider the dictum of Parmenides and to inquire whether we should not say that, in a certain sense, 'what is not' is, and 'what is' is not (241 d).

A modern reader approaching this discussion for the first time is apt to think either that Plato is about to propound a wanton paradox or that his mind is obsessed by the spectre of some fantastic 'metaphysical' conception of Non-being. That is, firstly, because he is using the language of his time, a language which he did not invent and for which he is not responsible. If he had been writing for us, he would no doubt have formulated the problem in another way. As it was, the Megarics had inherited from Parmenides the doctrine that 'what is not' is not (a doctrine which, in the mouth of its author, had a purely cosmological significance), and they had imported it into Dialectic, with the result that they were led to deny the possibility of significant negation. In the second place, the extreme simplicity with which the problem is stated is disconcerting to the modern mind. That is characteristic of Greek philosophy as a whole, and is one of the things that makes it worthy of study. There is nothing like stating difficulties in their baldest form to ensure that they will not be evaded. The modern reader would feel no difficulty if Plato had announced a discussion of the possibility of significant negative judgements, and that, as a matter of fact, is the subject of this dialogue.[1] It is a good thing, however, to study it in its simplest form and stripped of conventional terminology.

§ 206. In reality, the Stranger proceeds, the reason why we find such difficulties in 'not being' is just that we do not know what is meant by 'being'. Earlier philosophers have not taken the pains to think out clearly the import of certain elementary terms, the meaning of which appears to be obvious, but is really very far from being so. That is why they have only been able to tell fairy tales. Some say the things that are (τὰ ὄντα) are two or three or some other number. Others maintain that what is is one; others, again, seek to combine these views. But no one has asked what we mean by saying of anything that it *is*. This is shown by a criticism of the Pythagoreans, who said things were two, and of the Eleatics, who said they were one.

If all things *are* two (*e.g.* hot and cold), how is the 'being' which this implies related to the two? Either it must be a third thing besides them, or it must be identified with one of them, in which case the other would not be. Or, if we say that 'being' is true of both in the same way, they will be one and not two (243 d — 244 a).

If all things *are* one, then 'being' and 'one' are the same, and only two names for the same thing. But, apart from the absurdity of having two names for the same thing, how can there be a name at all? If the name is other than the thing, they are two and not one, so that, if all things are one, there can only be a name which is a name of nothing, or the thing itself will be a name, and its name the name of a name (244 b–d).

But they also say that the one which *is* (τὸ ὂν ἕν) is a whole. But a whole has parts and is therefore other than one, which as such is indivisible. If, then, 'what is' is a whole, it is a many. On the other hand,

---

[1] It is precisely the problem discussed in Bosanquet's *Logic*, Bk. I. chap. vii., which will be found to throw light on the *Sophist*.

if it is not a whole, it is not the whole of what is, and it can neither come into being nor be; for what comes into being or is comes into being or is as a whole (244 d — 245 d).

This is, of course, a summary of certain arguments in the *Parmenides*, and has a similar purpose. It is as hard to grasp the meaning of *is* as it is to grasp the meaning of *is not*. The difficulty is even greater when we turn from the *number* of what is to its *nature*.

§ 207. With regard to this there is a regular battle of the gods and giants between philosophers. Some identify reality or being (οὐσία) with body, that which admits of impact and contact (ὃ παρέχει προσβολὴν καὶ ἐπαφήν τινα), while others say that true being consists of certain intelligible and incorporeal forms or figures (νοητὰ ἄττα καὶ ἀσώματα εἴδη), while everything corporeal is only a stream of becoming (φερομένη γένεσις).

We must pause here and ask to whom the Stranger is referring; for this is one of the most pressing questions in the history of Greek philosophy. In the first place, it must be observed that the philosophers now under discussion are spoken of as if they belonged to a past generation. It can hardly be correct to suppose that the school of Demokritos are intended by the 'earth-born' (γηγενεῖς). Demokritos, who asserted the reality of the void, could not be spoken of as making impact and contact the test of being. We have seen, however, that the doctrine of Parmenides paved the way for materialism, and that Melissos, who was a very important figure in the latter part of the fifth century, definitely taught a materialistic monism (§ 68). As to the 'friends of the forms' (εἰδῶν φίλοι), of whom Plato speaks with such aloofness by the mouth of the Stranger, if our general view of the doctrine of forms is correct, we have seen that there is no difficulty in identifying them with the later Pythagoreans.[1] At any rate, they can hardly be the Megarics, as is often supposed; for they rejected the plurality of forms altogether, and identified the One and the Good (§ 129). It is worthy of note that the Stranger speaks of them as persons whom he understands, 'thanks to his intimacy with them' (διὰ συνήθειαν), and that suggests they were to be found in Italy. The language in which their doctrine is described is just that of the first part of the *Phaedo*, and they may therefore be identified with the 'we' of that dialogue.

[1] As we have seen (p. 91, *n*. 1) this identification is made without hesitation by Proclus, and is presumably the Academic tradition.

§ 208. The corporealists are hard to deal with; but, if we imagine them for the moment to be more reasonable than they are, we may get them to admit that by reality or being (οὐσία) they in fact mean force (δύναμις).

They must admit that there is such a thing as a mortal animal, and therefore as an animate body, and therefore as a soul. They must further admit that a soul may be good or bad, wise or foolish, and therefore that goodness and wisdom, the presence or absence of which make it one or the other, *are*. Very likely they may say that the soul is body, but they will hardly say that goodness or wisdom are bodies (though it is to be feared the real earthborn would). But, once they admit that a single incorporeal thing *is*, they must accept a definition of being which will apply equally to it. Perhaps they may accept as a definition of what *is* that it is anything that has the least power of acting and being acted upon, that, in fact, being is force (246 e — 247 e).

It is to be observed that the Stranger does not put this definition forward as one satisfactory to himself. Indeed, he says expressly that we shall very likely take a different view later.

If we turn now to those superior persons, the 'friends of the forms', we may expect them to be more tractable, and more ready to admit that what *is* is what can act and be acted upon. As a matter of fact, however, we shall find them even less amenable to argument than our reformed corporealists. They remain in the sky and do not answer us at all, though the Stranger knows from his intimacy with them that they regard us with contempt. They will not ascribe any kind of motion at all to reality or being (οὐσία), and therefore they will not speak of acting or being acted upon in connexion with it.

The 'friends of the forms' distinguish being (οὐσία) from becoming (γένεσις) and say that our souls participate in constant being by means of thought, and our bodies in variable becoming by means of sense. But this participation surely implies that being has a power of acting and being acted upon; for the thought that knows being must, in so doing, either act or be acted upon or both, and the being that thought knows must accordingly either act or be acted upon or both.

To this we may suppose them to reply that being is constant and immovable, and cannot therefore either act or be acted upon. But they must admit that we know being, and knowledge implies soul, and soul implies life and motion. If these are excluded from being and referred to becoming, there can be no knowledge at all. It is equally true, however, that being would be unknowable if it were only variable and in motion; for knowledge implies constancy, and that implies rest (248 a — 249 d).

We have not been able to get any answer out of the 'friends of the forms'; but our discussion with them has suggested that knowledge is impossible unless being is both in motion and at rest. But, as motion and rest are opposites, they cannot be united. On the other hand, they both *are*, and therefore being must be a third thing over and above them. From this it follows that being *per se* is neither at rest nor in motion. What are we to make of this? We see, at any rate, that it is just as hard to say what is meant by *is* as to say what is meant by *is not*, and this gives us a ray of hope. If we can only discover what *is* means, the other difficulty may be got rid of at the same time.

§ 209. We must start from the fact that, when we speak about a thing, we not only name it, but apply many other names to it. When we speak about a man, for instance, we apply to him the names of colours, forms, sizes, virtues and so forth. Of course there are youthful logic-choppers and elderly amateurs (Antisthenes?) who say we have no right to do this. Man is man, and good is good; but, if we say 'the man is good', we are confusing the One and the Many. Such theories are sufficiently refuted by the fact that they cannot be stated without contradiction. Those who forbid us to say that A is B in virtue of A's 'participation in being affected by'[1] B (252 b) have themselves to use such terms as 'is', 'apart from', 'from others', 'by itself', and thus carry about with them an inner voice that refutes their theory.

We must say (1) that all things are incapable of participating in one another, or (2) that all things are capable of participating in one another, or (3) that some things are capable of participating in one another and others are not. In the first case, rest and motion cannot participate in being, and so cannot be. That makes havoc of all the theories we have considered hitherto. In the second case, it will be possible for motion to rest and for rest to move. Only the third case is left, namely, that some things can participate in one another and others cannot (252 e).

We shall find that these simple considerations suggest the solution of the difficulty we have been dealing with.

This solution is briefly that *is* and *is not* have no meaning except in judgements or predications (λόγοι). In one sense, this doctrine is not new. In the *Phaedo* Plato made Sokrates formulate the

---

[1] The phrase κοινωνία παθήματος ἑτέρου is derived from the use of πεπονθέναι to express the relation of a subject to a predicate. Cf. *Parm.* 139 e.

method of seeking for truth in judgements (ἐν τοῖς λόγοις), and there too we have the terminology which represents the subject as 'partaking' in the predicate, and also the way of speaking according to which the subject 'is affected by' (πέπονθεν) the predicate.[1] What is new here is that, whereas in the *Phaedo* it is the particular things of sense that 'partake in' the forms, we are now discussing the participation of the forms or 'kinds' (γένη) with one another. The need for such discussion has been shown in the *Parmenides* (§§ 194, 199). It is to be observed further that these forms or 'kinds' of which we are now speaking are just the common predicates (κοινά) of the *Theaetetus* (§ 186). We may say, if we like, that these are the Platonic forms as distinct from the Pythagorean or the Sokratic.

§ 210. We have found that some forms or kinds will participate in one another and others will not, just as some letters will go with one another and others will not. The vowels, in particular, pervade all combinations of letters, so that without a vowel there cannot be any combination at all. In the same way, some notes in the octave are concordant and others are not. In these two cases we have the arts of Grammar and Music to direct us, and so we require an art which will show us what forms will harmonise with one another and what forms will not, and especially whether there are any kinds which (like the vowels) pervade all combinations and disjunctions (*e.g. is* and *is not*). That is just the art of Dialectic, and the man who possesses that will be able to distinguish what forms can enter into combination and what will not.

> In particular, he will be able to distinguish (1) a single form pervading many single and separate things, (2) many forms distinct from one another but comprehended from without by one, (3) a single form pervading in turn many such wholes and binding them together in one, while many other forms are quite separate and apart from it (253 d).

This passage gives us the foundation of Plato's Logic. The following points in it should be noted:

(*a*) He distinguishes clearly between (1) genus and (2) species, though he uses the terms form and kind (εἶδος, ἰδέα, γένος) indifferently of both.

(*b*) The single forms described under (3) are the 'highest kinds' (μέγιστα γένη), such as Being, Rest, and Motion. These are all of

---

[1] *Phaed.* 104 a.

them 'manners of participation', or, as Aristotle called them, 'forms of predication' (σχήματα τῆς κατηγορίας). They have no meaning except in a judgement.

(c) In the *Phaedo* the question was what particular things admit a given form as their predicate; here the question is one of the compatibility or incompatibility of the 'highest kinds' or forms with one another. Is it possible for any of these to be predicated of one another; and, if so, which can be so predicated and which can not?

(d) As Being is only one of the categories, though the most pervasive of all, it has no meaning except as entering into a judgement. By itself the word 'is' means nothing; it is only the bond that unites a subject to a predicate. We may put this by saying that Plato for the first time discovered 'the ambiguity of the copula', though, for reasons which will appear, he would certainly not have put the thing in that way.

§ 211. To avoid confusion, let us select only a few of the 'highest kinds' (μέγιστα γένη) and consider (1) their nature, and (2) which combine with which and to what extent. In this way we may be able to discover some sense in which we may safely say that there really is such a thing as 'not being'. To begin with, Rest and Motion exclude one another, but both of them *are*, and therefore combine with Being. That gives us three kinds, but each of the three is other than the other two and the same as itself. That gives us a fourth and a fifth kind, Same and Other; for we cannot identify these with any of the first three.[1]

For (1) if we identify either Rest or Motion with any common predicate of both, then it will be predicable of the other, so that Motion will rest or Rest will move. But Same and Other are common predicates of Rest and Motion, therefore neither Rest nor Motion can be identified with Same or Other. Again, (2) if we identify Being and Same, then, as Rest and Motion both *are*, they will be the same. Lastly, (3) we cannot identify Being and Other; for Other is essentially (τοῦτο ὅπερ ἐστίν) relative (πρὸς ἕτερον) and Being is absolute (καθ αὑτό). Therefore Other is a fifth kind (255 a–d).

Now Other pervades all the rest, just like Same and Being; for each of them is the same as itself and other than the rest, and this amounts to saying that each of them *is* itself and *is not* any of the others.

[1] Cf. *Theaet.* 185 a *sq.* (above, p. 247).

Thus Motion, being other than Rest, *is not* Rest, but it *is* Motion. Motion, being other than Same, *is not* Same, but it *is* the same as itself. (We must not mind the apparent contradiction. If we had not shown that Motion and Rest exclude one another, we might even have to say that Motion was at rest.) Again, Motion, being other than Other, *is* Other in a sense and *is not* Other in a sense. Lastly, Motion, being other than Being, *is not* Being, but it *is* Being because they all partake in Being. Motion, then, is really both Not being and Being, and the same thing will apply to all the other kinds, since each of them is other than Being and each of them *is* (255 e — 256 e).

We may say, then, that each of the kinds, in virtue of its otherness, has much Being and infinite Not being. And, as Being itself is other than all the rest, we must say that Being *is not* just as many times as there are other things, and they are innumerable. Not being these, it *is* just itself, but it *is not* the rest innumerable times.

§ 212. But this Not being which we have discovered is not the opposite of Being (like the Not being Parmenides spoke of). The negative term (ἀπόφασις) produced by prefixing 'not' to a word only signifies something *other than* the word which follows the negative, or rather than the thing that word denotes. Now otherness is subdivided into as many parts as knowledge, so, just as there are many sciences and arts with names of their own the parts of otherness will have names of their own. The part of otherness opposed (ἀντιτιθέμενον) to the beautiful is the not-beautiful, which is not other than anything else but beauty, and the not-beautiful *is* just as much as beauty, and so of the not-great, the not-just, and so forth. It is in this combination with a particular part of Being that Not being really *is*; it is 'not being so-and-so', and it *is* just as much as what it is not. We need not trouble ourselves further, then, about the question whether Not being as the opposite of Being can be thought or spoken of or not. In the sense we have now given it, it certainly *is* and is all-pervasive. It is merely childish to separate Being from Not being, and to argue that a thing must either be or not be. The two forms are inseparably bound up with one another, and this is what makes rational speech possible (διὰ γὰρ τὴν ἀλλήλων τῶν εἰδῶν κοινωνίαν ὁ λόγος γέγονεν ἡμῖν 259 e).

What has been proved so far is (1) that everything that is positively determined is also negatively determined, and (2) that negative terms are an expression of reality (δηλώματα τῆς οὐσίας).

It has been shown further, (3) that the reality expressed by a negative term is not the contrary of the corresponding positive term, but its contradictory. On the other hand, it has been shown (4) that, as the negative term must always be understood in relation to the corresponding positive, the reality it expresses is always a particular part of reality, so that 'not-great', for instance, does not include 'beautiful' or 'just', but only 'small'.

§ 213. In the course of the foregoing discussion the remark was thrown out that we have found the Not being which was necessary to justify our account of the Sophist. This is not explained further, but the point is quite simple. We called him an image-maker, and he replied that there was no such thing as an image, since an image is really not real. We now see that there is nothing in this objection; for the art of image-making, like all other arts, includes a part of Being and a part of Not being. The image is not the reality, indeed, and the reality is not the image, but that involves no difficulty. We are dealing with a particular art, that of Image-making, and in it 'not real' has a perfectly definite and positive signification. The 'not real' is not the unreal, but just the image, which *is* quite as much as that of which it is the image.

Even admitting this, however, the Sophist may still say that it is impossible to say or think what is false. Though we have shown that Not being *is*, or in other words that it combines with Being, we have not shown that it combines with speech. But, unless it does so, falsehood is impossible, and so therefore is deceit. We must, therefore, scrutinise carefully (1) speech (λόγος), (2) judgement (δόξα), and (3) appearance (φαντασία), with the view of seeing whether Not being and consequently falsehood can enter into them or not.

We must begin, as we did in the case of letters, by considering whether all words combine with with one another, or whether some will and some will not. There are two kinds of words that are expressions of reality (δηλώματα τῆς οὐσίας) nouns (ὀνόματα) and verbs (ῥήματα). The latter express *action or inaction* or *the reality of being or not being* (*i.e.* the reality expressed by a positive or negative term); the former express the *agent*, or *what is or is not so-and-so*. A statement (λόγος) cannot consist of nouns alone or of verbs alone; the very simplest must have one of each, *e.g.* 'man learns'. Further, every statement must be 'of some one or something' (τινὸς εἶναι), and it must have a certain quality (ποῖόν τινα εἶναι), *i.e.* it must express something which is or becomes in the present, past or future (τῶν

ὄντων ἢ γιγνομένων ἢ γεγονότων ἢ μελλόντων).[1] Now let us make
a simple experiment. If I say 'Theaitetos is sitting', that is a statement
which is 'of Theaitetos', and it has the quality of expressing something which really *is at the present moment*. But, if I say 'Theaitetos,
to whom I am talking *at the present moment* (νῦν), is flying', that is also
a statement which is 'of Theaitetos', but it has the quality of saying
something of him which, though expressing a real action, is something
other than what is real with regard to Theaitetos *at the present moment*.
It is, therefore, possible to speak of what is not as being, and that is
what we mean by falsehood (261 d — 263 d).

In fact, what we call truth and falsehood are not to be found in
terms, whether positive or negative, but only in the proposition,
which is a copulation (συμπλοκή) of terms.

§ 214. It will be observed that significant negative judgement is
explained as the affirmation of a negative predicate (ἀπόφασις),
but it would be altogether wrong to identify this with what
Aristotle calls an 'indefinite' predicate (ἀόριστον ῥῆμα), that is, a
predicate which may be truly predicated of everything alike,
whether existent or non-existent. In the present case, for instance,
'is sitting' excludes every other form of Rest, and therefore 'is
sitting' implies the negative judgements 'is not lying', 'is not
standing', and whatever other forms of Rest there may be. In the
second place, 'is sitting' excludes all the forms of Motion, which
cannot have any communion with Rest, and therefore implies the
negative judgements 'is not walking', 'is not running', 'is not
flying'. The significance of the negative judgement depends, in
fact, on the system of kinds and forms to which it refers, what we
should call a 'universe of discourse'. Plato held that there was a
perfectly definite number of such forms in each kind, which it is
the business of the dialectician to discover. That is why he insists
that 'not being' is subdivided into as many subdivisions as the arts,
and that each 'part' of 'not being' can be understood only in
relation to the corresponding 'part' of 'being'. The negative
predicate 'is not flying' does not include 'is beautiful' or 'is just'.

In the present case, the predicate 'is flying' expresses a real form
of action, a real form of the kind Motion, and it is 'of Theaitetos',
who is a real agent. The reason why the statement 'Theaitetos is
flying' is not true is just that, *at the present moment* (νῦν), Theai-

---

[1] That 'quality' really means tense seems to follow from the context, and
especially from the emphasis on 'to whom I am talking at the present moment'
in the illustration which follows.

tetos 'is sitting', and that predicate excludes 'is flying'. It does not exclude 'was flying' or 'will be flying', and that is why we must attend to the 'quality' of the statement.[1]

§ 215. But, if it is possible to say what is false, it is also possible to think what is false; for thought only differs from speech in this respect, that it is 'the conversation of the soul with itself taking place without voice', while speech is 'the vocal stream issuing from the soul through the lips'. Now we know that positive and negative predication (φάσις and ἀπόφασις) are found in speech, and, when the same things occur silently in the soul, we call them judgement (δόξα). Again, when affirmation and negation take place in the soul, not in virtue of its own activity, but through the agency of sensation, we call that appearance (φαντασία). It follows that, as thought (διάνοια) is mental speech, and judgement (δόξα) is 'the completion of thought', and appearance (φαντασία) is a mixture of sensation and judgement, the truth and falsehood which are possible in speech will also be possible in judgement and in appearance.

Now that he has shown the possibility of false judgement and false appearance, the Stranger goes on to give his final definition of the Sophist. That is of no particular importance for us here, though we may note some interesting points. Of these the most significant is the way in which advantage is taken of the division of productive art into divine and human to assert in impressive language the doctrine that what we call natural objects are the work of God and not of Nature or of Chance. We shall see presently that this thought was occupying Plato's mind at the time, and that he was already trying to work out a rational justification of theism.

---

[1] Most commentators understand by 'quality' the truth or falsehood of the statement, but that would make the argument puerile. There is no point in asking how we know that Theaitetos 'is sitting' now. We see him, of course.

XV

Politics

THE STATESMAN

§ 216. The dialogue entitled the *Statesman* (Πολιτικός) is in form a sequel to the *Sophist*. The characters are the same and the leading part is still taken by the Eleatic Stranger. There is no reason to suppose that the two dialogues are separated by any considerable interval of time.

The discussion begins by an attempt to find the definition of the Statesman by the method of division, and it is easier to trace the connexion of this with the principal theme of the dialogue than it was in the case of the *Sophist*. The first definition we reach represents the King as the Shepherd of Men, as he is already called in Homer. There is good reason for believing that this was the Pythagorean view. The King to them was an 'image' of God upon earth; for God was the shepherd of the world.[1] This is, in fact, the theocratic ideal of kingship. The Eleatic Stranger points out, however, that it rests on a confusion between God and man, and could only be realised if God were in person our ruler. That is the point of the myth related by the Stranger. The course of the world was once directed by God himself, but we are not living in that age. There are seasons when the captain of the world-ship (a Pythagorean conception)[2] retires to his conning-tower and leaves the ship to itself. At those times the world goes round in the opposite direction to that which God had given it, and all natural processes are reversed (an idea which may have been suggested by Empedokles). We are living in one of these periods, and there can be no question for us of a divine ruler. There is a curious hint that, after all, the ideal of mankind as a flock or a herd fed by the hand of God may not be the highest. If the men of those days, who had no need to take thought for the morrow, and who found everything

---

[1] See Campbell's Introduction to the *Statesman*, p. xxv *sq.*
[2] *E. Gr. Ph.*[2] p. 342.

bountifully provided for them without any labour on their part, spent their time in gathering wisdom, and made use of their power to communicate with the beasts in the interests of philosophy, then indeed they were happier than we are. But if they and the beasts spent their time in telling fables to each other such as have been handed down by tradition to our own days, it is not hard to form a judgement as to that either (272 c). This passage is very important. It is plain that the theocratic ideal of the Pythagoreans had little attraction for Plato. He did not think we could get rid of problems by simplifying them out of existence.

§ 217. Let us turn, then, from the divine ruler to the human. He will not be the feeder of his flock, but only its tender (275 e). He will have complete knowledge of what is good for his subjects, and he will secure it for them with or without their consent, just as the doctor who knows what is good for the body will cure his patients whether they like it or not. He will have no need of laws. No law can take account of the infinite variety of particular cases; it can only lay down certain principles in a rough and ready way. If the ruler were able to attend to every case in person, and if he could always be present, it would be absurd for him to trammel himself with laws. If he had to go away for a time, he would no doubt make laws to guide his subjects in his absence, just as a doctor might leave behind him written instructions for his patient. But, when the doctor came back, it would be ridiculous for him to insist on keeping to these instructions. He would feel quite free to alter the treatment if he saw fit. In the same way, if the philosopher king were ever to appear on earth (as he may have done in the past), there would be no need of laws. At present there is no appearance of his return, so we must do as well as we can without him. We must try to frame laws as nearly as possible in accordance with what he would approve, and we must insist upon their being scrupulously observed. If men found they were being badly treated by the practitioners of the arts of medicine and navigation, they would insist upon a code of rules for these arts being drawn up, and upon all transgressions of these being punished, and that is the true place of law in the state. It is only a makeshift ($\delta\epsilon\acute{v}\tau\epsilon\rho os \ \pi\lambda o\hat{v}s$); but, as things are, it is indispensable. It is in this way that Plato deals with the philosopher king of the *Republic*. His rule is still the ideal, but there is no immediate prospect of it being realised. The use of such an ideal is nevertheless very great. In the first place, it gives us a standard by which we can judge existing or possible institutions, and in the second place, it will save us from the mistake of attaching too high a value to these, and refusing in consequence to contemplate any alteration of them. The true point of view from which to regard existing laws and institutions is to look on them as more or less tolerable expedients. They are all alike open to criticism when compared with something higher, and ultimately with the rule of the philosopher king. We may say, then, if we please, that the purpose of the *Statesman* is to determine the provinces of realism and idealism in politics. We must not put the ideal too high, as the theocratic ideal did, but we may make it as high as we please, so long as we take account of human nature. The analogy of the beasts of the field is inapplicable to mankind.

§ 218. Plato goes on to give a classification of constitutions from this point of view, and, as might be expected, it is quite different from that of the *Republic*. There are six constitutions altogether, the rule of the philosopher king being excluded as *hors concours*. The basis of division is twofold. The rulers may be one, few, or many, and they may rule according to law or lawlessly. Of the legal constitutions, kingship comes first, aristocracy second, and democracy third; for the possibility of political knowledge is inversely proportional to the number of rulers. But, when we come to the lawless constitutions, the order is reversed. There is only one name for a constitutional and a lawless democracy, but they are quite different in principle. Of all possible constitutions democracy can do the least good and the least harm, so that, while a constitutional democracy is inferior to aristocracy and still more to constitutional monarchy, even a lawless democracy is far superior to a lawless oligarchy, and still more to a lawless tyranny. Such is the view of Plato, but it would be very hard to imagine Sokrates accepting any such doctrine. Even the Periklean democracy is not harshly treated. It is, of course, a lawless democracy, but it is not condemned so bitterly as it was in the *Gorgias* and the *Republic*. If it cannot do much good, it does relatively little mischief. The legal democracy is more or less the Athenian democracy of Plato's own time, and is placed just below true aristocracy. All this is quite in keeping with what we have learnt as to Plato's political upbringing and experience (§ 158), and it agrees very well with what he says about his political attitude in *Epistle* vii. It was impossible to maintain the Sokratic condemnation of all democracy after the events which marked the end of the fifth century.

But that is not all. Plato does not insist in a doctrinaire fashion on any rigid classification of constitutions. One of the chief functions of the true ruler is just to unite the various elements in the state, as the weaver unites the warp and the woof of his web, and there is room for a number of mixed constitutions as well as for the six types already described. In the *Laws* Plato's final conclusion is that, as things are, and in the absence of the philosopher king, the best constitution will be a combination of legal kingship with legal democracy.[1] He is thus able to take an extremely practical view of political questions, and he is able to do so without abating one jot of his idealism. That is where he goes beyond Sokrates, whose political teaching had not, we have seen (§ 145), been an unmixed blessing to his country.

PLATO AND DIONYSIOS

§ 219. Plato's political teaching in the Academy had an enormous influence through his pupils; for the foundations of Hellenistic civilisation were mainly laid by them. His personal intervention in the politics of the Hellenic nation, which was already coming into being, was in some ways a failure, as the world counts failure. He expected it to be so, and he entered upon it with great misgiving; but it seemed worth trying, nevertheless. It was just possible that he should succeed, and friends of his who were in a position to form a judgement were confident that he would, so he felt unable to shirk the task offered to him. To decline would have been treason to philosophy (*Ep.* vii. 328 e). If he had succeeded, the course of European history would have been altered, and we shall see that his failure was due to causes beyond his control.

In 367 B.C. Dionysios I. of Syracuse died at the age of sixty-three, after a reign of thirty-eight years. He was in many ways a great man, but he had failed in the main purpose of his life, which

---

[1] In the *Laws* the best constitution is a mean between Persian monarchy and Athenian democracy (756 e). Apparently Plato would have been an admirer of the British Constitution. It is also worthy of note that his ideal is not very unlike that of the speech of Perikles in Thucydides, and is just what might be expected of the stepson of Pyrilampes. That does not, of course, imply approval of Periklean democracy with Perikles left out. The illustration from the art of weaving is common to the *Statesman* and the *Laws* (734 e *sqq.*).

was to drive the Carthaginians from Sicily. He had been defeated by Hanno the year before his death, and a peace was now concluded on the basis of the *status quo ante bellum*. His successor, Dionysios II., was nearly thirty years old, but he was quite unfit to take up the reins of government. His father had always been jealous of sharing his power with anyone, and had even sent his ablest minister, Philistos the historian, into exile at Adria, near the mouth of the Po. For the same reason he had purposely kept his son at a distance from all public affairs, and encouraged him to find amusement in such pursuits as amateur carpentry and turning. The young man was not, we are told, without natural gifts, and it seemed to Dion, who was his father's brother-in-law and a devoted admirer of Plato, that something might still be made of him. It was too late to send him to the Academy at Athens, which by this time was the recognised institution for the training of rulers and princes, so Dion conceived the scheme of bringing Plato, now sixty years old, to Syracuse. There was nothing in the least chimerical in the project, and the problems Syracuse had to face made it essential that she should have an enlightened ruler. The great question of the day was once more how Hellenism could maintain itself against the pressure of Persia on the one side and Carthage on the other, and far-sighted statesmen saw clearly that the only hope lay in taking the offensive. We hear most, as is natural, of Persia. The conditions imposed by the King's Peace of 387 B.C., which left the Greek cities of Asia under Persian rule, were humiliating and intolerable. That side of the problem was successfully dealt with later by Alexander, and it was from the Academy that he derived his inspiration;[1] but the situation in Sicily was quite as serious. The Carthaginian question was only another aspect of the Persian question, and it is at least an instructive tradition that represents the battles of Salamis and Himera as having been fought on the same day.[2]

§ 220. Plato refused, however, to let things be rushed. Dionysios had a great deal of ground to make up, and it was necessary for him to go through a serious course of higher study before he could be

---

[1] Plut. *adv. Col.* 1126 d. Delios of Ephesos, an associate (ἑταῖρος) of Plato, was sent to Alexander by the Hellenes who lived in Asia, and did most to enflame him and stir him up to engage in war with the barbarians.

[2] It is interesting to note that the struggle between Hellenes and Semites had also been going on in Cyprus, the other great 'meeting-place of races'. Isokrates played a similar part there to that which Plato played in Sicily, — in his own way, of course.

trusted to make even a beginning with schemes of reform and liberation.[1] Unfortunately he was rather old for this. According to Plato's own principles, he ought to have begun these studies at the age of twenty, so it was natural enough that, after the first enthusiasm had passed, he should feel them irksome. That was the opportunity of the opposition who still clung to the principles of the elder Dionysios. Philistos (or, as Plato calls him, Philistides) had been recalled from exile, and he set himself at once to undermine the influence of Dion and Plato. The somewhat masterful and haughty temperament of Dion also played into his hands, and it was not hard to persuade Dionysios that his kinsman was taking too much upon himself. Only four months after Plato's arrival Dion was banished, and Plato saw it was all over with the project of reform. On the other hand, Dionysios had no idea of losing Plato, to whom he had become deeply attached. He had, in fact, been jealous of Dion's intimacy with him, and hoped to have him more to himself now Dion was out of the way. It was not to be expected that Plato would give up his friend, however, and he pressed his claim in season and out of season. A situation which threatened to become impossible was ended by the outbreak of war. Dionysios had to interrupt his studies, and Plato was free to return to Athens. The understanding was that at the conclusion of the war Dion should be restored to his old position, and that then Plato would return. On his way home he visited Archytas at Taras.

§ 221. It is not very likely that Dionysios was sincere in his promise to become reconciled to Dion, but he was determined to get Plato back at all costs. He tried to carry on his mathematical studies in his absence, and made the subject quite fashionable at court. At first Plato declined to return unless Dion was reinstated, but he was urgently entreated to do so by Dion himself and by

[1] Grote thinks Plato was wrong here, but that seems very doubtful. If he was not to give Dionysios a regular training like that of the Academy, what was the use of his coming to Syracuse at all? Possibly the men of those days believed too much in science, but their belief in it was perfectly sincere. Prof. Bury's view is even more remarkable. He thinks (vol. ii. p. 247) that Plato should have contented himself 'with inculcating the general principles which he has expounded with such charm in the *Republic*', in which case 'Dionysius would in all likelihood have attempted to create at Syracuse a dim adumbration of the ideal state'! In that case, we may add, the Carthaginians would have annexed Syracuse. Plato was no utopian dreamer, and the notion that he proposed to introduce the arrangements of the *Republic* at Syracuse (of all places) is quite unsupported by any sort of evidence.

Archytas, the most successful statesman of the day. He ought
certainly to have been a good judge of the situation, and he assured
Plato that Dionysios was really enthusiastic about philosophy, and
that everything would now go smoothly. With great reluctance
Plato accordingly made up his mind (361 B.C.) to 'recross
Charybdis' (*Ep*. vii. 345 e); but he soon discovered that Dionysios
had not the slightest intention of doing anything for Dion, and a
breach became inevitable. Plato wished to go home, but Dionysios
would not let him. No ship captain would venture to take him as a
passenger in the circumstances, and he had to wait a whole year.
At last a violent quarrel broke out on the occasion of a military
revolt. Dionysios made Herakleides, one of his officers, responsible
for it, and Plato with great difficulty got him off.[1] Dionysios could
not forgive the way in which he had been shamed into an act of
clemency, and bitterly reproached Plato with having hindered
him in the work of reform and the liberation of the Hellenic cities
under Carthaginian rule. Instead of that he had made him learn
geometry! Plato was excluded from the court and practically kept
a prisoner, until, on the intercession of Archytas, he was at last
allowed to return to Athens (360 B.C.). Even then there was no
final breach. Dionysios kept writing to Athens for explanations of
difficult points, and Plato answered him. He even wrote a book,
much to Plato's annoyance, in which he professed to disclose the
Platonic philosophy. It is clear that Archytas and Dion were not
wrong in believing he had some natural gifts, but they had not
been cultivated early enough. He was vain and petulant, no doubt,
but his attachment to Plato was obviously sincere, and we cannot
help feeling a little sorry for him, when we remember what he
might have been if his father had given him a chance when he was
young enough to profit by it.[2]

§ 222. At this point Plato's personal responsibility for the affairs
of Syracuse ceases, but Dion was still to be reckoned with. He was
not the sort of man to wait for ever, and he began to collect
adherents all over Hellas. He had determined to assert his rights
by force of arms. Plato would take no part in the adventure, but
the young hotbloods of the Academy were eager in the cause of

[1] We gather from the *Epistles* that Plato was very unpopular with the mercenary troops. These wild Keltic warriors knew very well that if Plato had his
way their day was over.
[2] This may be why Dion had tried to secure the succession for the sons of
Dionysios I. by Aristomache. They were much younger.

their fellow-student, among them Plato's nephew, Speusippos, and Eudemos of Cyprus, the friend after whom Aristotle named his dialogue on immortality.[1] All preparations were completed by the summer of 357 B.C., but difficulties began at once. Herakleides, who had gone into exile after the incident described above, would not subordinate himself to Dion and remained behind. With only 800 men Dion set sail for Sicily. Philistos was waiting for him in the Adriatic; but Dion eluded him by sailing straight across the sea instead of following the usual coast route. Once landed in Sicily he received accessions of strength from every side. Dionysios, who had not expected an attack in this direction, was in Italy, and Dion made himself master of Syracuse. All might now have been well had Dion been a little more conciliatory. Herakleides arrived on the scene and had to be given a share in the government, but this proved a constant source of weakness, and led at one time to the temporary deposition of Dion. This is not the place to recount the wretched details of the three-cornered struggle between Dionysios, Dion, and Herakleides; it will be enough to indicate its result. Herakleides was murdered at the instigation of Dion, and Dion himself fell by the dagger of Kallippos, an Athenian and a member of the Academy, who had been his most confidential adviser. Kallippos only held power for about a year, when he was once more expelled by Dion's partisans.

Plato felt deeply the discredit which the treachery of Kallippos had brought upon Athens and the Academy, but he never wavered in his belief in Dion's integrity. He was well aware of the defect in his character which has been pointed out,[2] but he continued to regard him as perfectly sincere and disinterested in his political action. In support of this estimate it may be observed that it would have been comparatively easy for Dion, who was closely related to the royal house, to brush Dionysios aside at the beginning of his reign and seize the power for himself. Instead of that he did his best, in conjunction with Archytas, to fit the young prince for the position he was called upon to occupy. If he was embittered by the return he received for this act of self-abnegation, we can hardly

---

[1] Eudemos lost his life in one of the combats round Syracuse.

[2] In his letter congratulating Dion on his success (*Epistle* iv.) Plato tells him that some people think him too deficient in complaisance, and warns him against this fault (321 b). He is very anxious that the rule of Dion should do the Academy credit. He reminds him that the 'you know whos' (τοὺς οἶσθα δήπου 320 c) are expected to surpass others even more than grown men surpass children.

wonder at it. His property had been confiscated, and his wife had been compelled to marry another man.

§ 223. The overthrow of Kallippos was the occasion of Plato's last endeavour to do something for Sicily. The partisans of Dion asked him for advice with regard to the settlement of the constitution, and this gave him the opportunity of writing the two open letters to which we owe all our knowledge of these affairs. The first (*Epistle* vii.) is a dignified defence of his own political attitude throughout life, and it bears witness at once to his disappointment in men whom he had trusted, and to his unshaken confidence in his principles. He is willing to advise the partisans of Dion, if they are really sincere in their desire to realise Dion's plans. He clearly does not feel sure of them. In the second letter (*Epistle* viii.) he suggests, however, a scheme for the government of Syracuse, in which Dionysios himself was to be asked to take a share, if he would accept it, along with Hipparinos, his brother, and Hipparinos, the son of Dion. It need hardly be said that this proposal was too statesmanlike to be accepted by embittered party men, and so the Syracusan Empire broke up for the time being. As Plato saw, it was in danger of falling into the hands of the Carthaginians or the Oscans.[1]

We have seen how very nearly Plato came to succeeding. At the very least he might have done for Dionysios what the Pythagorean Lysis did for Epameinondas. It was said at the time that the prosperity of Thebes at this date was due entirely to the philosophers.[2] And he might have done even more with more promising material. If it had been an Alexander of Macedon that Plato had to deal with instead of a Dionysios, a Greek king would have been ruling at Carthage before many years had passed. As it was, it was left for the Romans to carry out the task which seemed to fall naturally to the ruler of Syracuse,[3] and that brought about the division between Eastern and Western Europe which, to all appearance, will be the great political problem of the immediate future.

---

[1] *Ep.* viii. 353 e.

[2] Alkidamas said: Θήβησιν ἅμα οἱ προστάται φιλόσοφοι ἐγένοντο καὶ εὐδαιμόνησεν ἡ πόλις (Ar. *Rhet.* 1398 b, 18).

[3] The First Punic War broke out just eighty years after the final expulsion of Dionysios II. from Syracuse by Timoleon. Plato did not live to see either the brief restoration of Dionysios (345 B.C.) or his final overthrow (344 B.C.). After that Dionysios lived the life of a dilettante at Corinth, where Aristoxenos saw him, and asked him the cause of his quarrel with Plato. Dionysios answered that no one tells a tyrant the truth, and that he had been robbed of Plato's goodwill by want of frankness in his so-called friends (Plutarch, *Timoleon*, 15).

THE LAWS

§ 224. It must not be supposed, however, that Plato's attempt to make a constitutional ruler of Dionysios bore no fruit, even at the time. It was the immediate occasion of his undertaking his longest and most comprehensive work. It is true that a credible tradition represents the *Laws* as having been published after Plato's death by Philip of Opous, and it is likely enough that he never gave the finishing touch to the work. That is quite consistent, however, with its having been begun a good many years earlier. It is a treatise which goes into great detail, and which must have called for considerable study of existing codes of law. Now in *Epistle* iii. (316 a), writtern shortly after 360 B.C., we are told expressly that Plato had been working with Dionysios at the 'preambles' (προοίμια) to laws during his second visit to Syracuse. This is explained by a passage in the *Laws* itself (722 d *sqq.*), where we are told that the legislator ought always to preface his laws by a 'prelude' (προοίμιον) in which he explains their motive. That gives us some insight into Plato's method of teaching politics and jurisprudence, which is quite in accordance with the doctrine of the *Statesman*. In order to frame a code of laws on any subject, we must first of all lay down clearly the general principles which are to guide us, and then go on to embody these in detailed enactments. The general principles will as far as possible be such as would be approved by the ideal ruler who can dispense with laws altogether; the particular enactments will take account of the circumstances of the state for which they are intended.

The fiction of the dialogue is that a colony is to be established in Crete on a deserted site, and the magistrate of Knossos who is charged with the duty of legislating for it is represented as consulting an Athenian Stranger and a Spartan on the subject. The very first questions asked before legislation in detail is attempted are whether the new city is on the coast or inland, whether the soil is fertile or not, and the like (704 a *sqq.*). There is no attempt to legislate for a city in the abstract; we are dealing with a particular colony, and we have to take account of all the special circumstances affecting it.

§ 225. There is no work of Plato's which has been so little appreciated as the *Laws*, and yet it contains much of his maturest thought which we should otherwise know nothing about, and embodies the results of a long and varied experience of human life. It is, of course, impossible to summarise it here; all that can be done is to suggest certain points which may help the reader to a juster view of what Plato himself probably considered his most important work.

He still believed, in spite of his disappointment with Dionysios, that the co-operation of a tyrant with a philosopher would result in the greatest blessings for the Hellenic nation, and he reasserts this conviction emphatically (709 e). Failing that, however, much might be hoped from the influence of philosophy on law-givers and framers of constitutions. He did not, therefore, think it an unworthy use of his last years to codify what seemed best to him in Greek Law, public and private, and especially in the Law of Athens, supplementing it with legislative proposals of his own. To understand this we must try to realise the condition of the Greek world at the time. We are not accustomed in this country to systematic legislation (what the Greeks called νομοθεσία), though such things as the Code Napoléon may give us a notion of what is meant, but it was very familiar to the Greeks. Every colony had a written constitution and a code of laws, and the task of framing these was regularly entrusted to a single individual or a small commission. The situation presupposed in the *Laws* was of almost everyday occurrence, and there is nothing extravagant in the idea that a man like the Athenian Stranger — who is more or less Plato himself — should be able to give valuable assistance in such circumstances. It is certain, indeed, that many of the men who gave laws to the Greek States at this time were members of the Academy, and that several States applied to the Academy for an expert legislator when they were amending their constitutions.[1] The purpose of the *Laws* is, therefore, an eminently practical one, and the work is designed to meet a real need of the time.

§ 226. No doubt it may seem strange to a modern reader that Plato should devote so much attention as he does to minute police regulations about water-supply and the picking of ripe fruits by the passing wayfarer. As to that, there are two remarks to be made. In the first place, one of Plato's most deeply rooted convictions is that all human affairs are very insignificant in comparison with the

[1] Plut. *Adv. Col.* 1126 c Πλάτων δὲ τῶν ἑταίρων ἐξαπέστειλεν᾽ Ἀρκάσι μὲν᾽ Ἀριστώνυμον διακοσμήσοντα τὴν πολιτείαν, Ἠλείοις δὲ Φορμίνα, Μενέδημον δὲ Πυρραίοις. Εὔδοξος δὲ Κνιδίοις καὶ᾽ Ἀριστοτέλης Σταγειρίταις, Πλάτωνος ὄντες συνήθεις, νόμους ἔγραψαν᾽ παρὰ δὲ Ξενοκράτους᾽ Ἀλέξανδρος ὑποθήκας ᾔτησε περὶ βασιλείας.

immensity of the world, and that the events of the day are only an incident in the history of mankind through countless ages. Sometimes he feels that Man is perhaps no more than a plaything of God, and that human life is not after all a serious thing. Unfortunately, whether it is serious or not, we have got to take it seriously (803 b), but it is absurd to suppose there is much to choose between one department of it and another in point of worth and dignity. Nothing is too humble, as nothing is too exalted, for the philosopher's attention.

Closely connected with this is his belief that homely examples are often the best to illustrate important principles. He had learnt that from Sokrates, and he had discussed the matter in the *Statesman*. This is particularly the case in jurisprudence. Jurists, who presumably know their business, do not quarrel with the *Institutes* for their minute discussions of the ownership of stray animals and swarming bees. It is not to be supposed that these questions were treated entirely for their own sake by the Roman lawyers; it is because such simple instances are the best for the purpose of bringing out the fundamental principles of law.

This brings us to another very important point. We have seen that many of Plato's associates became lawgivers, and it is hardly too much to say that his work is the foundation of Hellenistic Law. That explains the fact, which was perfectly well known to some of the older jurists like Cujas, though it is often overlooked at the present day, that many features of Roman Law are derived from this source.[1] The direct influence of Greek philosophy on Roman Law has probably been overestimated, but its indirect influence has hardly been done justice to. The way in which this came about was as follows. When the Romans came into closer contact with non-Roman peoples, that is to say, especially with the Greek communities of Italy and Sicily, it was found that the principles of their civil law could not be applied easily to the relations between Romans and foreigners or to the relations of foreigners with one another. Hence arose the *jus gentium*, which, in its origin, was a sort of common law of Italy. This was administered by the *praetor peregrinus* and embodied in his edict, which was simply an announcement of the principles on which he intended to decide

---

[1] See Cuiacii Comm. in lib. xlix. Pauli ad Edictum, ad § *ad Namusam et seq.*: *multa . . . auctores nostri ex Platone mutuati sunt.* Examples are given in Observationum lib. xxiv. c. 24.

certain cases. The edict was handed down from praetor to praetor with such modifications as were required from time to time, and ultimately became a regular body of law, the *jus honorarium*. It was inevitable that many of its provisions should be modelled on the laws of the Hellenic states with which the Romans came in contact, and these in turn were profoundly influenced by the jurisprudence of the Academy. Now that Hellenistic law is becoming better known from the papyri, we may confidently anticipate some valuable discoveries in this field.

EDUCATION

§ 227. In the next chapter we shall be dealing with the most abstract aspect of Plato's philosophy, so it will be well to give here a brief sketch of the educational system recommended in the *Laws*. This will keep us in mind that these highly abstract speculations went hand in hand with the most intense interest in concrete detail. It will also be useful from another point of view. The educational theories of Plato are chiefly known from the *Republic*, and it is often forgotten that there is a much fuller and more practical treatment of the subject in the *Laws*.

The first thing to secure is that babies shall be straight (788 d), for everything depends on the start. A human being may go on growing till he is twenty, but quite half of this growth is accomplished in the first five years. Now growth implies nourishment, and the nourishment of babies is very great in proportion to their size. It follows that they must have a great deal of bodily exercise up to the age of five. The simplest way of putting this is to say that babies should live as if they were always at sea. Even nurses know that from experience, for when they wish to put babies to sleep they employ action, not rest, for the purpose. They shake them up and down in their arms, and they do not use silence, but sing to them. The Korybantic purifications depend on the same principle (790 d).

The next point to notice is that small babies scream and kick, while larger ones shout and jump about in a disorderly fashion. For three years babies can only express their wants by crying; and as three years is a considerable portion of a human life to spend well or ill, education must start from this fact, and build upon it. Pleasure and pain are the only feelings young children know, and we might suppose it the right thing to give them all the pleasure and save them all the pain we can. That, however, is wrong. What we wish to train them to is that state of calm which is as far removed from positive pleasure as from pain. In order to do this we must take advantage of the fact that from the very earliest age children take pleasure in tune and time. These two things must therefore be our chief educational instrument for the first three years of life; for, by developing this instinct, we can gradually transform the natural screams and shouts into song, and the kicks and jumps into dance. Punishment should begin at the age of three, but we must be careful not to employ forms of punishment which will produce anger and sullenness. As to games, they are instinctive at that age, and when a few small children are brought together, they will invent them of their own accord. It is best to leave them to do so.

From three to six children should be taken to the religious services of their village, and this at once raises the thorny problem of nurses. There must be a committee of twelve ladies appointed by the head of the Education Department to supervise all the nurses. They will divide the country into districts, and each will visit all the temples and celebrations in her own district, at least once a year, to see that the nurses behave. It is a good plan for the grandparents to live at some distance and have the children sent to visit them. In that way it is possible to make sure that they really do get the outing they are supposed to get.

The education of boys and girls should be separate from the age of six, for at that age they begin actual lessons. The boys are to be taught riding and archery and the use of the sling. The girls are also to be taught the use of arms as far as possible. We must also get rid of the superstition of mothers and nurses that the right hand is to be preferred to the left. It makes us only half able-bodied.

The chief instruments of education at this stage will be music and gymnastics, for which we have prepared the children by the use of time and tune and by shaking them when they were small. Gymnastics has two main divisions, dancing and wrestling. Music has two functions — one the accompaniment of the noble words of the poets, the other the accompaniment of dances and other exercises of the limbs. We must not teach the children anything elaborate or professional, but only simple physical drill with simple songs, taking as our model what is required in war and the service of the gods. The question of games and toys becomes more important at this age. The main thing is that each generation should play the same games and have the same toys as the last, for only so can the spirit of the constitution be preserved. The greatest of all revolutionaries is the man who invents new games and finer toys, for the boy who has played different games in youth will grow up a different sort of man. In things which are not in themselves bad change is dangerous, and therefore the preservation of the old games is a fundamental interest of the state. As to music, we must take it as our guiding principle that rhythms and melodies are imitations of character. They are the most direct imitation there is of anything — far more direct than painting and sculpture, for instance — but what they imitate is not the outward appearance but disposition of soul. These, then, must be preserved unaltered too. New melodies and rhythms will destroy the spirit of the constitution. Tragedy will be excluded, of course. We cannot allow competing choruses to blaspheme in the immediate neighbourhood of the altars.

The difficult task of selecting songs and dances will be left to a jury consisting of men over fifty, who will accept or reject the old ones, or, if necessary, call in expert assistance to correct their melody and rhythm. If the children are once accustomed to the sober and ordered Muse, when they hear the opposite kind of music, the sweet kind, they will think it only fit for slaves. On the other hand, if they have been habituated to the sweet Muse in early life, they will find true music cold and harsh. There must be separate songs for boys and girls, differing in pitch and time. The boys' music will imitate the proud and brave character, the girls' the modest and pure. Gymnastics must be taught to girls also. There is no reason for supposing that riding and gymnastics are suitable for boys and not for girls. It is true that women are not so strong as men, but that is no reason for their not being made to do what they can. A state that makes no call upon its women for military service is not much more than half as strong as it might be made at the same expense. It would be better that they should be relieved to some extent from household occupations, which might be simplified by the introduction of co-operative methods. At any rate, the human race should be freed from the disgrace of being the only one in which the females are incapable of defending the life of their young.

We have not yet touched on the manner in which these things are to be taught. It is not merely a technical one. Everything depends on the object we have in view. Just as a shipbuilder constructs a ship with a view to a certain kind of voyage, so our educational methods must be determined by a view of the best way to make the voyage of life. Perhaps it does not matter from the point of view of God, but we must at least play the game if it is one, and who knows but it may be more. Even if men and women are God's playthings, that is, after all, the best thing about them. The trouble is that people draw the distinction between jest and earnest, work and play wrongly. They suppose, for instance, that war is earnest and peace is not. That is wrong. Peace is more earnest than war, and a great deal that is taken for play is really the highest kind of work.

The question of school buildings is of great importance. The teachers must have salaries, and therefore (this is very Greek) they must be foreigners. Education must be compulsory. It cannot be left to the fathers of families to educate their children or not as they please, for they belong even more to the state than to their fathers. So far we have been dealing with what we should call elementary education, which was all the education most men had in Plato's time.

§ 228. But now comes the question what our young people are to do now that their preliminary training is finished. Is there something further, or are they to live the life of cattle being fattened for the market? Certainly not. Now is the time for real hard work; all the rest, including the military training, has really been play. There is no time to lose. In very truth every day and night of our lives, if devoted to that alone, is barely sufficient for a complete, or even an adequate education. The employment of each day must therefore be carefully ordered from one sunrise to the next. It would be unseemly for the legislator to enter into domestic details, but we may say at once that it is monstrous for those who are to guard a city to sleep all night, and that it is not proper for the mistress of a house to be wakened by her maids. She should be up first and see that the maids are up. A man who is asleep is worthless, and he who cares most to be alive and thinking keeps awake longest. It is wonderful how little sleep we need when we get into the habit of doing with little. The boy must therefore go to school before sunrise. He wants careful watching; for he is the most awkward of beasts to handle. That is just because he has what other beasts have not, a native spring of thought in him which is not yet settled or clear. Boys will now study things written, and not all of them in metre. Along with that will go at first the tuning of the lyre (not necessarily the playing of it), so much reckoning as is useful for war and housekeeping, and a certain amount of astronomy, enough to make the calendar intelligible. These things are not to be confused with the sciences, which come later.

The question arises how far a man who is to be a good citizen must go in these subjects. A boy should begin reading and writing at the age of ten and spend three years on them; music need not be begun till he is thirteen, and should be continued for three years. These times should be made compulsory whether the boy or his father has any taste for the subjects or not. It will be enough if the boys can read and write intelligibly; it is only in cases of special talent that we should encourage a higher degree of excellence. The time and trouble it takes are better spared for the higher studies.

That the boys will read poetry of the right sort is a matter of course, but prose seems a very dangerous thing. Even as to poetry there is the question whether it should be read in masses and whole poets learnt by heart, or whether we should use books of extracts and make our pupils commit these to memory. But, as has been suggested, the real difficulty is the educational use of prose. Books about the principles of legislation may certainly be read, but the works of philosophers and scientific men are not safe at this stage. All these things will be regulated by the head of the Education Department, but he will have expert advice on technical questions. He will not allow the experts to dictate to him on general principles, but will consult them as to the methods of carrying them out.

§ 229. We come now to the higher studies, beginning with Mathematics, in its three chief divisions of Arithmetic, Geometry, and Astronomy. Only a small number will pursue these studies to the end, those, namely, who show themselves fit to become members of the Nocturnal Council, but the prevailing ignorance of them can only be described as 'swinish' (819 d). And that is not the worst. Most teachers treat mathematical subjects in the most perverse manner, and the greatest evil is not total ignorance, but much learning and knowledge misdirected. Most people take it for granted that all lengths, breadths and depths are commensurable, whereas it is really the problem of incommensurability that should hold the first place in mathematical education. The study of questions arising out of this is a far better game than backgammon. The teaching of astronomy must be reformed on similar lines.

We may easily miss the significance of Plato's proposals as to the education of boys and girls from the age of ten onwards. We must remember that in his day there were no regular schools for young people of that age. They were taken to one teacher for music-lessons and to another to be taught Homer, and there was no idea of coordinating all these things in a single building under a single direction with a regular staff of teachers. By founding the Academy Plato had invented the university, and now he has invented the secondary school. In consequence we find such schools everywhere in the Hellenistic period, and the Romans adopted it with other things, quaintly translating the Greek term σχολή by *ludus*. That is the origin of the medieval grammar school and of all that has come out of it since. It will be seen that the *Laws* is not a work we can afford to despise if we wish to understand Plato's influence, but it is time to turn to a very different side of his activity.

XVI

The Philosophy of Numbers

§ 230. It is by no means easy for us at the present day to interpret the central doctrine of Plato's philosophy. As we have seen (§ 162), he did not choose to commit it to writing, and we are almost entirely dependent on what Aristotle tells us. What makes matters worse is that Aristotle is a very unsympathetic critic of Plato's teaching, and that he looks at it too much in the light of certain results to which it had led in the Academy of his own day. In one place he complains that the men of his time (οἱ νῦν) had replaced philosophy by mathematics.[1] That was repugnant to him as a biologist, and he made the teaching of Plato responsible for it. We shall have to see how far he was justified.

In dealing with Aristotle's evidence, it is necessary to make two distinctions. We must, in the first instance at least, distinguish (1) between doctrines attributed to Plato by name and doctrines vaguely stated to be those of 'some', a way of speaking which may include Pythagoreans and the contemporary Academy. We must also distinguish even more carefully (2) between statements as to facts which must have been well within Aristotle's knowledge and his interpretation of these facts. When he tells us, for instance, that Plato held numbers to be unaddible, we are bound to believe him. He could not have made such a statement unless it was true and was known to be true by his contemporaries. On the other hand, when he tells us what Plato really meant by this, we have to remember that he is one of those people who always know what another man means better than he knows himself. Above all, when he describes the historical origin of any doctrine, we must bear in mind that he is speaking of things he could know nothing about except from inference or hearsay. These obvious distinctions are often ignored. Speculations as to the influence exercised on Plato by Sokrates and Kratylos years before Aristotle was born are quoted

[1] *Met.* A. 9, 992 a, 32: γέγονε τὰ μαθήματα τοῖς νῦν ἡ φιλοσοφία.

as evidence of fact, and at the same time a philosophy is expounded as Plato's, which differs in the most important points from that which Aristotle says he heard from his own lips.

One thing, at any rate, seems clear. Aristotle knows of but one Platonic philosophy, that which identified the forms with numbers. He never indicates that this system had taken the place of an earlier Platonism in which the forms were not identified with numbers, or that he knew of any change or modification introduced into his philosophy by Plato in his old age.[1] That is only a modern speculation. Aristotle had been a member of the Academy for the last twenty years of Plato's life, and nothing of the kind could have taken place without his knowledge. We may be sure too that, if he had known of any such change, he would have told us. It is not his way to cover up what he regards as inconsistencies in his master's teaching. If the 'theory of Numbers' had been no more than a senile aberration (which appears to be the current view), that is just the sort of thing Aristotle would have delighted to point out. As it is, his evidence shows that Plato held this theory from his sixtieth year at least, and probably earlier.

§ 231. It is certain, then, that Plato identified forms and numbers; but, when we ask what he meant by this, we get into difficulties at once. In the last two books of the *Metaphysics* (M and N), which deal expressly with the objects of mathematics (τὰ μαθηματικά) and with forms and numbers, the name of Plato is only mentioned once (1083 a, 33), and the doctrine there attributed to him is that numbers 'are not addible to one another' (οὐ συμβλητοὺς εἶναι τοὺς ἀριθμοὺς πρὸς ἀλλήλους). In an earlier passage (1080 a, 12 *sqq.*) three versions of the doctrine that numbers are 'separate' (χωριστά) and the first causes of things are given as the only possible ones, but no names are mentioned. We are even told (1081 a, 35) that one of these versions had never been held by anybody, which does not prevent Aristotle (if he is the author of these books) from refuting it as vigorously as the other two. Obviously we cannot make anything of this for the present, and it is unsafe, at least in the first instance, to use these books as evidence except for the single doctrine attributed in them to Plato by name.

---

[1] In M. 4. 1078 b, 9 *sqq.*, it seems to me impossible to identify those who 'first said there were forms' with Plato, though it must be admitted that things are said of them which are said of Plato in A. 6. The explanation is, I think, that in both cases Aristotle is thinking primarily of the εἰδῶν φίλοι in the *Phaedo* (cf. p. 280).

§ 232. There is, however, a chapter in the First Book of the *Metaphysics* (A. 6) which seems more hopeful. It is the only place where Aristotle professes to give a careful statement of Plato's philosophy, attributing it to him by name and distinguishing it from other systems. The method he adopts is to compare Platonism with Pythagoreanism, which, he says, it followed in most respects (τὰ πολλά), though it had two peculiarities (ἴδια Πλάτωνος) which distinguished it from 'the Italic philosophy'. These two points of difference were as follows: (1) The Pythagoreans said that numbers were things, while Plato held not only that sensible things were distinct from (παρά) numbers, but also regarded the objects of mathematics as distinct from both and intermediate between them. (2) The Pythagoreans held the matter of numbers to be the Unlimited and their form the Limit; Plato regarded the elements of number as the One and the dyad of the Great-and-Small.

These two points are all that Aristotle regards as really peculiar to Plato; for he looks upon the substitution of the term 'participation' for 'imitation' as a merely verbal difference. Both the Pythagoreans and Plato left it an open question (ἀφεῖσαν ἐν κοινῷ ζητεῖν) what imitation or participation of things in forms could be. That is the outline of the chapter, but it is somewhat confused by a long parenthesis intended to show that the first difference between Plato and the Pythagoreans was due to the influence of Herakleitos (through Kratylos) and Sokrates. That may or may not be correct, but Aristotle's statements on this subject do not stand on the same level as his account of the peculiarities themselves, which he must have heard Plato expound.

I. FORMS, MATHEMATICALS AND SENSIBLES

§ 233. The first of these peculiarities is, then, that, while the Pythagoreans said numbers were things, Plato regarded sensible things as distinct from numbers, and made the objects of mathematics intermediate between the two. It is important to observe that Aristotle is here contrasting Plato with the Pythagoreans and not with Sokrates, who is only introduced to explain his divergence from the Pythagorean theory of numbers. It is also to be noted that by 'Sokrates' Aristotle means, as he usually does, the Sokrates of the *Phaedo*. We are expressly told (987 b, 29) that the distinction made between numbers and the sensibles and the 'introduction' (εἰσαγωγή) of the forms was due to the practice of 'considering things in statements' (διὰ τὴν ἐν τοῖς λόγοις ἐγένετο σκέψιν) and that is as clear a reference as can be to the new method introduced by Sokrates in that dialogue (99 e sqq.). We are also told that the predecessors of Sokrates were unversed in dialectic, and that is explained by what has been said above (987 a, 20) about the Pythagoreans. They began, we are told, to discuss the 'What is it?' of things (τὸ τί ἐστιν;), and to define them, but in a naïve and superficial way. Sokrates introduced universal definitions and busied himself with ethical matters instead of with nature as a whole, and it was Plato's acceptance of his method that made it impossible for him to follow the Pythagoreans in identifying numbers with things. He had convinced himself of the Herakleitean doctrine that sensible things were in flux, and he saw that the definitions of Sokrates could not apply to them, so he gave the name of forms to something other than sensible things, and said that sensible things were distinct from these (παρὰ ταῦτα) and were called after them; for the multitude of things sharing the same name as the forms were what they were in virtue of their participation in these forms. It will be observed that in this passage Aristotle insists rather on the distinction of sensible things from the forms than on that of the forms from sensible things, and he implies that this is what distinguished Plato from Sokrates. We have seen reason already for believing that Sokrates recognised no reality in sensible things apart from the forms, and Aristotle's language here confirms this view. Of course it is equally true to say, as Aristotle usually does, that the forms are distinct from the sensible things, but it is significant that, when he first has occasion to mention the point, he emphasises the other side of the distinction.

§ 234. Closely connected with this separation (χωρισμός) of sensible things is what Aristotle calls the 'introduction' (εἰσαγωγή) of the forms. This term does not imply that Plato invented them. The metaphor is, I believe, derived from the use of the word for bringing on the stage or 'producing', and the suggestion appears to be that the ethical inquiries of Sokrates had made it necessary to assume certain universals which were not numbers, and these, of course, would be separate from the things of sense just as the numbers were. The Pythagoreans had defined Justice, for instance, as a square number, but Sokrates had shown that we must postulate a special form of Justice (αὐτὸ ὅ ἐστι δίκαιον). That is not mentioned as an innovation of Plato's. The only difference which is implied between Sokrates and Plato is that the latter separated sensible things from the forms while the former did not. That is stated in so many words in the Tenth Book (1078 b, 17), though it is also said (1086 b, 3) that Sokrates gave the impulse to (ἐκίνησε) this separation. He is commended for not going further, and it is implied that his doctrine was much the same as Aristotle's own. That can hardly be historical, but Aristotle may have thought it a legitimate interpretation of the second part of the *Phaedo*, where the forms are certainly *in* things. It seems to me a far more serious anachronism to represent Sokrates as seeking for universals (τὰ καθόλου), a term not yet invented, than to represent him as seeking for 'forms'. It is worse still to make him talk about 'concepts'.[1] Realism is prior ro Conceptualism, and I doubt very much whether anyone ever 'hypostatised concepts'. As we have seen (§ 195), Conceptualism is tentatively put forward in the *Parmenides* as a solution of the problem of participation, but it is rejected at once.

§ 235. This parenthesis, then, is at best Aristotle's speculative reconstruction of history from his own point of view, and throws very little light on his definite statement that Plato not only made numbers distinct from sensible things, but also made the objects of mathematics intermediate between them. It is that statement of Aristotle, and not his historical notes upon it, which we have really to interpret. He tells us further that the objects of mathematics differed from the things of sense in being eternal and immovable and from the forms in being many, whereas each form is one and unique (αὐτὸ ἓν μόνον). If we can interpret that, we shall know what Plato's 'separatism' (χωρισμός) really meant.

The difference between the objects of sense and the objects of mathematics is a simple matter, and is fully dealt with in the *Phaedo*. The mathematician is not really speaking about the sensible diagram he traces in the sand. The sensible circle is only a rough 'image' (εἴδωλον) of what he really means. In the *Phaedo*, however, the objects of mathematics are certainly regarded as forms, and we have now to ask what is meant by distinguishing them from the forms. It cannot, of course, be meant that mathematical forms are on a lower level than others. That is the last thing Plato would think of, and the point is rather that they are on

---

[1] The term λόγος cannot possibly mean 'concept'. So far as there is any Greek word for 'concept' at this date, it is νόημα.

a higher level. The object of the mathematician's reasoning is not, indeed, the sensible circle, but neither is it *the* circle, the form of circularity. He speaks of circles of greater or smaller radius, and even of two circles intersecting one another. Mathematical reasoning, then, has to do with many circles, whereas *the* circle is one and one only. In the same way, the triangle about which we reason is either equilateral, isosceles or scalene, but *the* triangle is none of these. In fact, it is really the circles, triangles, etc., of which the geometer speaks that are the 'many' which partake in the forms.[1] And this is even truer of numbers than of figures, the spatial character of which has something of the sensible about it. We speak of adding two and two to make four, as if there were many twos. It is clear that we do not mean by these twos the pebbles or counters we may use to symbolise them, but neither do we mean the number two. There is only one number two, the form of two or the dyad. The arithmetician's twos, however, are even less like things of sense than the geometer's circles; they are the nearest approach we can get to the purely intelligible. From this point of view, Plato's separatism is a good deal less arbitrary than Aristotle seems to think.

§ 236. This distinction, moreover, furnishes the real explanation of the doctrine Aristotle attributes to Plato by name, that numbers are 'unaddible' (ἀσύμβλητοι).[2] When we say 'two and two is four', we mean that two units of a given kind added to two units of the same kind are equal to four units of that kind; we do not mean that the number two added to the number two is the number four. That would be nonsense; for the number two does not consist of two units nor does the number four consist of four units. Each number is a universal, and every universal is one and unique. The units we call 'two' somehow partake in the number two, but it is not identical with them. There is only one number two. From this it follows further that the relation between the numbers themselves is not one that can be expressed by any additive formula. The number five is not the number four *plus* a unit. The relation of four and five is simply one of priority and posteriority. What, then, are

[1] There is a hint, perhaps unconscious, of this doctrine in the *Phaedo*, where Sokrates speaks of αὐτὰ τὰ ἴσα (74 c). These are not identical with the more or less equal things of sense nor yet with αὐτὸ τὸ ἴσον. Probably such things as the two angles at the base of an isosceles triangle are meant.
[2] I am much indebted here to Professor Cook Wilson's article in the *Classical Review*, vol. xviii. (1904) pp. 247 *sqq.*

the 'two and two' which we say make four? The answer will appear if we remember that the particulars of the mathematical sciences are objects of thought just as much as the universals. We can think particular 'twos' without regarding them as inhering in any sensible substratum, so that the 'two and two' which 'make four' are distinguished on the one hand from the 'two and two pebbles' which make four pebbles, and on the other from the unique universal, *the* number two.

It is clear, then, that numbers are unique forms, and we have seen some reason for thinking that they are forms in a pre-eminent sense. That is certainly the doctrine Aristotle attributes to Plato, but we cannot understand it completely till we have discussed the relation of the forms of number to the other forms. That brings us to what Aristotle regards as the second peculiarity (ἴδιον) of Plato's philosophy.

II. THE ONE AND THE INDETERMINATE DYAD

§ 237. The Pythagoreans had regarded the Limit (πέρας) and the Unlimited (ἄπειρον) or Continuous as the elements of number, and therefore as the elements of things. Plato substituted for these the One and the dyad of the Great-and-Small. The only difference, according to Aristotle, is that the Pythagorean Unlimited was single, whereas Plato regarded the 'matter' of numbers, and therefore of things, as dual in character. It also follows, as Aristotle points out elsewhere, from Plato's separation of numbers and things that there will be what he calls 'matter' in the numbers as well as in things. This is called the Indeterminate dyad (ἀόριστος δυάς)[1] to distinguish it from the Determinate dyad, which is the number two. From this dyad the numbers are generated as from a sort of matrix (ἐκμαγεῖον).[2]

§ 238. Now it is at least clear that the term Indeterminate dyad

[1] The use of this term is not attributed to Plato by name, but *Met.* 1091 a, 4 seems to imply that he used it.

[2] Aristotle's account of the way in which the numbers are generated is extremely obscure. Mr. George A. Johnston has suggested a most interesting explanation of the matter, which I have his permission to quote. We have seen (p. 53, *n.* 1) that the ratio between the sides of successive oblong numbers (*i.e.* the sums of the series of even numbers) is always changing. It is a dyad, because it is always a ratio between two numbers; it is indefinite because the ratio is always changing. The one, on the other hand, is the square root of the successive oblong numbers, $\sqrt{2}$, $\sqrt{6}$, $\sqrt{12}$, etc., which are means between the sides of 2 (2 : 1), 6 (3 : 2), 12 (4 : 3), etc.

is a new name for Continuity, and it expresses more clearly than the old term Unlimited its twofold nature. It not only admits of infinite 'increase' ($a\check{v}\xi\eta$), but also of infinite 'diminution' ($\kappa\alpha\theta\alpha\acute{\iota}\rho\epsilon\sigma\iota\varsigma$).[1] That is why it is also called the Great-and-Small. The new idea which Plato intended to express was that of the infinitesimal, the *infiniment petit*. The introduction of this conception involves an entirely new view of number. That need not surprise us; for we have learnt from the *Republic* that it is the business of Dialectic to 'destroy the hypotheses' of the special sciences, and also that the hypothesis of Arithmetic is the series of natural integers, each consisting of so many equal and indivisible units, and each either odd or even. From our present point of view, these units and their sums belong to the 'intermediate' region. They are not sensible, indeed, but neither are they numbers in the true sense. The destruction of this hypothesis allows us to extend the conception of number so as to include quantities which are not a sum of units ($\mu o\nu\acute{\alpha}\delta\omega\nu\ \pi\lambda\hat{\eta}\theta o\varsigma$), and which are neither odd nor even. We have seen that it was the study of incommensurables that made this extension necessary. That is indicated by the prominence given to the study of quadratic surds in the *Theaetetus*. If 'irrationals' are once regarded as numbers, the old hypothesis of Arithmetic is destroyed.

This is not, as I understand it, tantamount to making the numerical series itself continuous; for in that case number would be identified with the mere potentiality of *plus* and *minus*, which is the Indeterminate dyad. It does, however, get rid of the indivisible unit, which was the source of all the trouble about irrational numbers. We may now regard the origin of the numerical series, not as 1 but as 0, and there is no reason for refusing to call such quantities as $\sqrt{2}$ and $\sqrt{5}$ numbers. The best proof that this was really the step which Plato took is that Aristotle always insists against him that there is no number but number made up of units ($\mu o\nu\alpha\delta\iota\kappa\grave{o}\varsigma\ \grave{\alpha}\rho\iota\theta\mu\acute{o}\varsigma$). It follows that Plato maintained there was.

§ 239. The hypotheses of Geometry were, of course, submitted to a precisely similar criticism. The new view of number had really broken down the barrier which Zeno had erected between

---

[1] Not necessarily by division ($\delta\iota\alpha\acute{\iota}\rho\epsilon\sigma\iota\varsigma$). The term $\kappa\alpha\theta\alpha\acute{\iota}\rho\epsilon\sigma\iota\varsigma$ is more general, and covers subtraction ($\grave{\alpha}\phi\alpha\acute{\iota}\rho\epsilon\sigma\iota\varsigma$). It is used in the extract from Hermodoros given below, p. 330.

Arithmetic and Geometry, and the old view of the point as 'a unit having position' (μονὰς θέσιν ἔχουσα) was superseded. Aristotle has preserved a very important piece of information as to Plato's oral teaching on this subject. He tells us that Plato objected altogether to the conception of a point as being a mere 'geometrical dogma', and preferred to speak of 'the origin of a line' (ἀρχὴ γραμμῆς).[1] That implies the view that the line is generated from the point by what we know from other sources was called 'fluxion' (ῥύσις).[2] This corresponds to the doctrine that the numerical series has zero, not the unit, for its origin. In the same way, the plane is a fluxion of the line and the solid of the plane. On the other hand, Aristotle adds, Plato often postulated indivisible lines.[3] Aristotle says it is easy to refute this doctrine, and the later commentators throw no light upon it. No doubt the term is paradoxical, but not more so than 'infinitesimals'. What Plato meant was clearly that, if you postulate indivisible units and regard 1 as the origin of the numerical series, you are also committed to indivisible or infinitesimal lines as the spatial unit. All this brings us very close to Newton and Leibniz, and the historical connexion can still be traced.[4]

§ 240. When we look at geometry in this way, we see that its spatial character tends to become irrelevant. It becomes a form of Arithmetic, dealing with continuity in general, whether spatial or not. This view is fully developed in the *Epinomis*, where we are told (990 d) that Geometry (which is said in passing to be 'a very absurd name') is really 'an assimilation by reference to surfaces of numbers not similar to one another by nature'. That is just the development of what we read in the *Theaetetus* (148 a), to the effect that certain numbers are incommensurable 'in length' (μήκει), but commensurable 'by means of the surfaces of which they are roots' (τοῖς ἐπιπέδοις ἃ δύνανται). In precisely the same way Stereometry is said to be the art by which certain numbers not

---

[1] *Met.* A. 992 a, 1: τούτῳ μὲν οὖν τῷ γένει (sc. τῷ τῶν στιγμῶν) καὶ διεμάχετο Πλάτων ὡς ὄντι γεωμετρικῷ δόγματι.

[2] Simpl. *in Phys.* p. 722, 28 (Diels): ἡ γραμμὴ ῥύσις στιγμῆς, Proclus *in Eucl.* i. p. 97, 6 (Friedlein).

[3] *Met.* ib.: τοῦτο δὲ πολλάκις ἐτίθει τὰς ἀτόμους γραμμάς.

[4] The recently discovered *Discourse on Method* by Archimedes has thrown unexpected light on the development of the method of infinitesimals among the Greeks. See Milhaud, *Nouvelles études*, pp. 134 *sqq.*, and especially p. 154. Cavalieri's 'method of indivisibles' is the connecting link between Greek and modern higher Mathematics. Newton and Leibniz got their knowledge of the former from Wallis and Barrow. Wallis translates ῥύσις by *fluxus*.

naturally similar can be assimilated by being raised to the third power. Aristotle strongly objects to what he regards as the confusion of Geometry with Arithmetic. He insists that the proper hypotheses of each science must be left undisturbed, and that it is illegitimate to prove a geometrical proposition by Arithmetic. We may infer that Plato held otherwise.

There is also a fragment of Plato's friend Archytas which puts the matter very clearly, and proves this was really the direction mathematical thought was taking at the time. He says (fr. 4):

I think that in respect of wisdom Arithmetic surpasses all the other arts, and especially Geometry, seeing it can treat the objects it wishes to study in a far clearer way.... Where Geometry fails, Arithmetic completes its demonstrations in the same way, even with regard to figures, if there is such a thing as the study of figures.[1]

§ 241. In the last resort, then, geometrical figures are reduced to numbers, and these in turn are generated from the One and the Indeterminate dyad. What is new here is the assumption of a material element even in the forms, though that element is nothing more than abstract continuity. The importance of this is that it tends to make the intelligible forms less disparate from the things of sense. It will be observed that it is precisely because Plato 'separated' numbers from sensibles that it became possible for him to justify the world of appearance. This cannot be fully explained till the next chapter; all we have to note at present is that the One combines with the Indeterminate dyad to generate the numbers, just as the forms combine with the Great-and-Small to generate sensible things. In that sense the elements of numbers were the elements of things. That is how Aristotle states it, and by great good fortune we possess a dialogue which must have been written while he was a member of the Academy, and which, though it deals primarily with another subject, and avoids the doctrine of form-numbers altogether, contains nevertheless some indications of Plato's thought at the time. I refer to the *Philebus*, one of his maturest works.

---

[1] Diels, *Vors.*³ i. p. 337, 6 καὶ δοκεῖ ἁ λογιστικὰ ποτὶ τὰν σοφίαν τῶν μὲν ἀλλᾶν τεχνῶν καὶ πολὺ διαφέρειν, ἀτὰρ καὶ τᾶς γεωμετρικᾶς ἐναργεστέρω πραγματεύεσθαι ἃ θέλει... καὶ ἃ ἐπιλείπει αἱ ἁ γεωμετρία, καὶ ἀποδείξιας ἁ λογιστικὰ ἐπιτελεῖ καὶ ὁμῶς, εἰ μὲν εἰδέωι τεὰ πραγματεία, καὶ περὶ τοῖς εἴδεσιν.

THE PHILEBUS

§ 242. From certain discussions in Aristotle's *Ethics* we get a hint of how the *Philebus* probably came to be written. Eudoxos had introduced into the Academy the heresy that Pleasure is the Good, a doctrine he probably received from the school of Demokritos, as Epicurus did at a later date. This raised considerable discussion, as was natural, and Speusippos in particular opposed Eudoxos vehemently, going so far as to maintain that Pleasure was an evil. Plato was interested, of course, and he did what he had not done for years; he wrote a Sokratic dialogue on the subject. It was quite an appropriate theme for Sokrates to discuss, and there is little in the greater part of the dialogue which the Sokrates of the *Gorgias* or the *Phaedo* might not have said. On the other hand, Plato's dramatic power is no longer what it was, and the characteristic touches of the Sokratic manner are fewer than in the earlier dialogues, though more than is often supposed. Undeniably, too, the voice is sometimes that of the Stranger from Elea and sometimes that of the Athenian Stranger in the *Laws*, and in those cases we are justified in thinking that we have a hint at least of Plato's personal thought. I propose, for the present, to summarise only that portion of the dialogue which bears directly on the subject we are now discussing; the general theory of Pleasure, though of the highest importance in itself, can only be adequately treated in connexion with the views of Eudoxos and Speusippos and of Aristotle's criticism of these. We get the impression from the *Philebus* that we are dealing with a dispute between the younger members of the Academy, in which Plato condescends to take part, though, by transferring the conversation to the fifth century and by making Sokrates the chief speaker, he avoids committing himself too much.

§ 243. Before the opening of the dialogue, Sokrates and Philebos (a youth of whom nothing is known) have been discussing the Good. Philebos has stated the position that the Good is Pleasure (ἡδονή), while Sokrates has identified it with Thought (φρόνησις) or Wisdom. Philebos declines to argue the question, and Protarchos (another young man of whom nothing is known)[1]

---

[1] He is addressed as 'son of Kallias' (19 b), but there is no ground for identifying him with one of the two sons of Kallias son of Hipponikos, mentioned in the *Apology* (20 b) as pupils of Euenos in 399 B.C.

undertakes to replace him as the advocate of Pleasure. It is not a little remarkable that the dialogue should be called after a personage who takes practically no part in it.

The two positions are more distinctly stated thus. That of Philebos is that Pleasure, understood in its widest sense as including joy, delight, and so forth, is the highest good for all living beings without exception.[1] That of Sokrates is that Thought, understood in its widest sense as including memory, right belief, true reasoning, and so forth, is the highest good for all living beings that are capable of it. The two positions agree in this, that both make Happiness ($εὐδαιμονία$) a habit ($ἕξις$) or disposition ($διάθεσις$) of soul.[2] It is further pointed out that there may prove to be a third habit of soul which is better than either Pleasure or Thought, in which case we must give the preference to whichever of these two is most nearly akin to it (11 a — 12 a).

§ 244. Sokrates begins by calling attention to the fact that pleasures may be very unlike and indeed opposite, so that we cannot apply the same predicate to all of them, but it soon appears that it will be necessary to go deeper than this. We cannot, in fact, make any advance without coming to an understanding on the troublesome old question of the One and the Many. By this we do not mean the puzzle about the predication of opposite attributes like great and small, heavy and light, of the same subjects. That is child's play, and the solution has long been public property. Nor do we mean the question arising from the fact that every sensible thing has parts, and is therefore both one and many. The real difficulty is with regard to such units (*monads*, *henads*) as horse, ox, beautiful, good (*i.e.* the 'forms' of the *Phaedo* and the *Republic*). With regard to these we have to ask (1) in what sense we are to hold that each of these units really is, (2) in what sense we are to hold that each of them being *one*, and admitting neither coming into being nor ceasing to be, nevertheless *is* that one,[3] (3) in what

[1] This seems to refer to the argument of Eudoxos that Pleasure must be the Good, since all things, rational and irrational, aim at it (Arist. *Eth. Nic.* 1172 b, 9 *sqq*).
[2] The terms $ἕξις$ and $διάθεσις$ are taken from medicine. A 'habit' is a more lasting 'disposition' (Arist. *Cat.* 9 a, 8). The doctrine that Happiness is a habit of soul is characteristic of the Academy; Aristotle made it an 'activity' ($ἐνέργεια$). See my edition of the *Ethics*, p. 3.
[3] The sense of the second question (15 b, 2–4) has been much disputed. I think that, if we read it with an emphasis on the first $μίαν$ and on $εἶναι$, we shall see that it refers to the difficulty that arises when we predicate 'being' of 'one',

sense we are to hold that these units can be present in the innumerable things of the sensible world, whether (a) in part, or (b)
as wholes, so that (what seems quite impossible) they should be
identical both in their unity and in their plurality (12 c — 15 c).

This section serves to link the *Philebus* to the *Parmenides*. At the
beginning of the latter dialogue, the question of the One and the
Many, so far as it refers to the predication of opposite attributes,
and to the relation of whole and parts, is disposed of by the
participation of sensible things in the forms, and it is then shown
that the real difficulty lies in the union of One and Many in the
forms themselves. If we say that the One *is*, it seems to become
two on our hands; while, if we say that sensible things participate
in it, it is either broken up into parts and so becomes infinitely
many, or the whole form must be present in each of the participants,
so that we have an infinite number of ones alongside of the one
One. No direct solution of this difficulty is given in the *Parmenides*,
but a hint was thrown out that a solution was possible. We shall
see that the *Philebus* puts us on the way to it.

§ 245. The difficulty that a thing turns into a one and many
whenever we speak of it, really pervades all statements (λόγοι) or
propositions we can make about anything whatsoever. It is 'an
affection of propositions in our minds (ἐν ἡμῖν) that never dies
nor ages'. It is this that gives rise to all eristic disputation, and we
cannot get rid of that till we have formed a sound theory of it. The
only way to reach one is a way of which Sokrates has always been a
lover (ἐραστής), though it has often left him stranded, and it is the
way in which all inventions and discoveries in the arts have been
made. It is this.

The gods once revealed to mankind, and the ancients, who were
of a higher nature and nearer to the gods than we are, have handed
it down as a tradition, that everything we say at a given moment
(ἀεί) *is* consists of one and many, and has Limit and Unlimitedness
innate in it. What we have to do, then, is first to find a single form
(ἰδέα) in the thing we say *is*, and then to look in that for two
subordinate forms, or three, or whatever number there may be.
After that we must look at each of these new units and see how
many forms are in them, until we are able to say of the original
unit, not only that it is one and many, but also how many it is.

that is, when we speak, not merely of τὸ ἓν ἕν, but of τὸ ἓν ὄν. When we do that
the One at once seems to become two. That is a chief *crux* of the *Parmenides*.

We must not predicate the Unlimited (τὴν τοῦ ἀπείρου ἰδέαν) of the manifold, before we have gained a clear image of the number which is intermediate between the Unlimited and the One. Then, and not till then, may we give it up and let the manifold slip into the Unlimited. That is the genuine revelation of the gods, but the wise men of to-day are both too quick and too slow in setting up a One and a Many, and the middle terms (τὰ μέσα) escape them. That is just the difference between dialectical and eristical discussion (15 d — 17 a).

Voice, for instance, is both one and many, but to know that does not make you a 'grammarian' (phonetician). To become that, you must know also how many and of what nature the indefinite manifold is. In the same way, he is not a musician who can only say of a note that it is high or low or of the same pitch (as the keynote); he must know also how many intervals there are and of what nature, and what are the terms (ὅροι) of the intervals (i.e. the numbers, such as 12, 9, 8, 6, which express them), and how many scales these give rise to. Further, he must know to how many rhythms and metres the motions of the body when measured by numbers give rise (17 a — 17 e).

Just in the same way, when we have to start from the side of the Unlimited, we must not go straight to the One, but must carefully note the number of the intermediate terms.

If we start from sound, which is unlimited, we find first that there is a certain number of vowels, and then a certain number of liquids (μέσα) and a certain number of mutes, and considering all these we bring them under the single unity of letters (στοιχεῖα). Then, and not till then, do we see clearly that the art of grammar has letters for its province, and not merely sound (18 a — 18 d).

A good example of the premature introduction of the Unlimited is afforded by the early Pythagorean treatment of the scale. If we were right in holding that they only determined the intervals of the fourth, the fifth, and the octave, referring all the internal divisions of the tetrachord to the Unlimited (§ 30), that is just the sort of thing Plato means here. It is the more likely he had this in mind that we know Archytas and Plato busied themselves with this very problem of the division of the tetrachord. We must also observe carefully that we do not eliminate the Unlimited altogether, but reach a point where we can no longer introduce number. That, too, can be illustrated from the musical scale, where we come ultimately to intervals which cannot be expressed as the ratio of one whole number to another. So far as we have yet gone, there is a point where division must cease.

§ 246. To illustrate what he means by the Unlimited, Sokrates takes the example of 'the hotter and colder', and this enables us to elucidate his meaning with the help of the distinction between heat and temperature, a distinction historically connected with the Pythagorean doctrine, since, as we have seen, 'temperature' is a translation of κρᾶσις.

If we consider the sensation or quality of heat, we see at once that it varies in intensity. Water may be much hotter than our hand or only a little hotter, or nearly as hot, or not nearly so hot. In other words, heat 'admits of *plus* and *minus*' (τὸ μᾶλλον καὶ ἧττον). On the other hand, these degrees of intensity are quite indefinite. We cannot attach any clear meaning to the statement that one sensation of heat is equal to another, or that one sensation of heat is the double of another. These considerations explain what Plato meant by 'the dyad of the Great-and-Small', which was his own name for what he calls the Unlimited in the *Philebus*. It is the possibility of indefinite continuous variation in both directions from a fixed point. The Limit, on the other hand, does away with this indefinite 'more and less'. Its simplest form is 'the equal and the double' ($\frac{1}{1}$ and $\frac{2}{1}$), and in general it is everything which 'has the ratio of one number to another or one measure to another'. This is the conception of quantity as distinct from that of quality, and its chief characteristic is that it enables us to speak with perfect clearness of *equality* and of *addition*, the simplest form of the latter being 'the *double*'. What enables us to do this is the introduction of a unit, in terms of which we may measure degrees of intensity. We cannot attach any clear meaning to the statement that it is twice as hot to-day as yesterday, but we do understand what is meant by saying that 60° is twice 30°. That implies further that a zero of temperature has been fixed, all temperatures above which are *plus* and all below it *minus*. The conception of negative quantity is thus clearly formulated for the first time in the history of science.

§ 247. Aristotle tells us further that the Great-and-Small was identified with 'not being'.[1] This doctrine is not attributed to Plato by name, but we fortunately possess a fragment of Hermodoros[2] which leaves no doubt upon the subject and also suggests the explanation. He says:

[1] *Phys.* 192 a, 6 *sqq.*   [2] See Simpl. *in Phys.* p. 247, 30 *sqq.* (Diels).

Those things which are spoken of as having the relation of great to small all have the 'more or less', so that they can go on to infinity in the direction of the 'still greater' and the 'still less'. And in the same way, the broader and narrower, the heavier and lighter, and everything which is spoken of in that way can go on to infinity. But what is spoken of as equal and at rest and attuned has not the 'more and less' as their opposites have. There is always something more unequal than what is unequal, something more in motion than what moves, something more out of tune than what is out of tune. [The text of the next sequence is corrupt]. . . . So that what is of this nature is inconstant and formless and infinite, and may be called 'not being' by negation of 'being' (κατὰ ἀπόφασιν τοῦ ὄντος).

If we have read the *Sophist* aright, the meaning of this is plain. It is not meant that the indefinite continuum of the more and less is *nothing*, but rather that it is *not anything*. We predicate of it the significant negative term (ἀπόφασις), 'not being', not a blank negation which has no meaning.

§ 248. From all this it appears that we shall have to assume a third 'kind' in addition to the Limit and the Unlimited, namely, the Mixture of both. We see this both in Medicine and in Music, where health and 'harmony' are produced by the due mixture of the two. We see the same thing in climate; for a temperate climate is produced by such a mixture. The same explanation may be given of all goodness whether of body or soul, beauty of body and order of soul, and indeed all good things are due to such a mixture (25 e *sqq.*).

The thought here is obviously Pythagorean; it is just the tuned string once more. But there is a fundamental change in the point of view. The Pythagoreans had identified the Limit with good and the Unlimited with evil, but here we are distinctly told that, so far as human life is concerned, good things are all to be found in the Mixture. It is just for that reason that the 'mixed life', which includes both Thought and Pleasure, is found to be superior, not only to the life of Pleasure alone, but also to the life of Thought alone.

§ 249. Closely connected with this is the new sense in which Plato uses the term 'being' (οὐσία) in this passage. The Pythagorean doctrine simply identified the Form with being and the Unlimited with becoming, but Plato distinctly states that the Mixture alone is truly 'being'. The process of mixing is indeed a 'becoming' (γένεσις), but it is a becoming which has being for its result (γένεσις εἰς οὐσίαν) and the mixture itself is being, though a being which has become (γεγενημένη οὐσία). Just in the same way we are told in the *Timaeus* (35 a) that being (οὐσία) is a blend of the Same and the Other. These are only hints, and there are no others of the same kind in the dialogues, where they would be out of place, but they supplement what Aristotle tells us in the most interesting way. As the form-numbers are themselves a mixture, it follows that even sensible things may be real in spite of the fact that they are mixtures. In other words, the mature philosophy of Plato found reality, whether intelligible or sensible, in the combination of matter and form, and not in either separately.

§ 250. There has been considerable discussion as to the 'kind' to which the 'ideas' or forms belong in this scheme. The traditional view was that they were represented by the Limit, and that is, of course, in accordance with the earlier Pythagorean version of the theory. It would be quite correct to refer the forms of the *Phaedo* and the *Republic* to this kind. Professor Jackson, on the contrary, maintains that the forms belong to the Mixed kind, and we have seen that the forms were certainly regarded by Plato as a mixture. On the other hand, it is surely plain that the Mixture of the *Philebus* is the world of sense, and the forms must, therefore, be referred to the Limit. The difficulty arises, I think, from the fact that Plato refrains from giving his full doctrine on the subject in this dialogue. From the point of view here taken, the forms belong to the Limit, but that does not alter the fact that they themselves are in turn a mixture. In the sensible world, their function is to limit, but in the intelligible world they themselves appear as a limited continuum, as a blending of matter and form, of the One and the Indeterminate Dyad.

§ 251. Now this new view of reality clearly implies not only the categories of Being and Not-being, Same and Other, but also that of Motion, which was already associated with these in the *Sophist* (§ 211), and this not only in the sensible but also in the intelligible world. We could only explain the generation of lines, planes, and solids by the help of this category (§ 239), and if the sensible world is also a mixture, there must be a cause of the Mixture. That will be a fourth 'kind' (27 b), and we must now go on to consider what Movement implies. Unless we can give an intelligible account of this, we have failed to explain the world we know.

XVII

The Philosophy of Movement

THE SOUL

§ 252. It was his theory of Soul that enabled Plato to account for Motion. Apart from that, we should have nothing but a string of what we may best represent to ourselves as algebraical formulae. The early Pythagoreans had grasped the conception of Soul as something more than the mere ghost of popular belief, but their later tenet that the soul is an 'attunement' of the body made them lose hold of it again. Sokrates had insisted on the reality and eternity of the soul; but Plato was the first to attempt a scientific justification of this belief. It is significant that the argument which seemed decisive to him does not occur in the *Phaedo*, though Sokrates is made to state it in the *Phaedrus*. In that dialogue we are told (245 c) that what moves another thing, and is in turn moved by something else, may cease to be moved and therefore cease to move anything else; but what moves itself will never cease to move. It is the source and beginning of motion (ἀρχὴ κινήσεως). Now such a beginning can never have come into being; for everything that comes into being must have a beginning, while this is itself a beginning. Nor can it have any end; for, if it perished, everything would come to a standstill. Such a beginning is the soul; for it is the self-moved (τὸ αὐτὸ ἑαυτὸ κινοῦν), and is therefore without beginning and without end.

§ 253. If this doctrine occurred only in the *Phaedrus*, it might be set down as mythical, though, despite the enthusiasm of the passage, the language is curiously technical and scientific. It might also be said that it only proves the eternity of soul in general or of the world-soul, not that of the individual soul. In fact, however, the phraseology of the *Phaedrus* remained in use, and the question of the 'first mover' continued to be a fundamental one. All doubt on the point is set at rest by the perfectly matter-of-fact treatment of the subject in the *Laws*, where we have an indication of Plato's mature thought on the subject.

He begins (893 b) by distinguishing ten kinds of motion, of which the ninth and tenth alone concern us at present. The ninth is the motion that can move other things but cannot move itself, and the tenth is that which can move both itself and other things. It is really, Plato says, the first, since it is the beginning of motion (ἀρχὴ κινήσεως) to the other nine. Now we do not find motion of this kind in earth, fire, or water, but only in what lives, that is, in what has a soul; and if we ask for a definition of the soul, we can only say that it is 'the motion which of itself can move itself' (τὴν αὑτὴν αὐτὴν δυναμένην κινεῖν κίνησιν). The other motions all belong to body, and soul is therefore prior to body (896 b).

But, if soul is prior to body, it follows at once that all the attributes of soul, such as characters, wishes, reasonings, beliefs, forethought, and memories are prior to the attributes of body, such as length, breadth, depth, and strength; and, if this is so, soul alone can be the cause of good and bad, fair and foul, righteousness and wickedness, and all other such opposites. There are such things as bad habits and bad reasonings, so there must be at least two souls, one that does good and the other that does the opposite (896 e).

This passage is generally supposed to assert the existence of an evil world-soul as well as of a good one, but it is important to observe that this does not follow from the words of Plato. He does not say that there are two souls, a good and a bad one, opposed to one another, but that there are not less than two. It is as illegitimate to infer that there is only one evil soul, as it would be to infer that there is only one good soul, and it is rather implied that there is a plurality of souls, some good and some evil. We shall see presently that there is one pre-eminently good soul, namely God, but there is no suggestion of a pre-eminently evil soul, and that view is expressly rejected in the *Statesman* (270 a). The main point is rather that, since evil exists, there must be a plurality of souls; for evil as well as good must be caused by a soul, whether by one soul or many. That is the important thing. We can no longer refer evil to body or matter; the philosophy of movement requires us to attribute it to soul just as much as good.

GOD

§ 254. Now, if we look at the motions of the heavenly bodies, we see at once that they must be caused by a good soul or souls, and indeed by the best, since they are the most regular of all motions. That is due to their circular character, which must have been given them by a good soul, since, if left to themselves, things do not move in a circle but in a straight line.[1] These souls are what we call gods, if there are many, or God, if there is one only, or one which is the best of all. It is in this way that Plato reaches what he believes to be a scientific proof of the existence of God, and it is only when he has done this that he can explain the world. There can be no sort of doubt that Plato regarded this as the central thing in his philosophy, and we shall understand that just in proportion as we realise this fact. At the same time, we must note at once that, though he believes this line of argument sufficient to demonstrate the existence of God, it tells us no more about him than that he is the self-moving source of good motions. Even so this is something quite different from anything the earlier philosophers had meant when they spoke of God. The Ionians had called fire, air, water and the like gods, but that only meant there were no other gods but these. Anaximander and Xenophanes had called the worlds or the World gods or God, but that was at most a sort of pantheism, as it was also with Parmenides. Belief in God was doubtless part of the Pythagorean religion, but it was hardly a part of Pythagorean science. Plato brought the idea of God into philosophy for the first time, and the form the doctrine took in his mind was that God was a living soul and that God was good. So much as that, but no more, he believed himself to have established by strictly scientific reasoning.

We must not assume, therefore, that Plato meant by God exactly what a modern theist would mean by the word. Plato's God is certainly a 'personal' god, as we should put it; for he is Mind ($\nu o\hat{u}s$) existing in a living soul, but it does not follow that he is the 'supreme being'. We have seen (§ 171) that Plato continued to

---

[1] This was rightly insisted upon by the Platonist Atticus (2nd cent. A.D.) as the fundamental distinction between the theories of Plato and Aristotle. Aristotle made the circular motion ($\kappa\upsilon\kappa\lambda o\phi o\rho\iota a$) natural to the heavens, while Plato held that it must have a cause. We call this cause Gravity, and we know much more than Plato did of the way in which it acts, but we know no more than he did of its nature. Plato knew there was a problem here; Aristotle denied that there was any.

lecture on the Good to the last, and it is clear that his deepest thought was expressed in this lecture, so far as it was expressed at all. The way in which one of his followers after another, including Aristotle himself, endeavoured to publish an authentic report of it proves that it was regarded as fundamental. The question that arises, then, is whether we are to identify God with the Good or not; and, if we are not, what relation we are to understand God to have to the Good. This question is not so simple as it appears; indeed, it is highly ambiguous. If it is asked whether the Good is to be identified with the conception of God as held by modern theists, the answer is that it is certainly included in that conception, though it by no means exhausts it. If, on the other hand, it is asked whether the Good is to be identified with the God whose existence Plato believed himself to have proved by the argument just explained, the answer must certainly be that it is not. The Good is not a soul, but a 'form'. That is just how Plato avoids pantheism, which he regards as equivalent to atheism.

§ 255. This conception is not without its difficulties, as Plato was well aware. In the *Timaeus* he says (28 c) 'To find the maker and father of this universe is a hard task; and, when you have found him, it is impossible to speak of him before all people.' That is a sentence of unquestioned authenticity, and fully explains the enigmatic manner in which Plato speaks of the same difficulty to Dionysios (who imagined he had solved it) in the *Second Epistle* (312 e). It also explains why he never wrote or published the Lecture on the Good, and why in the *Laws*, which was written for publication, he always speaks of God and never of the Good, though the *Laws* must be contemporary with that very lecture. The problem continued to be discussed wherever there was living Greek thought. Some later writers regarded the Good as the supreme God, and made the Creator of the world subordinate to him, and there were many other attempted solutions. The difficulty is, in fact, the source of the controversies which were ultimately settled by authority at the Council of Nicaea, though this did not prevent it from continuing to trouble the minds of original thinkers. That does not concern us here. All we have to make clear is that Plato's God is not a form but a soul, and that he is the self-moved mover of the best motions. The Good is not a soul, but it is independent of God, and even above him, since it is the pattern by which he fashions the world.

It is equally certain that God is not the only self-moved mover but simply the best of them. No doubt the subordinate gods of the *Timaeus* belong to the mythology of that dialogue, and we can hardly doubt that Plato was a monotheist. The question, however, of monotheism or polytheism was not an important one to the Greeks, and Plato might have admitted other gods, so long as they were strictly subordinate. The main point is that human souls, though inferior, exist just as truly as the divine soul, and that in this way Plato thought it possible to reconcile the existence of evil with the absolute goodness of God. Here too we are faced by a difficulty which continues to trouble mankind. Are individual souls in any sense created by God, or is their existence entirely independent of him? In the *Timaeus* there is a hint of a possible solution of this question. We learn there that individual souls are indestructible, not in their own nature, but because to destroy what he has made is inconsistent with the goodness of God. How far such a solution would really express the mind of Plato cannot be determined till we have come to a conclusion about the principles on which the *Timaeus* is to be interpreted.

THE WORLD

§ 256. The *Timaeus*, which was certainly written long after the *Republic*, professes to describe a meeting which took place the day after Sokrates repeated the conversation narrated in the earlier dialogue, and consequently two days after that conversation itself. That makes a busy three days, especially as the *Timaeus* was to be followed at once by the *Critias*, which Plato has left unfinished, and by the *Hermocrates*, which was never written at all. We learn for the first time in the *Timaeus* that the audience to which Sokrates repeated the *Republic* consisted of Plato's great-grand-father, Kritias,[1] Timaios the Lokrian, Hermokrates, and an un-named fourth person who is prevented by illness from being present the next day. It is not very profitable to speculate who he may have been, but it is at least certain that he was a Pythagorean;

---

[1] See Appendix. It is made perfectly clear that this Kritias is not the Kritias who was one of the Thirty, but his grandfather, though the two are hopelessly confused by modern writers. He is a very old man, who can hardly remember what he was told yesterday, but remembers the scenes of his boyhood clearly (26 b). At that time the poems of Solon were still recent (21 b). It seems clear to me that most of the poetical fragments ascribed to the younger Kritias are really his grandfather's.

for Timaios is represented as his understudy and agrees to replace him. If a name has to be given, I would suggest that of Philolaos, and I should explain his absence by the consideration that the *Timaeus*, though certainly based on his system, in several points goes beyond what we can reasonably attribute to him. If that is so, we can understand the origin of the famous scandal that Plato plagiarised the *Timaeus* from the 'three books' of Philolaos which had come into his possession.[1]

However that may be — and I only offer the suggestion for what it is worth — the elaborate *mise en scène* must surely have some significance. If Plato took so much trouble to attach the *Timaeus* to the *Republic*, he must have meant the later dialogue to supplement the earlier in some way, and this must be connected with the startling fact that Sokrates begins by giving a recapitulation of the *Republic* which includes Book V., but ignores Books VI. and VII. altogether. We are not allowed to attribute this to an over-sight; for Sokrates asks Timaios whether the summary is complete, and receives the answer that nothing is lacking (19 b). This can only mean that the *Timaeus* and its projected sequels were intended to replace in some way the later books of the *Republic*. The fact is that the central books of the *Republic* do not, except in the matter of solid geometry, go materially beyond what Sokrates might have learnt and probably did learn, from his Pythagorean associates, and Plato now wishes to make a further advance. For the same reason, Sokrates is no longer the chief speaker. The new views, however, are introduced with great reserve and somewhat obscurely expressed, so that there has been much dispute as to the meaning of some of the most important passages. Plato does not forget that the dialogue is supposed to take place in the fifth century.

§ 257. The *Timaeus* professes to give an account of the creation of the world, and the question at once arises whether this represents Plato's own doctrine or not. It is quite certain that Xenokrates and other early Platonists held it did not. The world, they said, was represented as having a beginning in time only for purposes of exposition ($\delta\iota\delta\alpha\sigma\kappa\alpha\lambda\iota\alpha\varsigma$ $\chi\acute{\alpha}\rho\iota\nu$), just as the construction of a diagram may be the best way to exhibit the properties of a figure. Aristotle thought it necessary to argue against this principle of interpretation, and we may say that, on the whole, the Platonists regard the *Timaeus* as mythical, while the Peripatetics take it

[1] *E. Gr. Ph.*[2] § 140.

literally. That, however, is impossible for anyone who has grasped the central doctrine of Platonism. We can infer the existence of the soul and of God from the fact of motion, but we cannot give any scientific account of the way in which they act. The world of experience is only, after all, an image, and it belongs to the region of becoming, and we can therefore do no more than tell 'likely tales' (εἰκότες λόγοι) about it. Cosmology is not, and cannot be science, any more than Theology or Psychology. It is only a form of 'play' (παιδιά). Science, in the strict sense, must be mathematical. And yet Cosmology is not mere play either, for our account of the world will be related to the truth in the same way as the world is related to reality. It will be truth in the making, just as the sensible world is the intelligible world in the making. The appropriate vehicle for half-truths of this kind is myth, and here we must note once more that myth expresses something lower than science, and not something higher. That is fundamental for the interpretation of Plato. The matter is put quite clearly in the *Timaeus* itself. We are dealing with what is always becoming and never is, not with what always is and never becomes (27 d). The former is an image (εἰκών) of the latter (29 b), and the work of ordering the sensible world after the pattern of the intelligible is assigned to God. No description of this process can have a scientific character, for we are dealing with what cannot be an object of knowledge, but only of belief (29 b–c), and knowledge is higher, not lower, than belief.

§ 258. We are first told that God found a visible mass moving in a disorderly fashion, and resolved to bring it out of disorder into order. If we ask why he did so, the answer is 'He was good, and the good has never at any time a feeling of jealousy towards anything, so he wished everything to become as like himself as possible' (29 e). This he brought about by creating a soul of the world, into which he introduced mathematical and harmonic relations (35 a *sqq.*).

We note here, in the first place, the phrase 'as like himself as possible'. This reservation is called for because Mind (νοῦς) is confronted by Necessity (ἀνάγκη), and cannot, therefore completely effect its purpose (47 e). We must, then, consider the 'errant cause' (πλανωμένη αἰτία). In particular, we must explain how the elements came into being. For these cannot be ultimate. So far from being 'letters' (στοιχεῖα, *elementa*), they are not even syllables.

The conception of Necessity to which we are here introduced is not by any means an easy one. It is certainly not what we call physical necessity, for we are told that it can be 'persuaded' by Mind. We are even told that it is a cause, and a cause 'subservient to' the divine. It is a 'concomitant cause' (συναίτιον) of the goodness of the world, which could not be realised without it. This idea is as old as the *Phaedo*, where the *concausa* as distinct from the *causa* as defined as 'that without which the cause would never be a cause' (99 b). We learn further that this 'concomitant' or 'subservient' cause is corporeal, and that most people make the mistake of confusing it with the true cause, explaining everything, as they do, by warming and cooling, rarefaction and condensation, and so forth. The true cause is Mind and Mind alone, and the corporeal is a hindrance as well as a help. Mind could do nothing without something to work on, but that of itself stands in the way of it carrying out its purposes completely. We learn also that these secondary causes 'are moved by something else, and then of necessity move something else', as contrasted with the primary cause, which is self-moved. That is to be understood in the light of the doctrine of soul discussed above (§ 256). It may help the reader to appreciate the account Plato makes Timaios give of Mind and Necessity if he will compare it with the theory of Leibniz that this is the best of all possible worlds. The difference is that Plato regards his explanation as a myth, while Leibniz considered his to be an adequate solution of the difficulty.

§ 259. This purely mythical character of the cosmogony becomes still more evident if we consider its details. In particular, motion is ascribed to the disordered mass before the world has received a soul, and that is in flat contradiction to Plato's doctrine that soul alone is self-moved. Plutarch, one of the few Platonists who took the *Timaeus* literally, can only get out of this difficulty by the help of the evil world-soul supposed to be assumed in the *Laws* (§ 256). That, according to him, is eternal, and is to be identified with Necessity; only the good world-soul was created. But, even supposing Plutarch to be right in finding an evil world-soul in the *Laws*, there is certainly nothing said about it in the *Timaeus*, and it is impossible to suppose it would not have been mentioned if so much depended upon it. Besides that, we have seen that Necessity is 'subservient' to Mind. A similar difficulty arises when we consider what is said about Time. In the *Timaeus* it is spoken of as

a 'moving image of eternity' (37 d), and we are told that it comes
into being 'along with the heavens' (38 b), that is to say, after the
creation of the world-soul, which does not, therefore, take place
in time. That gives us the explanation of the necessarily mythical
character of the whole story. We can only think of motion as in
time, for time is just the measure of motion. On the other hand,
knowledge is of the eternal and not of the temporal. It follows that,
when we have to speak of motion, our language is perforce unscientific and pictorial. It can only convey an 'image' of the truth,
since time itself is only 'a moving image of eternity'. This does not
mean, as we shall see, that time is subjective, but only that we fail
to grasp its true nature. It is really the continuum implied in the
conception of motion, but that cannot be known in abstraction
from motion itself.

§ 260. But, besides being temporal, the 'errant cause' is spatial.
This is also hard to express in words; for space is apprehended
neither by thought nor by sense, but by 'a sort of bastard reasoning'
(λογισμῷ τινι νόθῳ). It is a sort of 'receptacle' (ὑποδοχή) or 'nurse'
(τιθήνη) of all things (49 a). To understand this, we must go back
to the elements, which we have already denied to be primary. We
see that they pass into one another by rarefaction and condensation,
and it is safest not to call any of them 'this', but only 'such' (49 d).
The only thing which can be called 'this' is that 'in which' (ἐν ᾧ)
they all appear to arise and pass away (49 e).

This may be illustrated by an example. If we were to make all
sorts of forms out of gold and keep constantly changing them, the
only answer to the question 'what is that?' would be 'Gold'. We
should not speak of the transient forms it assumed as 'things' (ὡς
ὄντα) at all. It is the same with 'the recipient of all things' (τὸ
πανδεχές), the matrix (ἐκμαγεῖον) on which the forms are 'impressed'
(ἐντυποῦνται). It has itself no form, but remains always the same,
taking on with complete indifference the forms that 'pass in and
out of it' (τὰ εἰσιόντα καὶ ἐξιόντα), and these in turn are 'imitations
of what is ever' (τῶν ὄντων ἀεὶ μιμήματα). They are, in fact, the
elementary triangles and their products the regular solids, and we
know from Aristotle, though we are not told so in the Timaeus, that
they are imitations of numbers. We must, therefore, distinguish
three things, the Form, which is the father, the Recipient, which is
the mother, and the offspring of the two (the Mixture of the
Philebus), which is the Corporeal. The Recipient is altogether

K   B.G.P.

formless; all we can say of it is that it is an invisible, all-receptive something, partaking in a mysterious way in the intelligible. It is, in fact, space (χώρα).

§ 261. That the so-called 'primary matter' of the *Timaeus* is space of three dimensions and nothing else is really quite certain both from Plato's own language on the subject and from the statements of Aristotle. Nor is there any occasion in the system for any other kind of 'matter'. The 'elements' of the corporeal are completely accounted for by the regular solids, and they in turn can be constructed from the elementary triangles. Plato undoubtedly means to say that the corporeal can be completely reduced to extension geometrically limited. Indeed, he goes a great deal further than that, though he only gives us a few hints of his real meaning here. We do not perceive space at all by the senses; we only infer it by a species of reasoning, and that reasoning is a 'bastard' one. It is 'in a dream' that we say everything must be in a place and occupy a space (52 b), and when the elementary triangles are discussed, it is said that the principles (ἀρχαί) which are higher than these God knows, and of men he who is dear to God (53 d). Space is only one aspect of Continuity, and not an essential one. These considerations, however, take us beyond the mythology of the *Timaeus*, for which space is ultimate.

§ 262. The Corporeal world, then, is in space and time, and for that reason it can only be described in mythological language. That does not, however, exhaust Plato's teaching on the subject. What we say of the world is not, indeed, the truth, but it may be more or less like the truth, and it is our business to make it as like the truth as possible. The boundary-line between the intelligible and the merely sensible is not a fixed one, and the sensible may be made progressively intelligible. It will, I think, be admitted that this is the doctrine to which all the dialogues from the *Theaetetus* onwards naturally lead up, and I believe we shall find proof that Plato held it. Unfortunately, however, his followers were not able to rise to this point of view, and Plato has been generally credited with an absolute dualism. Xenokrates confined the province of science to the things 'outside the heavens', and made the heavens themselves the objects of belief (δόξα). They were intelligible by the help of astronomy, but they belonged to the sensible world as being visible. If this report does justice to him, he made absolute a distinction which for Plato was merely relative. At the same time,

it is just possible that this report may be only a distortion of what
we shall find to be the true Platonic doctrine. There is no doubt
about Aristotle, however. It is certain that he introduced for the
first time the fatal notion that the nature of the heavens was quite
different from that of the sublunary world. It is this doctrine,
generally known as that of 'the incorruptibility of the heavens',
that the Platonist Galileo was chiefly concerned to disprove by
calling attention to such phenomena as the new star in Sagittarius,
and it is strange that Aristotle, who condemned Plato's perfectly
legitimate separation of forms from sensible things, should himself
be responsible for a much more questionable 'separation' ($\chi\omega\rho\iota\sigma\mu\acute{o}s$)
like this. There is no trace of anything like it in Plato. He certainly
assigned an exceptional position to Astronomy and its sister-
science Music in his philosophy, but that was simply because, in
his own day, these were the sciences in which the intelligible was
most obviously advancing at the expense of the merely sensible.
Even in the *Republic* (530 d) it is hinted that there are more
sciences of motion in space than these two, and we can see from
the *Parmenides* (130 e) that a complete science would have to
account for 'hair, mud and dirt' as well as for the planetary
motions. It is, however, from his astronomy alone that we can gain
a clear idea of the relation Plato held to exist between the sensible
and the intelligible. It would be out of place to discuss it fully here;
it will be enough to look at a single branch of it, and I shall select
one which is commonly misunderstood.[1]

§ 263. The great problem of the day was that of the planetary
motions. For the senses these are hopelessly irregular, and that is
probably why we hear in the *Timaeus* of the 'errant cause'
($\pi\lambda\alpha\nu\omega\mu\acute{e}\nu\eta$ $a\grave{\iota}\tau\acute{\iota}a$). In the first place, since the paths of the planets
are oblique to the equator, their apparent courses are spirals
($\H{\epsilon}\lambda\iota\kappa\epsilon s$), not circles. In the next place, Mercury and Venus at one
time travel faster than the Sun, so that they get in front of it and
appear as morning stars; at another time they lag behind it and
appear as evening stars. In fact, these three bodies are always
'overtaking and being overtaken by one another' (38 d). The other
planets behave even more strangely. Sometimes they seem to
accelerate their velocity so as to appear stationary among the fixed
stars or even to get some way ahead of them; at other times, they

---

[1] This applies even to the recent discussion of it in Sir T. L. Heath's *Aristarchus of Samos*, which in other respects is an excellent guide in such matters.

are retarded and seem to have a retrograde motion. There is a further irregularity in the Sun's annual course. The solstices and equinoxes do not divide it into four equal segments as we should expect them to do.

Now this irregularity cannot be ultimate. If we ask why not, the only answer is that the Artificer created the world on the pattern of the Good, and disorder of any kind is opposed to the Good. That is the ultimate ground of the rule that hypotheses are not to be needlessly multiplied. The postulate of simplicity and regularity which still guides scientific research is at bottom teleological,[1] and we probably come nearest to Plato's thought about the Good if we say that, according to him, reality must be a system. There is something to be said, however, for his simpler way of expressing this. At any rate, it does not admit of doubt that Plato conceived the function of Astronomy to be the discovery of the simplest hypotheses which would account for the apparent complexity of celestial phenomena. We know as a fact that he propounded the solar anomaly as a problem to his scholars (§ 174).

§ 264. Now we know further that Eudoxos invented a beautiful hypothesis, that of concentric spheres, to account for all these irregularities on the assumption of the earth's central position,[2] and we know also that Plato did not accept his solution as satisfactory. The assumption of twenty-seven spheres did not seem simple enough, and fuller study showed that still more were required. Kallippos added to their number, and Aristotle had to add still more. Finally, the concentric spheres were replaced by eccentric spheres and epicycles, and what we call the Ptolemaic system was the result. Besides this, Aristotle transformed the geometrical hypothesis of Eudoxos into a mechanical system of material spheres in contact with one another, and all that arrested the growth of a true astronomy for nearly two thousand years.

§ 265. Plato, on the other hand, saw clearly that the geocentric hypothesis was the source of the trouble. The later Pythagoreans had taught that the earth revolves round the Central Fire, and it was in this direction that a solution was to be looked for. Here again we have direct first-hand evidence. Theophrastos (who came to Athens before the death of Plato, and was almost certainly a

---

[1] It is worth while to note that this term is derived from τέλειον, 'complete', not immediately from τέλος. It has no implication of an external end.

[2] For a clear account of this, see Heath, *Aristarchus of Samos*, pp. 190 *sqq.*

member of the Academy) said that 'Plato in his old age repented of having given the earth the central place in the universe, to which it had no right'.[1] This is unimpeachable testimony, and no interpretation which ignores it can be accepted.[2] It does not follow from it, however, that Plato adopted the heliocentric hypothesis.

§ 266. Now there is a sentence in the *Timaeus* (40 b) which can only refer to the same doctrine, if we adopt the best attested reading.[3] The only admissible translation of this is 'earth, our nurse, going to and fro on its path round the axis which stretches right through the universe'. The choice of a word which properly means 'to go backwards and forwards'[4] is specially significant; for it is just that aspect of the terrestrial motion which accounts for the apparently retrograde motion of the planets. This is enough for our present purpose, and I do not propose to discuss here the vexed question of whether the heliocentric hypothesis was mooted in the Academy or not. I believe it was, but in any case Aristarchos of Samos, who did propound it, must have got his inspiration from the Academy and not from Eudoxos.

§ 267. Now let us see what light all this throws on Plato's philosophical position. In the first place, it is the phenomena of the visible heavens that furnish the problem for solution, and the assumption throughout is that it is possible to give an intelligible account of these. There is no attempt to shirk the difficulty by

---

[1] Plut. *Quaest. Plat.* 1006 c: Θεόφραστος δὲ καὶ προσιστορεῖ τῷ Πλάτωνι πρεσβυτέρῳ γενομένῳ μεταμέλειν ὡς οὐ προσήκουσαν ἀποδόντι τῇ γῇ τὴν μέσην χώραν τοῦ παντός. In the *Life of Numa*, 11, Plutarch says, doubtless on the same authority: Πλάτωνά φασι πρεσβύτην γενόμενον διανενοῆσθαι περὶ τῆς γῆς ὡς ἐν ἑτέρᾳ χώρᾳ καθεστώσης, τὴν δὲ μέσην καὶ κυριωτάτην ἑτέρῳ τινὶ κρείττονι προσήκουσαν.

[2] Sir T. L. Heath (p. 186) says Theophrastos got the statement 'from hearsay'. No doubt, but he probably heard it from Plato himself, and certainly from his immediate disciples.

[3] This is: γῆν δὲ τροφὸν μὲν ἡμετέραν, ἰλλομένην δὲ τὴν περὶ τὸν διὰ παντὸς πόλον τεταμένον. Everything here depends upon the word τὴν, which is quite distinctly written in Par. A, though omitted in all printed texts before by own. It can only be explained on the principle of τὴν (sc. ὁδόν), and we must 'understand' περίοδον or περιφοράν. No 'scribe' could have invented such a reading, which is also that of at least one other first-class MS. It is true that Par. A has εἰλλομένην for ἰλλομένην, but that is an everyday confusion, and the agreement of the MSS. of Aristotle, Plutarch and Proclus with other Plato MSS. turns the scale of evidence.

[4] The verb ἰλλεσθαι (which cannot be etymologically connected with εἴλλεσθαι) has no other meaning than this in classical Greek literature. It is used by Sophokles (*Ant.* 340) of ploughs going backwards and forwards in the furrow, and Xenophon (*Cyn.* 6) speaks of κύνες ἐξιλλοῦσαι τὰ ἴχνη, going to and fro till they find the scent. If Apollonios Rhodios confused ἴλλω and εἴλλω, that proves nothing. Aristotle certainly understood the word to mean motion of some sort (*De Caelo*, 296 a, 5), and this is confirmed by the use of the present participle. It is quite incredible to me that Aristotle should have misnuderstood or misrepresented Plato's teaching on a subject like this.

referring the irregularity of the planetary motions to the short-comings of the sensible world, or to 'matter' or to an evil world-soul, as popular Platonism did later. Nor is there any attempt to represent the phenomena as illusory; on the contrary, the whole object of the inquiry is to 'save' them. The appearances remain exactly what they were, only we now know what they mean. The gulf between the intelligible and the sensible has so far been bridged; the visible motions of the heavenly bodies have been referred to an intelligible system, or, in other words, they have been seen in the light of the Good. If we ask why they should appear to us as they do, the answer must be on the same lines. It is because we are placed on a spherical earth which revolves round the axis of the universe, and that is because it is good that we should be so placed, though we cannot clearly see why in the present state of our knowledge. That, I take it, is how Plato laid the ghost of the two-world theory which had haunted Greek philosophy since the time of Parmenides, and that is what he meant by saying that the sensible world was 'the image of the intelligible'. He had shown already in the *Sophist* that to be an image was not to be nothing. An appearance *is* an appearance, and is only unreal if we take it for what it is not.

CONCLUSION

§ 268. The account just given of Plato's mature philosophy is of necessity meagre and in a measure hypothetical. As to that, I can only say that in this case the phenomena to be 'saved' are the writings of Plato himself and the statements of Aristotle and others who knew him, and the only proof or disproof the hypothesis admits of is its efficacy in accounting for them. It cannot be otherwise tested. Personally I have found this hypothesis efficacious during a course of Platonic study extending over twenty years at least. I claim no more for it than that, and also no less.[1] I do not pretend to impose my conclusions on the reader, who must make the experiment for himself. He will certainly find it worth while.

There is another point still. It must be admitted that Plato's

[1] It is nearly a quarter of a century ago that I found the current views of Sokrates and Plato leading me into a hopeless scepticism and resolved to see what could be done with the hypothesis that Pluto really meant what he said. Since then I have edited the whole text of Plato, and an editor necessarily reads his text through minutely many scores of times.

immediate follower's fell very far short of the ideal I have attributed to their master. Aristotle was impatient with the mathematical side of the doctrine and did not even trouble to understand it. The result was that this did not come to its rights for nearly two thousand years. Even those men who were really carrying out the work Plato began felt bound to put their results in a form which Aristotle's criticism would not touch. The *Elements* of Euclid are a monument of that position.[1] Xenokrates confused Plato's philosophy of numbers with his philosophy of motion, and defined the soul as a 'self-moving number'. Speusippos held that the Good was not primary, but only arose in the course of evolution. The Neoplatonists did more justice to Plato's doctrine of the Good and of the Soul, but they failed to remember his warning that the detailed application of these could only be 'probable tales' in the actual state of our knowledge. Yet these very failures to grasp Plato's central thought bear witness to different sides of it and justify the attempt to reconstruct in such a way as to explain how it could be misunderstood in so many different ways. After all, these 'broken lights' are also among the phenomena which have to be 'saved', and for this reason many sides of Plato's philosophy will only appear in their true light when we have seen how it fared in the hands of his successors, and especially in those of Aristotle.

[1] Perhaps the most significant touch is that he calls the axioms κοιαὶ ἔννοιαι or 'innate ideas'. That is a stoic formula which enables him to avoid discussing the true nature of hypothesis.

APPENDIX

This table of Plato's family is based on that given in Kirchner's *Prosopographia*, nr. 11855, but it has been adapted to the conclusions stated in the text of this volume.

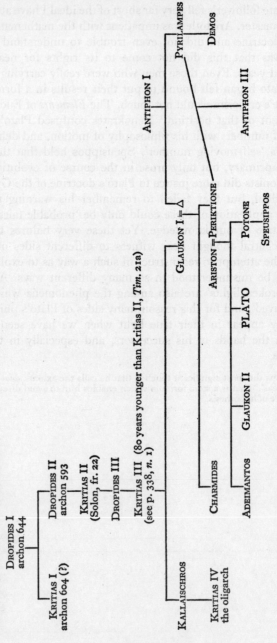

NOTE.—Alexander of Aphrodisias rightly distinguished Kritias III and Kritias IV (Diels,[3] *Vors.* ii. p. 312, 32). The former was celebrated in a poem by Anakreon, and it is therefore natural to ascribe the panegyric of Anakreon (fr. 1) to him. It will be observed that this affords a further ground for making Adeimantos and Glaukon considerably older than Plato, and for regarding the supposed date of the *Timaeus*, and therefore of the *Republic*, as previous to the departure of Polemarchos for Thourioi.

INDEX

PRINTED IN GREAT BRITAIN
BY ROBERT MACLEHOSE AND CO. LTD
THE UNIVERSITY PRESS, GLASGOW